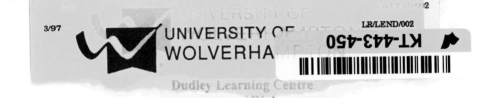

CHALLENGING WOMEN'S ORTHODOXIES IN THE CONTEXT OF FAITH

HEYTHROP STUDIES
IN CONTEMPORARY PHILOSOPHY, RELIGION & THEOLOGY

Series Editor
Laurence Paul Hemming, Heythrop College, University of London, UK

Series Editorial Advisory Board
John McDade SJ; Peter Vardy; Michael Barnes SJ; James Hanvey SJ;
Philip Endean SJ; Anne Murphy SHCJ

Drawing on renewed willingness amongst theologians and philosophers to enter into critical dialogues with contemporary issues, this series is characterised by Heythrop's reputation for openness and accessibility in academic engagement. Presenting volumes from a wide international, ecumenical, and disciplinary range of authors, the series explores areas of current theological, philosophical, historical, and political interest. The series incorporates a range of titles: accessible texts, cutting-edge research monographs, and edited collections of essays. Appealing to a wide academic and intellectual community interested in philosophical, religious and theological issues, research and debate, the books in this series will also appeal to a theological readership which includes enquiring lay-people, Clergy, members of religious communities, training priests, and anyone engaging broadly in the Catholic tradition and with its many dialogue partners.

Published titles
Radical Orthodoxy? – A Catholic Enquiry – Edited by Laurence Paul Hemming

Forthcoming titles include:
Biblical Morality – Mary Mills
Postmodernity's God – Laurence Paul Hemming
God as Trinity – James Hanvey
Religion Within the Limits of Language Alone – Felicity McCutcheon
Reading Ecclesiastes – Mary Mills

Challenging Women's Orthodoxies in the Context of Faith

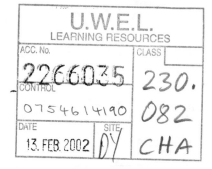
Edited by
SUSAN FRANK PARSONS

Ashgate

Aldershot • Burlington USA • Singapore • Sydney

Published by
Ashgate Publishing Ltd
Gower House
Croft Road
Aldershot
Hants GU11 3HR
England

Ashgate Publishing Company
131 Main Street
Burlington, VT 05401-5600 USA

Ashgate website: http://www.ashgate.com

British Library Cataloguing in Publication Data
Challenging women's orthodoxies in the context of faith. -
   (Heythrop studies in contemporary philosophy, religion and
   theology)
   1. Feminist theology 2. Feminism - Religious aspects -
   Christianity 3. Woman (Christian theology)
   I. Parsons, Susan Frank
   230'.082

Library of Congress Control Number: 00-134430

ISBN 0 7546 1419 0 (Hbk)
ISBN 0 7546 1420 4 (Pbk)

Printed and bound in Great Britain by MPG Books Ltd, Bodmin, Cornwall

Contents

List of Contributors   vii
Acknowledgements   ix

Introduction   xi
Susan Frank Parsons

1   Accounting for Hope: Feminist Theology   1
     as Fundamental Theology
     Susan Frank Parsons

2   Theology and Earth System Science   21
     Anne Primavesi

3   Justification by Gender: Daphne Hampson's *After Christianity*   35
     Angela West

4   The Rehabilitation of Eve: 53
     British 'Christian Women's' Theology 1972–1990
     Jenny Daggers

5   When God Beheld God: 73
     Notes Towards a Jewish Feminist Theology of the Holocaust
     Melissa Raphael

6   Harmony in Africa: Healing the Divided Continental Self   89
     – Mercy Amba Oduyoye, Feminist and Theologian
     Carrie Pemberton

7   The Mute Cannot Keep Silent: Barth, von Balthasar,   109
     and Irigaray, on the Construction of Women's Silence
     Rachel Muers

8   Losing One's Life for Others: Self-sacrifice Revisited   121
     Kerry Ramsay

9   Touching upon the Soul: 135
      The Interiority of Transcendence after Luce Irigaray
      Lucy Gardner

10   On the Nature of Nature: 155
      Is Sexual Difference Really Necessary?
      Laurence Paul Hemming

11   The Grace of Being: 175
      Connectivity and Agency in John Macquarrie's Theology
      Georgina Morley

12   The Power of Christian Innocence: 191
      Revisiting a Classical Theme
      Anne Murphy

13   Healing the Wound: Discourses of Redemption   205
      James Hanvey SJ

Index   223

List of Contributors

Jenny Daggers is a practical theologian, who has recently completed her PhD on recent British feminist theology at the University of Manchester.

Lucy Gardner is Tutor in Christian Doctrine at St. Stephen's House, Oxford. She is a co-author of *Balthasar at the End of Modernity* (Edinburgh, T&T Clark, 1999), and a contributor to *Radical Orthodoxy? – A Catholic Enquiry* (Aldershot, Ashgate, 2000).

James Hanvey SJ is Head of Systematic Theology at Heythrop College, University of London. He is a member of the Editorial Advisory Board of *Heythrop Studies in Contemporary Philosophy, Religion, and Theology*, and a contributor to *Radical Orthodoxy? – A Catholic Enquiry* (Aldershot, Ashgate, 2000).

Laurence Paul Hemming is Assistant Dean of Research Students at Heythrop College, University of London. He is editor of *Radical Orthodoxy? – A Catholic Enquiry* (Aldershot, Ashgate, 2000), and of the series *Heythrop Studies in Contemporary Philosophy, Religion, and Theology*.

Georgina Morley is Director of Studies of the North East Œcumenical Course in Durham, and has recently completed her PhD on the theology of John Macquarrie at the University of Nottingham.

Rachel Muers is working on a PhD at the University of Cambridge focusing on the theme of silence in recent Christian theology.

Anne Murphy SHCJ is a Lecturer in the Pastoral Theology Department at Heythrop College, University of London. She is a member of the Editorial Advisory Board of *Heythrop Studies in Contemporary Philosophy, Religion, and Theology*.

Susan Frank Parsons is Director of Pastoral Studies at the Margaret Beaufort Institute in Cambridge. She is the author of *Feminism and Christian Ethics* (Cambridge, Cambridge University Press, 1996).

Carrie Pemberton is Ecumenical Minister of Cambourne, Cambridgeshire, and has recently completed her PhD on the work of African women theologians at the University of Cambridge.

Anne Primavesi is a theologian and writer living in Newbury. She is the author of *From Apocalypse to Genesis* (Tunbridge Wells, Burns and Oates, 1991) and *Sacred Gaia: Holistic Theology and Earth System Science* (London, Routledge, 2000).

Kerry Ramsay is a priest on the staff of Great St Mary's, the University Church, Cambridge and a research student at Heythrop College, London.

Melissa Raphael is Senior Lecturer in Theology and Religious Studies at Cheltenham and Gloucester College of Higher Education. She is the author of *Thealogy and Embodiment: The Post-Patriarchal Reconstruction of Female Sacrality* (Sheffield, Sheffield Academic Press, 1996), *Rudolf Otto and the Concept of Holiness* (Oxford, Oxford University Press, 1997) and *Introducing Thealogy: Discourse on the Goddess* (Sheffield, Sheffield Academic Press, 1999).

Angela West is a theologian and writer living in Monmouth. She is the author of *Deadly Innocence: Feminism and the Mythology of Sin* (London, Cassell, 1995) and of numerous articles.

Acknowledgements

This book is the outcome of a conference held, with the same title, at Heythrop College, University of London, in May 1999. I am grateful to the speakers for making their papers available for publication here, and for those additional contributors who wrote and offered papers for this book. We are grateful to John McDade SJ, Principal of Heythrop, for his encouragement and welcome to the conference, and for the hospitality of the College and its staff. My thanks to Gemma Simmonds IBVM, Chaplain at the College and Laurence Hemming, for their work in the planning of the conference, and to Gemma especially for her skill and good humour in chairing the day.

The Editor and Publisher would like to thank the following for permission to reproduce material used in this book: Sheffield Academic Press Limited for the article *When God Beheld God: Notes Towards a Jewish Feminist Theology of the Holocaust* by Melissa Raphael, originally published in *Feminist Theology*, 21 (May, 1999), pp. 53 ff., of which the chapter included here is an abridged version; T&T Clark for the article *Justification by Gender: Daphne Hampson's After Christianity* by Angela West, originally published in the *Scottish Journal of Theology*, 1998, Vol. 51 No. 1, pp. 99 ff., to which a new preface has been added here.

My thanks to Sarah Jane Boss of the Marian Study Centre at the Margaret Beaufort Institute in Cambridge for her help in locating the cover illustration. Thanks are also due to Laurence Hemming and to Tony Hemming for their help in the editing and preparation of the text.

Finally I would like to dedicate this book to my father, Eugene Maxwell Frank, Bishop of the United Methodist Church (USA) and co-founder of St Paul's School of Theology, Kansas City, Missouri – in honour of his service to the church and the gospel she proclaims, in gratitude for the sincere and heartfelt faith in which he nurtured me, and in love.

Eastertide 2000

Introduction

Susan Frank Parsons

In each time there is possibility for the revealing of God, and for the turning
into witnesses of those who find themselves caught up in its sudden radiance.
The stories that are treasured in Jewish and Christian traditions tell of these
moments of encounter with God in communal and individual lives, stories
recited and so re-enacted into the lives of those who are captured by the
hearing of them. One of these stories that serves as a founding moment is that
of Moses who comes upon a burning bush in the field, which would not let go
of his life until he too burned with its brightness.[1] In wondering whatever it
was that happened there, we may be brought before the possibility it tells and
made to stand with him on the holy ground of God's revealing, and so we
repeat it as a witness, a living sign. Another is that of Mary whose conceiving
of God to be born into the world opens to us the astonishing possibility of
human being as bearer of the divine, and of God as one who comes to be
enfleshed amongst us.[2] This story too is a source of continual amazement, for
it stretches our credibility to breaking point and delivers us into the intense
fragility of this moment of a meeting.

That there might be a connection between these two stories is the insight
that inspires the painting of an icon like the one on the cover of this book, and
that stirs in the meditation of Gregory of Nyssa upon the life of Moses.[3] For
in these renditions of divine-human encounter, separated by time and culture,
we are brought before the same fundamental questions of who God is and of
who we are to be. Their words speak us to the brink of an opening, where we
might become aware of the utter suspension of all that is within God's grace,

---

1 Exodus 3.
2 Luke 1 [26-38].
3 Gregory of Nyssa, *The Life of Moses*, translated and edited by Malherbe, A. J. and
   Ferguson, E. in *The Classics of Western Spirituality*, New York, Paulist Press, 1978, esp.
   pp. 59 ff.

and where we might receive the expectation that it is for our lives to disclose God's glory.

Such possibility for a revealing and a turning into witness is understood to be the place for the beginning of faith, the point of an origin from which all life is then to take its orientation, and with which the heart and mind are to be consumed in most completely coming alive. It ever seems to be the work of the theologian in these traditions to ponder the ways in which this faith takes root in the soul, which is to wonder how it is that faith happens, and to find in the articulation of the truth of faith the most demanding of intellectual challenges and commitments. How is all of this to be said in our time? How are we today to understand what it is to believe? For we come upon such moments, such epiphanies, as ones who have been shaped by the prevalent ways of thinking of our culture, and who find that this past determination ill fits the occasion that now greets us. We are quite at a loss for words. So it occurs to us that truth may not be that which is already known and grasped in our hands, so much as it is that which has yet to be disclosed, which lies ever ahead of us, and thus which must be sought with the most urgent desire for its appearance in ourselves. It is this handing over of a life to the coming of God which brings us to approach the place with bared and tender feet, and it is the effort to discern its meanings which draws us into a conversation with the divine that astonishes us in its boldness of address, and it is the desire to be formed as a faithful bearer of truth that causes us to be returned to its mystery over and over again. By this is the work of theological reflection held in its faithfulness to tradition, and moulded anew into an activity in which the apprehension of God comes to life.

Something of this spirit of the vocation of theology informs the book you are about to read. In it are gathered together the essays of thirteen theologians, whose attention has been caught by the shining forth of the divine, and who seek to turn their own thinking into a reflection of its brightness. Theirs are voices of faith, and so it is in the context of faith that this work is held. Precisely because of this, theirs too are challenging voices. For every articulation of faith in its own time bears a disturbance into the settled world of assumptions and prior commitments, and every effort to speak into the needs of the world as they come to be known in us takes trouble to engage at just the points of most sensitivity and pain. This is no work that can be done at a distance, nor merely put on for a show, but is rather done with life. There is then also in these pieces an expression of a faith that rises up into the time it is given to speak, and a concern for a world in anguish for redemption, a care that is held with all the passion of those who are likewise implicated in its suffering. This is where the most strenuous exercise of reason is taken up into the heart of faith, where critical reflection upon the inheritance of ideas and enquiry into the conditions and the boundaries of knowledge itself are joined inseparably to pastoral awareness. If this book may open one small way to step into the contemporary sunderance of faith and reason, with entire confidence in the revealing of God there, then it will have begun its work well.

There are few places where this self-involving nature of theology is quite so profoundly experienced today as in the discourse of gender. As a category of human self-understanding, as an attempt to formulate what it is to be woman and to be man, gender has become a focal point of many of the most precious, and so vulnerable, assumptions of modern thinking. The notions of being a subject with a distinct identity, of having a nature which is to be realised, of speaking in a different voice or of being differently embodied, of the capacity to act to fulfill one's potential – such notions have all been used in modern humanism to disclose woman and man in the space of their common life. With these notions the ethics and the politics of modernity have been shaped, as also by means of them, various kinds of feminism have sought to provide for the coming of woman most entirely into a life of her own. Thus, to engage in a careful reading of feminist theology/thealogy is to find a sincere and serious effort to locate the holy ground upon which the presence of God alights, bringing with it an empowering of speech and an encouragement of dignity and an emancipation into fullness of life. To stand at this place and to see these things are the gifts of feminism, with which many women have found themselves in faith and given their lives to its transforming grace.[4] Some of the pieces in this collection reflect a commitment to this project, which many believe ought still to be completed.

Yet this collection appears in the midst of the postmodern, and so in the context of the commodification of all things human, of the stylisation of gender as that which is worn, and of the exhaustion of the notions through which our self-understanding has been articulated by modern thought. Gender

---

4   See Carr, A. E., *Transforming Grace: Christian Tradition and Women's Experience*, San Francisco, Harper and Row, 1990, and LaCugna, C. M. (ed.), *Freeing Theology: The Essentials of Theology in Feminist Perspective*, San Francisco, Harper Collins, 1993.

has come to bear the anxiety of these events and of the unresolvable dilemmas it presents, and so it is a troubled discourse which in its own way calls out for the touch of redeeming. The entanglement of gender with power, with the holding and the withholding of power, discloses too this nihilism of the age, and carries its discomfort into every discussion.

Since the ways in which our understanding of what it is to be woman and to be man that have been formed in modernity are no longer entirely available to us, every attempt to hold them open in this time risks a rigidity of ideology and a nostalgia for values that once held good. So this is a challenging place in which to come to speak about what it is to be human, and about how the divine may be enfleshed in the one I am given to be, and to do so in friendship. For this is a place in which the voices of women and men are to be heard in conversation with one another, with old and new questions that concern us both, and with a common enquiry whose purpose is to articulate the appearing of God. It is in this sense that the work represented here is concerned with truth, and so with orthodoxy, and is inspired to ask its difficult questions in anticipation of charity.

Most of the papers here were given at a day conference held at Heythrop College. Its aim was to provide an occasion for the discussion of challenging women's orthodoxies in the context of faith. With little more than the title for the day, this diversity of topics appeared from those invited to give papers. In the morning, three speakers addressed the plenary session. Among these was Janet Martin Soskice, who read from her Stanton lectures, *Naming the Christian God*, delivered at the University of Cambridge, which are soon to be published, and so her paper could not be included here. In the afternoon, six newer scholars were invited to present their work during two seminar sessions. What became clear during this time is both that the interface of gender and theology is being approached with renewed vigour and seriousness, and that the particular but multi-faceted question of women and faith is one that is very much alive. For these are people who have listened to and engaged with the feminist critique, but are not bound merely to repeat it, and who find their questions to be deeply rooted in tradition and sharply focused on the requirement for its re-articulation in new situations. The many intersecting lines of approach to these matters, and the different intellectual commitments with which they were addressed, made for a lively discussion in the final plenary session with a panel comprised of all the speakers.

Subsequent to the conference, five people were invited or offered to provide papers for the collection, and so this is a very full volume indeed.

It comes into your hands now as an invitation, an invitation to enter into the debate that informs these papers, and to let your own thinking be challenged by the discoveries this may awaken. The book is an indication that gender matters in our understanding and living of faith, and that the way in which this is articulated is the way for a revealing of God in human form. Our hope is that, within its pages, you will catch glimpses of the calling of theology into the fractures of thinking that are manifest in the time of our lives. Then may you follow along in your own way to find that the end with which this task is always to begin is love.

Chapter One

Accounting for Hope: Feminist Theology as Fundamental Theology

Susan Frank Parsons

I

As one who has taken a special interest in the ethics that has both informed and been shaped by the various types of feminism, I have been drawn to consider anew the problematic of ethics that presents itself in our situation today. To say something about that situation, it seems there is a re-thinking of all that modernity has come to mean and all that it has promised to accomplish, a time in which what is after modernity already announces itself; and so we are living in a time both of modernity's intensification and of its potential demise. The risk of this situation, its uncertainty and its questions, speaks itself into all of our discourses, and finds a particular place for causing its trouble in ethics. The question of whether ethics can deliver what it has promised and the uncertainties that now accompany its own assumptions are delicate matters in ethical thinking today, so that in some cases there are renewed intensities of all that modern ethics has been about, and in others a willingness to live with the end of this ethics, its time being up. This problematic of ethics and of ethical thinking manifests itself in every dimension of our lives today, and therefore becomes an especially important responsibility upon those who are called to the work of philosophy and theology.

Feminist thinking finds itself in this situation too, for this is also a time of its intensification and its potential demise. In common with all modern ethics, feminist ethics have in different ways sought to provide a scheme of understanding our identity as human persons, our place in the overall order of things, and the ways in which the fulfilment of our humanity might come about. In each case, there is a provision for our humanity in which its completion may be attained, a framework of thinking which offers an explanation of our beginning and an expectation of our end. The language of these ethics has been taken up by women, who may or may not consider themselves feminist, so that women have come to speak about equality, about liberation, about difference, in ways that have provided openings for their entry into public life, that have helped in the overcoming of oppressive circumstances, and that have facilitated their own making sense of their lives. For some, this language has still to do its work, and there is a passion for bringing about its potential for good. For others, this language already speaks into a hollowness where it no longer reverberates with all that life has come to be, and where its sounds have become posturings in which is not heard truth, or burdens in which is no longer hope. How it is to be for feminist ethics and theology in such a risky time as this is part of the situation that informs this paper.

Which brings me to the particular question with which it is concerned. The Christian tradition has quite richly suggested that the moral life is to find its beginning and its end in faith and hope and love, the three theological virtues upon which an ethics is to be founded and in which it is to be completed. May it not be that the situation in which we find ourselves today is in readiness for a return to these theological moments, a turning into their significance and a reinterpreting of their presence in human life? May it not be that women of faith find themselves already poised with the treasures of a tradition borne into their lives, that comes now to be voiced in new ways in the muddle of our time? To take on this thinking, and to ask for this voice, is to enter deeply into the problematic of our time and to engage the fundamental things that matter there. Feminist theology as fundamental theology is shaped by this work. Here in this paper, we attend to the matter of hope, and ask in what ways hope might come to be a beginning and an end in those things with which feminist theology and ethics have been especially concerned. In this, may a speaking in hope come to matter anew in our time.

II

In each time, people of faith find themselves speaking of the hope that is in them, through their searching of heart in prayer and study, and through thinking with others in worship and in dialogue. To attend to this hope is to approach the meeting of God and myself as an ordinary human being, and thus to speak of it is to speak of the way by which God is known to come amongst us and of the way in which I am to become most entirely what it is human to be. In accounting for hope, I am to let hope get hold of my life and come to dwell in me, as I also reach out towards the unknown in an astonishing reliance upon a charity in whose midst I find myself already to be. It is a readiness to respond to any who call, encouraged by the epistle of Peter to early Christians that forms the beginning of a defence of the faith, a point of starting, a moment of risk in which faith is tested as it is reasonably explained, challenged as it is offered up in living.[1] Such is to become the responsibility that lies at the heart of theology, with which its thinking and writing is to be informed, so that Pope John Paul II in his encyclical letter *Faith and Reason* draws attention to the "specific character" of fundamental theology "as a discipline charged with giving an account of faith".[2] This work, to which each person of faith is called, is to be the special task of theology within the community of the faithful, a task in which theology finds itself touched by the urgent cries of an anguished world, as it is led into ever deepening understanding of its own most intimate beginning of faith.

In our time of turnings and openings, of proliferating interpretations and commodified representations, the context for explication of Christian faith is especially challenging, presenting itself in theological reflection in profound questioning of the self-understanding of theology and of its bearing of a tradition, and in assertions and positionings that compete for our loyalty. That this context is the occasion for stimulating argument and exciting new explorations is manifest, for example, in the debate surrounding the

---

1   "Always be prepared to make a defence to any one who calls you to account for the hope that is in you." 1 Peter 3 [15].
2   John Paul II, Encyclical Letter *Fides et Ratio*, Vatican, Libreria Editrice Vaticana, 1998. Translated as *Faith and Reason*, London, CTS, 1998, §67.

appearance of Radical Orthodoxy.[3] That it also presents a number of problematic sites which unsettle forms of theology that have become more entrenched and institutionalised is the less comfortable face of this context, as it disrupts typical assumptions and upsets predictable responses. It is here that feminist theology finds itself working, as it too is brought back critically into its self-understanding and is challenged to consider its own bearing of faith into the world.[4] For women of faith are caught up in the general turmoil of ideas and commitments, of persuasions and possibilities that now characterises the postmodern, and that calls for precisely the accounting for hope entrusted in a particular way to theological enquiry. Challenging women's orthodoxies in the context of faith is a moment for such speaking in hope, for attending to the beginnings and end of faith, a moment in which there is a turning to reflect upon the established orthodoxies of what have become feminisms and feminist theologies, and a turning into new forms of discourse that become challenging orthodoxies for our time.

This chapter is an attempt to reflect upon the ways of accounting for hope which are to be found within three paradigms of modern western feminist theology, to explore some dimensions of the theological and philosophical problematic in which these accounts now find themselves, and to consider in what ways an apology for faith might come to be embodied. In this exercise, there is an awareness that feminist theologies are and have been deeply informed by modern western culture, and that insofar as this inheritance is unravelled by cultural critique and philosophical reinterpretation, so too feminisms become subject to the very suspicion they also provoke. The awkwardness of this challenge is felt keenly by women, many of whom are torn between their reliance upon and indebtedness to feminist ways of thinking they now question, and their reluctance to abandon the language and the critical tools by which the concerns of women's lives have been so illumined and articulated. For women of faith, this dilemma is one that places them

---

3   See the papers in Hemming, L. P. (ed.), *Radical Orthodoxy? A Catholic Enquiry* in *Heythrop Studies in Contemporary Philosophy, Religion, and Theology*, Aldershot, Ashgate, 2000.

4   Feminist theology and theologians occupy different places within the established churches and institutions of higher education in Britain than in North America, a complex matter involving social location, employment and theoretical commitments that would bear closer investigation, and that surely influences the possibility and the enthusiasm for this self-critical stance.

along the rough edges of post-Christian feminist critiques of the church and its history, the authority of canonical texts, the morals of a living tradition in which submissiveness and self-sacrifice so centrally figure, indeed any theological thinking which silences, devalues or kicks over the traces of woman's thinking. How it is that those who are sustained in hope may offer reasonable explanation of this, and in so doing may show the fuller implications of the gender critique begun in feminism, is the work of feminism as fundamental theology.

III

It may be said that what is generally called feminism is a movement of thinking, of culture, and of politics that takes shape during the Enlightenment, and is thus deeply informed by the language, thought-forms, ideologies and theories of modern humanism. The relationship of feminist theologies in the West with this humanism has itself been a challenging place for women of faith to be. While there is expressed optimism in the openings humanism presents for women to consider their nature and the value of their lives, this has been accompanied from the earliest days by the realisation of a disturbing effect brought on by the mention of their particular interests *as women* within the schemes they seek to utilise. Thus feminism begins as a demand for inclusion in what appears as already and entirely inclusive, and is stirred to action in the application of basic humanist principles, also to analysis and to change of women's economic, social and political conditions.

At the same time, there is astonishment that these apparently obvious conclusions need to be demanded, a gap between theory and practice which is to be filled with explanations of patriarchal precedents and of structural sin. That such straightforward reasoning becomes characteristic of feminist theologies, which on the whole have been sadly lacking in a sense of irony, is one of the discomforts that challenging women of faith experience, whose hope is something altogether more strange than this scheme of understanding can accommodate. In this difference already are the roots of a turn from modernity.

Modern feminist theology has found three ways of accounting for hope, which might both demonstrate the reasonable basis of women's faith, and inspire practices that enhance the human dignity and worth of women.[5] One of these has been closely associated with the growth of liberalism in politics and in philosophy, and thus it speaks a language of equality of persons, based upon the positing of a God-given human nature by which we are endowed with capacities and corresponding rights. This equality was to be promoted as a guiding principle for social, economic and political interactions, from which has followed a long and increasingly complex course of implementation of equal rights and opportunities, equal pay and conditions of work, equal access, equal treatment in law, and equal representation in institutional and political life.

For feminist theologians, thinking in this way was taken up as a significant expression of the doctrine of the creation of humanity in the *imago dei*, whose original form, it was believed, is not barred to us by sin, but rather becomes an available prophetic principle of judgment that is to be appealed to and implemented in political and moral action. To believe this human form to be incarnated in the person of Christ, in whom is neither male nor female, promises an equality to be found here within the body of Christ, the Church, and to be fulfilled in the kingdom which is to come. This turning of the doctrine of creation into visible manifestations of describable attributes offers, as Rosemary Ruether recognised many years ago, a rather minimalist definition of what it is to be created in God's image, a reduction which provides the focus for a tremendous moral urgency, but which continues to haunt this form of feminist theology, whose hope is placed in something less.[6]

A second way of accounting for hope within feminism has drawn upon the critique of power that appears within modern social, political and economic analyses, especially influenced by Marxism. Here the liberal human ideal is turned over into history, as the physical and spiritual need of real individuals is understood to be the raw material out of which social institutions and practices are constructed and by which they are justified ideologically; and it

---

5   For a succinct rendering of these paradigms, which I call "liberal", "social constructionist", and "naturalistic", see Parsons, S. F., *Feminist Ethics*, in Hoose, B. (ed.), *Christian Ethics: An Introduction*, London, Cassell, 1998. For a fuller analysis and critique, see Parsons, S. F., *Feminism and Christian Ethics*, Cambridge, Cambridge University Press, 1996.

6   Ruether, R. R., *Sexism and God-talk: Toward a Feminist Theology*, London, SCM Press, 1983. Ruether herself provides what she considers a much richer and more complex understanding of *imago dei* in Ruether, R. R., *Dualism and the Nature of Evil in Feminist Theology* in *Studies in Christian Ethics*, 1992, Vol. 5, No. 1.

is in the disparity between these that seeds of change are deemed to lie. Recognition of the social construction of our humanity in any particular locations, and deconstruction of the language and practices of power by which this is maintained, yield the possibility for reconstructions to be considered and effected.

For those feminist theologians who understand themselves to be political theologians, this becomes a paradigmatic way of explaining what is meant in biblical accounts of the redeeming work of God in history, and of understanding the work of Christ who breaks open the principalities and powers of death, casting down the mighty from their seats and releasing the captives. The essence of redemption here is translated into the receiving of grace for the formation of right relationships with myself, with others and with God, for specific actions that repeat the drama of salvation by converting moments of inauthentic life into new openness for the future, and thus for orthopraxy that is determinedly to displace orthodoxy.[7] Its scepticism regarding fixed belief systems becomes an appeal to an empowerment by hermeneutics, making available a perspective that takes in the largest sweep of human history in a grand narrative, as it must also be located very precisely within specifiable prison walls where its truth is rooted and instantiated. The tension between the demand to be everywhere, but only from this particular standpoint, suggests an unresolved suspicion of the power of the discourse of power itself, and brings feminist theology to those self-critical questions posed by MacIntyre, "*Whose Justice? Which Rationality?*".[8]

Yet a third way of accounting for hope by feminist theologians has been found through an emphasis on sexual difference. The gender debate within modern humanism has been characterised by the polarity between a one-nature and a two-natures anthropology, such that "the idea that there is a single human nature shared by women and men now does combat with the notion of two distinct human natures, one superior and the other inferior".[9] The work of naturalistic feminists has been to revalue the difference that women are on

7   See, for instance, Grey, M., *Redeeming the Dream: Feminism, Redemption and Christian Tradition*, London, SPCK, 1989. For a sustained defence of orthopraxy in theology see Sölle, D., *Thinking about God: An Introduction to Theology*, London, SCM Press, 1990.
8   MacIntyre, A., *Whose Justice? Which Rationality?*, London, Duckworth, 1988.
9   See O'Neill, M. A., *The Mystery of Being Human Together* in LaCugna, C. M. (ed.), *Freeing Theology: The Essentials of Theology in Feminist Perspective*, San Francisco, Harper San Francisco, 1993, p. 149.

their own terms, and thereby to challenge representations of women in the western tradition. Political and cultural representations are included here, as the effort to reassess the closeness of women to the natural world, and to hear from the embodied experiences of women a different voice speaking values of nurture, of mutuality, of relatedness, and of care that have for too long been neglected or feared, reveals the impoverishment of a tradition and offers an alternative forgotten undercurrent of wisdom. This notion of a trans-historical nature that finds embodiment in particular women, that serves as source and resource for their lives, has been understood by some feminist theologians to be a way of speaking of God, here not as θειôς or as λóγος, but rather as θεία or as σοφία, and to be a way of encouraging growth in this wisdom, and indeed in holiness of life, as its spirit is manifest in the newness of self-affirmation it renders possible. There is here an inversion of Plato, by which the cave is reinterpreted as the place within which one is to find truth, abandoning the false projections and abstract visions of elsewhere that are spun out of man's anxieties, giving oneself instead to the power of cosmic life by which all that is is sustained.[10] Such an assertion of a new absolute becomes the means of dethroning the male god who has become an idol of Christian tradition, and the man of reason who shapes the philosophical one; yet like them, it too serves those seeking representation of their humanity who may find themselves reflected in its glory.

There are many feminist theologians who remain within these modern frameworks of understanding, and who seek to adapt the language that has been formulated there into the new situations of women in the world today. What lies before them is a two-fold task: of extension, so that more and more women may be reached with the hope which is spoken in these forms; and of discerning strategies, so that the practice of this hope may be shown to be both tangible and effective in improving the lot of women. Feminist theologians are drawn to this work in a commitment to the universal, with a conviction that ultimately it is the whole of humanity that is to be touched by that for which we hope, and therefore that nothing less than this global vision is the context for its theological and moral thinking. There is now a growing

---

10 See, for instance, Cavarero, A., *In Spite of Plato*, Cambridge, Polity, 1995. See the appreciative analysis of the potential of this cave by Gerard Loughlin, *Ethics in the Cave: Living in Plato's Cinema and Christ's Church* in *Studies in Christian Ethics*, 2000, Vol. 13, No. 1.

impatience with purely academic talking and a compelling towards the practical. In this is an urgency for bringing positive changes that are to make the difference between death and life, starvation and being filled, poverty and well-being. Feminisms generally have become attached to this renewed universalism in morality that seeks a just framework for the articulation and legitimation of special interests, motivated by a sense of urgency to secure the future against awful consequences. Somehow, *real* feminists are thought to belong here, and should model themselves on those in India who

> know that they live in the middle of a fiercely unjust reality; they cannot live with themselves without addressing it more or less daily, in their theoretical writing and in their activities outside the seminar room.[11]

Has feminist theology, as theology, anything to say in this discourse, or have its interests been translated entirely into the terms of ethical humanist debate? Is there any reserve? Is there any hesitation about the modernity of which it is the product, the horizon of which can no longer provide the bearings for the geography of its hope, so that there is left only an anxious fixing of things, and a sheer determination? And to what end?

IV

To ask these questions is to open up the question of orthodoxy anew for women of faith today, and to pose the problem of our relation to the theological and philosophical tradition in whose terms we are given to think. Ruether provides one way for such thinking in her historical account of women and redemption.[12] As she traces the shifting theological paradigms through which women have spoken of the hope that is in them, her book reveals the assumptions of modern feminism at work in her reading of the tradition and in her recommendations for feminist theological reflection today. The central question of her study is the one concerning Christ, the question she raised so many years ago, "Can a male saviour save women?" and the one

---

11 Nussbaum, M. C., *The Professor of Parody: The Hip Defeatism of Judith Butler* in *The New Republic*, February 22, 1999, p. 38.

12 Ruether, R. R., *Women and Redemption: A Theological History*, London, SCM Press, 1998.

which today still troubles feminist theology, as it seeks to understand "the Christian claim of a universal and inclusive redemption in Christ".[13] Ruether explains how this question divides women against themselves, requiring them to accept that their identity as women is to be found in the person of Christ who was a man, or to believe that their liberation from suffering is to be accomplished in the work of Christ who requires their continued self-sacrifice. These dilemmas trouble contemporary feminist theologies around the world, as Ruether documents, as they also have furnished the pretext for the withdrawal of post-Christian feminists from the work of this theological tradition.[14] In response to them, she proposes:

> I think it is not enough to say that Jesus represents both men and women because he was fully human, the sort of human we all want to be, if we cannot also say that women can be fully human and can represent the sort of liberative human we all want to be. Also one wants to be able to experience that sort of liberating woman in our own culture and ethnicity.[15]

For Ruether, such "radically new envisionings of redemptive hope" are precisely what the work of "ongoing revelation" entails, and she calls women into this "process of continuous reinterpretation".[16]

Ruether comes to this interpretative work with assumptions regarding what it is human to be and in what way it is human to act, assumptions which bear the marks of modern thinking, and which are in turn shaped by what she understands interpretation to be. These underlying assumptions are disturbed in the context of postmodernity, and in their disturbance we find too that we must ask anew what it is to interpret. Certainly, as much as feminism has been entangled with modernity, it has also helped to unravel it, poking bigger holes through the weak spots in the fabric, and pulling at the loose ends of substantive arguments. Some of this is rather gleefully proclaimed by feminists in cultural and critical theory, whose work across the boundaries of disciplines affords a kind of theoretical freedom to be disrespectful – indeed this is perhaps the performance that 'theory' has come to be – while on the

13 Ruether, R. R., *Sexism*, chapter 5; *Redemption*, p. 1.
14 See, for instance, Hampson, D.: *Theology and Feminism*, Oxford, Blackwell, 1990; *After Christianity*, London, SCM Press, 1996.
15 Ruether, R. R., *Redemption*, p. 278.
16 Ruether, R. R., *Redemption*, p. 280.

whole this dismantling has been more cautiously treated by feminist philosophers and theologians. The unsettling of these enterprises threatens altogether the deepest commitments of thinking.

Yet it is precisely here that we are called to think anew what it is to be orthodox, to be informed by a tradition and embodied in its thinking, and to engage in a work of apologetic theology for our day that is sensitive to the feminist critique. For this question now needs itself to be put in question, so that we begin to hear what it reveals and what it yet conceals from our attention. Such work, I want to suggest, requires of me as a theologian, not that I ask the same question Ruether poses, nor that I presume this question to have been the same throughout the Christian tradition only to be articulated in our time, nor that I deem this question to be the litmus test of true feminist believers. Rather this work requires of me that I think redemption anew, that I come before the matter of the hope that is in me, that I find myself at the meeting place of divine charity, and speak of its possibility. In this is a thinking that honours feminist theology, that risks an examination of even its own most treasured assumptions with confidence, and that knows its authentic speaking to be non-repetitive, which is to repeat only Christ.

Two of Ruether's assumptions can be mentioned, and questioned, here. Modern thinking has been particularly concerned with the representation of the human, with the philosophical formulation of general claims about the distinctive characteristics of human being, with the development of the human sciences which would investigate and corroborate these, and with political structures that would allow these representations to appear and to be effective in social life. While it is argued that such representations are not ideals in the Platonic sense, since they are grounded in our experience of the world or in our patterns of thought, and are tested in empirical studies, nevertheless they come to be generalities which somehow stand beyond us, universally applicable definitions in which our thinking gathers together what is taken to be common to all human beings individually. Much that has been the business of modern thinking has been the trying and testing of representations, and much that feminisms have from the earliest days protested has been that representations of the human are limited to, and written by, men. Women have spoken of this as a problem of their own identity, that is of not being able to find themselves represented here, and thus of being outsiders to the various and competing descriptions of identity offered in modern thought. So it is that gender too comes to be thought as something which is a representation, something which is characteristic of a 'human being' thought objectively, by which we can recognise one another and come to know ourselves too.

Representation has been a contested site for feminist critical thinking in all its forms, but it has been the witty genius of Luce Irigaray to take this to its logical conclusion. Knowing that some single definition of human being must figure in the debates about equality, she poses the playfully serious question, "égales à qui?" – and in the asking of it, the comparison that was not supposed to be a comparison came unstuck before us.[17] The absent figure of woman suddenly becomes obvious, the one who must insist that she belongs because she is not present there already, the one who exists in this sense only under erasure, who seeks by an effort of will to join what has been rendered asunder. Thus comes an ever-disappointed mood to hang over this adherence to posited representations, driving it on to try again, and again, to match up to a disappearing model.   Irigaray's proposal of a radical two-natures anthropology, in which women's separate nature is posited, a female essence upheld by a feminine divine in whose image women may know themselves reflected, has struck an ambivalent note amongst feminists, who are either drawn to the saving grace of a woman's appearance at last, or are offended by the blatant play of representations that risks idolatry. Given these alternatives, Ruether's appears as perhaps a modest middle ground, encouraging representation for a "growing plurality of women's voices in many cultural contexts". Yet can we live in this place without considering why it is that representation is what matters?[18] It has not always been the case that we have thought like this, that we have posited an abstraction as the way in which we come to know ourselves, nor has it always been assumed that to interpret means to find the matching elements. These things belong especially with modernity, and insofar as they become the touchstones of feminist theological reflection, not only in its thinking of *redemptor hominis* but also in its understanding of being created *imago dei*, then women of faith may not find a place there from which to speak of the hope that is in them.

17 Title of an article by Irigaray, L., in *Differences*, 1989, Vol. 1, No. 2, translated as *Equal to Whom?* in Berry, P. and Wernick, A., *Shadow of Spirit: Postmodernism and Religion*, London, Routledge, 1992.
18 Ruether, R. R., *Redemption*, p. 280.

Renewed thinking becomes possible in a postmodern culture of over-representation, in which the proliferation of images of ourselves and our world both materialises the modern myth that this is the way to get real, and commodifies our desire to be the most fulfilled possible material girl. The continuous spinning of variations on the human theme becomes the mirror in which a universal moral code is both revealed and mocked, its requirement being that the plurality of voices which it encourages in different cultural contexts be recognisable within a common frame of interpretation. This is the requirement now copied in a system of global capitalism which contains and disciplines these so-called differences by a common method of operation. The critique of the cultural story of modernity, as exemplified in Baudrillard, opens a way for thinking the human otherwise, and it does so by exposing the death of the human being we have assumed to be there.[19]

Our thinking is challenged to examine its reliance upon the supposed *a priori* of such representations, by turning our attention to the ways of their construction, and in this, the matter of our hope in the form of the human being, that treasure of humanism, is thrown into question. This is the issue too that now appears in gender theory as the problematic of identity, that supposed essence of woman or of man to which we are fitted up for living, to which a determined defensiveness within feminism responds with ever wider and more tolerant descriptions of the parameters within which the human is to be confined and controlled. Might this not be the moment however for self-critique, for a reflection that asks why these representations of the human appear now and to what end, a moment of pause in the relentless logic of humanism to consider what allows this kind of thinking to happen? And may women of faith not also find themselves at just such a moment?

A second of Ruether's assumptions calls for critical examination, in its entanglement with a certain understanding of power that comes to prevail, both in her descriptions of what it is for a human being to act, which becomes an exercise of power, and of what it is to be of human value, which becomes a significance conferred by power. At the beginning of her study, Ruether states her conviction that redemption has to do with this world, with its structures, its earthiness, and its peoples. The great work of feminist theologies has been to dismantle falsehoods about otherworldly hopes requiring ascent into "communion with a spiritual world", and to enunciate

19 See Baudrillard, J., Poster, M. (ed.), *Selected Writings*, Oxford, Polity Press, 1988.

"the true meaning of original and redeemed creation and reconciliation with God" as "egalitarian mutuality".[20] This context serves as the rationale for an action-centred approach to redemption as human work of liberation modelled after the actions of Christ. Herein is a conviction that it is in action that the human makes its distinctive mark upon the world, and it does so by effecting real changes that build good structures and relationships. It is not simply the language of making (and remaking) and of building (and rebuilding) that gives evidence of this, but finally Ruether's claim that redemption is something that is "done". Jesus, she argues, "does not and cannot do it for us", rather his is the root story of a process "in which we must all be engaged", and thus in her statement, "Redemption cannot be done by one person for everyone else" is the appearing of a discourse of power.[21] Certainly there is suspicion here of the power of a redeemer figure, acting from a high (and masculine) place upon passive (and feminine) recipients of this good work, a hermeneutic of suspicion that is now common feminist theological parlance. What does not seem to enter Ruether's self-reflection however in this externalisation of the matter is a consideration of the ways in which the terms of this discourse also shape feminist theology, and it is precisely here again that a challenging women's orthodoxy may appear.

To believe the human person to be an agent who exercises power in action, after a process of deliberation and of choosing between alternatives, is again a feature of modern humanism. It is this active agent who figures in the politics of modernity, shaped as it has been by movements of liberation, and whose value must be continually reaffirmed by what is believed to be empowerment. To be empowered is to know one's potential, to be granted the privilege of full humanity, to take up one's human being as the power to act, so that one may construct relationships and engage in practices that enable others to release this potential, this fullness of humanity, too. Such affirmations of human power in action and in value require to be sustained by some "root story" of liberation and empowerment, and so it is here that investigations of early Christian history become so critical to the argument. For this discourse of power rests upon a "reconstruction of Christian origins", an interpretation of an original moment of shared power between God and humanity – in this case between Jesus and an unnamed woman – a moment

---

20 Ruether, R. R., *Redemption*, p. 8.
21 Ruether, R. R., *Redemption*, p. 275.

when something was done in the conferring of value and in the empowering to act that is ours to remember by re-enactment today.[22] This is the moment of co-operation, divine and human, upon which Christian feminist theology comes so heavily to depend and wherein its most difficult attempts at interpretation of the doctrine of redemption are contested. So Ruether too wants women to be "agents of liberative action for themselves and other women (and men)", by which deeds they become "christomorphic"; for "his story can model what we need to do, but it happens only when all of us do it for ourselves and with one another".[23] At no moment does there appear to be any distance, any standing back from these proclamations to ask what makes them possible, any sense of irony that may wonder its own limits. Would this be deemed to constitute some humiliating act of giving up power?

Again we become aware of the context of the postmodern in which such matters have become problematic to us. For there is today such widespread anxiety over doing, such overworking of technique, such reinventing of strategies for the doing of things that can be devised beforehand as aims and objectives and assessed afterwards in measureable outcomes, such making and remaking, that we face exhaustion by, not to say subjection to, the power to act we have spoken. This increase of power for which we hope, and which we want to extend around the globe to people everywhere, now also threatens us, demanding that all our ideas be turned into practical outcomes, that may then be commodified. Isn't it good to be in control? Increasingly ethics is drawn into this pattern of thinking so that it too becomes a means of accomplishing things, having to justify itself as useful in some way beforehand for humanity. Are the hopes expressed in feminism to be drawn into this pattern too – so that successful feminist strategies are ones that facilitate the placement of more women into every level of an organisational structure, or require the presence and the speaking of each (how many?) diverse perspective in every decision that is made, or demand of women around the world that their interpretation of power be the same as that held by high-achieving white western women? Does the common measure of power here mask its hegemony? Is the doing of these things what feminism has come to perform in politics, in ethics, in theology? So feminism is challenged to explain why it cannot be dissolved

---

22 Schüssler Fiorenza, E., *In Memory of Her: A Feminist Theological Reconstruction of Christian Origins*, London, SCM Press, 1983.
23 Ruether, R. R., *Redemption*: p. 278; p. 275.

without residue into pragmatism, and herein lie some difficult questions about feminist collusions in a culture of technique, and in a theological and philosophical thinking the human person that fixes the horizon of our transcending at the limits of the technically possible, the do-able.[24]

And to speak of horizon is to hear the Nietzschean critique, and to understand this to be the time in which there has been a saying of the death of god and the thinking of the wiping away of the horizon of meaning. This is the time in which the performing of the will to power and the raising up of value in place of God has entered our understanding of what it is to be human. In its speaking of the hope that is in us, the dependence of feminist theology upon language of power, as alone that which will disclose and enact the human to be as real, and upon the necessity for repeated re-valuations (re-envisionings) as that thinking which will ensure the presence of the human as a force to be reckoned with – this dependence is put in question with the hearing of Nietzsche in postmodernity. In this hearing, we begin to ask after the sources of our ideas and our language; and in that genealogical work is an asking after what has appeared and what has been concealed in the forms of our knowing; and in that thinking is a transcending of the given and an approach to that beyond, which comes to make itself knowable and to give itself into our midst.

This is the site of a challenging orthodoxy, that would listen for that unrepresentable which is not said in our saying of redemption, and that would know itself to be in consequence of an act of passion, of dying and rising, in which is the world's un-doing. So that what is asked of feminist theology, or what is asked of an apologetic theology sensitive to the feminist critique by women of faith, is to think anew in what is our hope. Otherwise, in its presentation of itself, feminist theology may forget what is given to it, and in the requirement of obedience to its project of re-envisioning, its inclusivist and pragmatic orthodoxies may come to take the place of the conceiving of God in the human soul, which is, in the end, what it is to interpret.

---

24 See Rorty, R., *Feminism and Pragmatism* in *Radical Philosophy*, 1991, No. 59 (Autumn), and the response of Wilson, C., *How did the Dinosaurs Die Out? How did the Poets Survive?* in *Radical Philosophy*, 1992, No. 62 (Autumn).

V

To consider in what ways an apology for faith might come to be embodied, which is the final task of this paper, turns us into our context, asking that in our philosophical thinking we listen to what is being said in our time and for that which presents itself in this saying, and that in our theological thinking we may come to be receptive to divine love. In this is no divisive work, but a consistent discipline of reasoning that demands of faith its self-exposure both to its own foolishness and to its own desire to know God. It is in the spirit of this thinking that a renewed orthodoxy turns to reflect upon what is being said in feminisms, to listen for what makes this presentable in our time, and to ask that in its own speaking may be heard the coming of charity into the world. With this task in mind, one further thing needs to be said here to challenge feminist theology into its own best effort.

Feminist theology, so far as I am aware, has paid little attention to the matter of nihilism, and in this may lie something of the root of its failure to be self-critical. Nevertheless, without attention to this as the experience of the postmodern itself, and without regard for the effacements of nihilism, which is the masking of itself against its own unmasking, there is little that will be offered for a speaking in hope in our time. To be sure, nihilism shadows the writing of particular feminist theologians, as one senses it does Ruether's own writing on redemption. One can hear its voice almost being allowed to speak in, for example:

> Postmodernist thought has rejected the whole concept of universals . . . even the idea of an essential humanness . . . All such notions of an essential self and universal values are declared to be social constructions that veil the universalising of dominant cultural groups of men and women. We have to recognise infinite particularity.[25]

This thought is then left alone, though it might occasion a deeper thinking, in favour of a sustained defence in the book for the construction of "new and more authentic ways of reaching across these differences toward solidarity in struggle against systems of oppression that are global".[26] However, what a challenging orthodoxy wants to ask, and what should be quite poignantly

25 Ruether, R. R., *Redemption*, p. 10.
26 Ruether, R. R., *Redemption*, p. 10.

asked by women of faith, most especially by women, is whether any hope may be spoken at all which has not looked into the grave of God to find it empty. Without this move of faith, the moral exhortations of Ruether to establish a code of conduct based on some spurious notion of "solidarity in struggle" is itself a postmodern, and thus a nihilistic move, acknowledging, by what it refuses to speak, its own lack of anything at all to say in the face of the absence of God, and masking itself with humility. This is a difficult claim to make of a theologian whose work has been of the most profound importance for feminist theologians around the world, and who has herself moved through the developing thinking of feminisms with her own challenging questions. Nevertheless it is asked so that we may both be turned to the anguish of the world which waits with eager longing, and to the coming of God who raises from the dead and who calls us into a transcending thinking that may even lose the cloak of its own assumptions in its running for joy.

Lest Ruether bear the brunt of this argument, it should be said that nihilism more prominently features, and seems indeed to be welcomed, in a lecture series given in the early 1990's by Schüssler Fiorenza.[27] Utilising just the assumptions we have examined above, Schüssler Fiorenza sets about a higher thinking, an interpretation of feminist interpretations, with which she intends to establish a secure place for women who love wisdom to dwell, and to set out the framework of ideas within which such loving thinking is to be conducted. This is no modest undertaking, for she expects her thinking to provide an "alternative intellectual space" and in so doing, effectively to "instantiate the *ekklesia* of wo/men".[28] In what other context than the postmodern can these things be thought and this power be enacted, and in the face of what other experience than that of the death of God, whose absence is the emptiness that accompanies each word of her text? While she explicitly disowns the postmodern as "overspecialised academic postmodern language", she is unwilling to attend to its presence in all that she says, and thus she allows nihilism to mask itself behind the power that is said to be found in "sharing her word".[29]

---

27 These lectures are published in Schüssler Fiorenza, E., *Sharing Her Word: Feminist Biblical Interpretation in Context*, Edinburgh, T&T Clark, 1998. See also my review of this book in *Modern Theology*, 1999, Vol. 15, No. 4.

28 Schüssler Fiorenza, E., *Sharing*, p. xiii.

29 Schüssler Fiorenza, E., *Sharing*, p. 186.

Yet it erupts nonetheless into the text, into what I have called "the awesome litany to the 'nothing' of love", which I quote here in full.[30]

> Contrary to Paul's hymn to love and Luke's admonition to steadfast prayer, love does not patiently wait and endure everything. It does not accept and tolerate inequality, injustice, rejection, violence, abuse, and dehumanisation. Love and prayer are dangerous if they are not expressions of self-esteem, respect, dignity, independence, and self-determination. Love and prayer are nothing without engaging G*d's power to bring about the *ekklesia* of wo/men as the harbinger of a more just world. Love and prayer are nothing without the engagement for justice that upholds us in the political struggle for the well-being of everyone. Love is nothing without the imagination to create a sustaining spiritual vision for new forms of familial relationships and world communities with equal resources. Love is nothing without justice. Indeed, love must not endure everything.[31]

These are shocking words, the impact of which is physically felt as the most deadening of spirit and hardening of heart and steeling of nerve in the face of the harshest realism of postmodern power. There is nothing to say in the presence of such an awesome expression of nothing, for it has been said here for us, taking the words right out of our mouths into its vast emptiness. There is no joy here between the clenched teeth of this determination to engage, and certainly there is no hope in its miserable wandering through the wreckage of dreams that fail (always) to materialise. What is it that makes this speaking possible and that allows its recognition, not to say its acceptance, amongst women of faith? To what have we become subject in this proclaiming of the limits of our endurance? What is enacted through us in our refusal to wait patiently? These questions, these paradoxes will not leave us alone, and in the turning away from them is an abandonment of hope, a giving over of ourselves to the power of these thoughts, an assumption of the speaking of this world as if its words had already concluded all there is to say in the matter of God.

A renewed orthodoxy is an attentiveness to the suffering of soul that speaks this litany, a sensitivity, a pastoral concern if you like, for the common humanity known also in me that cries out as much in what it does not say as in what it does; and it is an endless patience of prayer that listens deeply into

---

30 Parsons, S. F., Review of *Sharing*, p. 518.
31 Schüssler Fiorenza, E., *Sharing*, p. 159.

the tradition for the formation of its longings into faith; and it is a searching of mind that finds itself informed and challenged in the body of Christ to meet again and again in worship the coming of God to matter and the turning of the soul into love. To attend to what comes to be known in our humanity, to listen for that vocation to be into which the soul is called, to find itself rising up into an exceeding of love – in all of these is a women's orthodoxy to be drawn into the life of God wherein is all its hope. So an apology for faith meets itself where it begins – in its own future, in hope.

Chapter Two

Theology and Earth System Science

Anne Primavesi

In February 1998, *Gaia*, the Society for Research and Education in Earth System Science, was founded 'to promote an integrated understanding of the Earth system through research and education'. At the inaugural meeting I asked myself what kinds of understanding were to be integrated. As the only professional theologian present (as far as I know) I had to ask myself whether or not they included theological understanding. The scientists there had already taken James Lovelock's Gaia theory as a framework for ongoing research projects and as a subject for scientific syllabuses. It is, after all, a scientific systems analysis of the structures and dynamics present in the chemical and physical evolution of the Earth system, and as one member of the Society wrote later, 'this systems–analytic approach becomes unavoidable once we perceive our planet as one unique entity driven by multiple internal and external forces towards ever higher degrees of complexity'. He sees the advancement within science of such a holistic perception as one of the great achievements of Lovelock and those who have worked with his presuppositions.[1]

Mary Midgley, who spoke at the Society's inaugural meeting, is also quite clear about the benefits for philosophy of pursuing a Gaian approach. The notion of the Earth system as an enclosing whole corrects, she says, a large and disastrous blind spot in our contemporary world view. It reminds us that we are not separate, independent, autonomous entities. Since the Enlightenment the deepest moral efforts of our culture have gone to establishing our freedom as individuals, and as a result we have carefully excluded everything non-human from our value system and reduced that system to terms of individual self-interest. "We are mystified – as surely no

---

1 Schnellhuber, H. J., *Earth System Analysis: Integrating the Human Factor into Geophysiology*, Gaia Circular, 1999, Vol. 2, Issue 3.

other set of people would be – about how to recognise the claims of the larger whole that surrounds us: the material world of which we are a part." The idea of Gaia, therefore, "is not a gratuitous, semi-mystical fantasy", but a cure for distortions in our current world view.[2]

This is not a new perception on her part. In 1983 she had written about the need for an environmental ethics which is not human-centred by re-examining the philosophical question of whether or not, when he was alone on his island, Robinson Crusoe had any duties. She pointed to various fallacies in the presupposition that duties only obtain as quasi-contractual relations between symmetrical pairs of rational human agents, concluding that while we have duties *as* farmers, parents, consumers etc, it is the business of each of us not to forget our transitory and dependent position, the rich gifts we have received and the tiny part we play in a vast, irreplaceable and fragile whole.[3]

The concept of non-human-centred duties is indeed a late arrival on the philosophical scene, for, since Socrates to the present day, orthodox views of duties or ethics have assumed that moral concern only extends to human-human relations. But over the past thirty years or so, notably since Arne Naess published his classic statement of the distinction between human-centred and non-human-centred ethics, although the latter obviously take cognisance of human interests and concerns, the discussion has moved beyond the boundaries of the former.[4] Briefly, this move results from philosophical reflection on the natural environment as displayed to us by science, our relationship with it and our effect upon it.

I was left, however, with my question of what a holistic world-view arising from Earth system science might mean for theology. I offer some provisional answers in my book *Sacred Gaia: Holistic Theology and Earth System Science.*[5] My question here centres on what it means for our theological self-perception to situate our relationship with God within rather than outside of Earth's history. Surely this accords with our linking the coming of the

2   Midgley, M., in a personal communication to me.
3   Reprinted as Midgley, M., *Duties Concerning Islands*, in Elliot, R. (ed.), *Environmental Ethics*, Oxford, Oxford University Press, 1995.
4   Naess, A., *The Shallow and the Deep, Long Range Ecology Movements: A Summary* in *Inquiry*, 1973, No. 16.
5   Primavesi, A., *Sacred Gaia: Holistic Theology and Earth System Science*, London, Routledge, 2000.

Messiah to an earth which shall be 'full of the knowledge of the Lord'.[6] The refusal to endorse this belief has resulted in a potentially disastrous 'blind spot' in our theological perspective, one which remains as long as Christianity continues to function as a self-referential religious system where communication with the sacred is reduced to two forms: revelation based on written texts, and personal or communal prayer. 'Nature' is presumed ignorant of and silent before God. So we relate to the non-human world as at best an object of pleasure but more and more as an object for exploitation.[7] The scientific progress and technological innovation which followed the Enlightenment did not have to initiate the secularisation of 'the environment' in order to exploit or devastate it. Science merely built on previous Christian secularisation of the non-human world.

Today theologians as well as philosophers and scientists live in a culture where our horizons of knowledge about the world are continually being widened through the application of scientific method. Most notably, we now have a view of the Earth from space which, while it calls for urgent research into key interactions between the Sun, the atmosphere, oceans, ice, land, marine and terrestrial ecosystems, does so in the context of the planet as an entity. Within that entity, as some scientists note, there have been and are significant interactions between all these systems and human societal, political and religious systems which have had significant effects on the Earth system as a whole. Some of these effects are quantifiable. Others are not. Another member of the Gaia Society, Chris Rapley, who heads the British Antarctic Survey, notes that roughly half the planet's land area has been transformed by us, principally through agricultural and forestry systems. This has changed the surface reflexivity and flows of wind and water, with major impact on nutrient flows, soil degradation and biodiversity worldwide. But how do we measure the effects of theological anthropocentricity? How does a human-centred religious system validate our increasingly deleterious impact on marine and terrestrial ecosystems, and how do we move beyond it to a geocentric world-view?

---

6   Isaiah 11 [9].
7   Luhmann, N., *Essays on Self-Reference*, New York, Columbia University Press, 1990, p. 153.

Freedom to develop theologically

In a benchmark article in 1964 entitled *The Problem of Religious Freedom*, John Courtney Murray defined the theological task as tracing the stages of growth of a tradition as it makes its way through history. The further task, he said, is discerning the 'growing end' of the tradition. This is usually indicated by the new question that is taking shape under the impact of the historical moment.[8] On this premise, such questions, and the search for answers to them, would themselves become part of that 'growing end'. In this way historical consciousness, which is the ability to discern what is of moment at a particular stage in our history, in some measure constitutes and also acts as a necessary spur to the exercise of theological freedom. Therefore the evolution of human history, recorded as change in human societies through time, is constitutive of the evolution of theological tradition, of its development through time. 'Stages of growth' within theology correspond in some measure to those discerned within history.

The historical theological moment for Courtney Murray was the Second Vatican Council and in particular its 'Declaration on Religious Freedom', not least because by recognising the historic legal principle of religious freedom it also sanctioned the development of doctrine. The Declaration establishes the right of members of the Catholic Church, as well as those of other religions, to the free exercise of their religion. This right, it is argued, is based on persons' growing awareness of their own dignity and of their active participation in society. The opening words of the Declaration, *dignitatis humanæ personæ*, translate as 'a sense of the dignity of the human person', and it is this sense which is invoked as justifying the demand that we should act on our own judgment, 'enjoying and making use of a responsible freedom, not driven by coercion but motivated by a sense of duty'.[9]

However, the demand made by the Vatican document is for 'the right of the person and of communities to *social and civil freedom* in matters religious' (my italics). It is assumed that in regard to society they have demonstrated their capacity to handle the responsibilities of freedom. If this were paralleled

---

8   Murray, J. C., *The Problem of Religious Freedom* in *Theological Studies*, 1964, No. 25, p. 569.
9   Abbott, W. M. (ed.), *Vatican Documents*, London, Geoffrey Chapman, 1966: p. 673; p. 675.

in theological freedom, it would establish the right of theologians, on the basis of their human dignity and of their being active members of society, to demonstrate their capacity to handle the responsibilities of their freedom to theologise. It would assume religious freedom in the sense I am arguing for: freedom to respond theologically to the stages of growth within history; to the widening of the horizons of understanding through scientific research so that 'the growing end' of the theological tradition might be shaped by the concrete exigencies of contemporary personal, scientific and political consciousness.[10]

It is now, I believe, also being shaped by a particular consciousness of ourselves as belonging to a global rather than a geographic or ethnic community, situating us within the known range of emergent species on Earth and, as comparative latecomers, dependent on those which emerged before us. At the personal level this self-perception is most visibly created/symbolised by the Internet. Access to it is still largely confined to those in the 'First' world, but we are all, potentially at least, 'world-wide-webbers'. At the global level, scientific space exploration and technology disclose the evolution of the physical, chemical and material earth systems which underpin our planetary interdependence and, through an ambitious satellite mapping programme, bring us brilliant pictures of our personal and planetary environments. The marvels revealed by the Hubble telescope offer differing and elusive perspectives on the evolution of our universe and the knowledge that in a certain sense 'we are stardust'. All of which not only widens our scientific horizons but changes our self-perception. Which change is itself part of the 'growing end' of contemporary theological consciousness.

Systemic consciousness

This means that since he wrote, the religious freedom argued for by Courtney Murray is now set within a changed, because expanded, historical consciousness. For our history is now situated within the history of the whole Earth household. This new historical setting also changes moral consciousness, for our necessary acknowledgment of human dependence on the other members of Earth's household is at the same time an acknowledgment of their intrinsic value to the ecosystems which sustain both

10 Murray, J. C., *The Problem of Religious Freedom*, p. 505; p. 523.

us and them. In an historic twist in self-perception, as we come to know more and more about the complexity and diversity of those systems, our own intrinsic value to them is increasingly put in question. Rapley's sober statistics about agriculture and forestry make the point, as does the fact that our year-on-year global economic expansion, for instance, and the resultant increase in carbon emissions (around 200 tons of carbon burnt to produce $1,000 income) has affected world climate so adversely that most governments have agreed to the Kyoto Protocol, an international agreement which would legally bind their countries to cut greenhouse gas emissions.[11] Those involved realise that it doesn't make sense if our economic growth causes more damage than benefit: damage not only to ourselves, but to the planet which has to sustain that growth. There are no extra-terrestrial resources available to us, and projects mooted for finding them, such as terra-forming Mars, would only use up even more of this planet's resource base.

The negative impact of our economic infrastructure and consumerist lifestyles undermines theological arguments for our supreme dignity and, for its theological corollary, our God-given right to dominate the Earth household. Our dysfunctional behaviour within that household ill accords with that responsible use of freedom which would reasonably accord with that dignity. Can we honestly argue that we are worth more than any other creature to a planetary household created and sustained over billions of years, and that it exists for our sole use and benefit? Can we claim a divine mandate for our species' increase in numbers to such an extent that we consume a totally disproportionate amount of the household's resources? Can we invoke a 'God-given' right to exploit and abuse other species by claiming that human communities alone, and their relationships with one another, are all that 'count' before God? In other words, can we make a convincing claim to our right to destroy our own life-support systems? Not unless, earth system science says, we are compiling the longest suicide note in history . . . and making God countersign it.

Systemically all our interrelationships, and those with whom we share them, count as part of an interconnected physical and moral order. We can no longer see our well-being or our dignity as divorced in any real sense from that of the whole Earth household. How we live affects all its members and,

---

11 Rapley, C., *Earth System Analysis: Integrating the Human Factor into Geophysiology*, Gaia Circular, 1999, Vol 2, Issue 3.

measured along different axes and time-scales, their lives affect ours. This growing ecological consciousness reflects a shift in western historical consciousness evident in legal/political foundations, in government ministries and programmes devoted to 'the environment', and in listings for university courses and school curricula which now include courses on environmental law, environmental health, environmental ethics and environmental justice movements worldwide.

Theological listings, however, remain almost exclusively focussed on 'human-only' concerns, as do undergraduate and further education courses targeted on clergy and religious communities. Why so? Briefly, in traditional theology, geocentricity only emerges as anthropocentricity, and the change in self-perception required by ecological consciousness requires a revolution away from anthropocentricity. And in the course of that revolution, the traditional theological centre cannot hold. The fears inspired by the loss of this theological anthropocentricity, or even the suspicion of its loss, explain the absence of ecology from theological syllabuses. But if this continues, what happens to theological relevance in an ecologically conscious society? What happens to any organism, person or tradition which refuses to grow, which refuses to evolve?

Evolutionary history

The ecosystems within which all living organisms interact with their environments have evolved over many millions of years. The term evolution, whether applied to physical, environmental, communal or social entities, is generally understood as meaning change through time, change through which new life forms and environments gradually emerge, and healthy ecosystems are sustained which nourish the life potential of the whole Earth household. After Darwin, evolution usually focusses on a scientific description of the processes whereby organisms and their environments come into being and pass away. No species, including ours, can live outside these co-evolutionary processes or fail to contribute to them, positively or negatively. The widespread use of the term evolution and evidence of its concrete exigencies in, for example, developments in genetics and biotechnologies, constitute literally and figuratively one of the most visible 'growing ends' in contemporary consciousness.

However, for many Christians today, Darwin and his theories constitute as great a threat to human dignity as did Copernicus or Galileo. For the facts of evolution in relation to all species – that is, that all of them now living, including our own, may and do evolve from and into other species – signal the loss of the biblical notion that we are special because there is a sharp distinction between our creation by God (in God's image) and that of all other beings. And since our God-given supremacy over other beings rests on that distinction, to lose it is to lose our supremacy. So in 1999, in a decision forced through by Christian religious conservatives and supported by Roman Catholic bishops, the state of Kansas voted to remove most references to the theory of evolution from its new standards for science education from kindergarten through to high school.

This particular denial of our inclusion in an expanded Earth household and its moral order is unusually public. It usually takes the form of denial by omission. A quick glance at the indexes of most theological manuals will find no references to ecological and/or evolutionary consciousness, and those which do discuss the evolution of life in the universe do so as if nothing new has been discovered about it. Noting this, Karl Schmitz-Moormann accounts for it by pointing to the change in perspective required if theologians take evolution seriously. The importance of the biblical text changes, he says, from absolute to relative, since knowing what the first man and woman did (as if we did know!) does not tell us much about human beings today. Our evolving universe is marked by the slow but constant emergence of new realities, and the new cannot be deduced from the old: "Nobody who studies the earliest stages of the universe could write an algorithm that would lead with certainty to the existence of humans".[12] There are, of course, those who claim that God did write such an algorithm, but then that leaves us facing another set of problems about freewill, contingency and determinism.

All this is unsettling enough, but for traditional theology there is a greater challenge still. Darwin moved the timescale inferred for the evolution of our species back beyond any individual 'Adam' to a shadowy and uncertain past where we, as one species among others, cannot point, in any strict sense, to a

---

12 Schmitz-Moormann, K., *Theology of Creation in an Evolutionary World*, Cleveland, Pilgrim Press, 1997.

precise starting point for our own. 'Adam' ('earthling') was not, however much we might want to believe otherwise, put into the Earth household by God at a particular moment in time, in a pre-specified form and subject to specific rules of conduct. Yet western Christian theology and its cultural descendants have remained focussed on the antithetical relationship postulated between this putative individual and Christ. The range of theological enquiry has been reduced to whatever has been deduced, imagined, interpreted, defined and taught about the relationship between them and its import for the whole of human history. Theology has officially and effectively been reduced to salvation history with all that has meant for Church life, order, teaching and authority. But, evolution asks, salvation from what? And for whom?

Anthropocentricity and salvation

We are, we are told, saved by Christ from the bodily inheritance (sin) bequeathed us by Adam. His sin marked and marred every human being born after him, and left us lacking the ability to rescue ourselves from its effects, the most notable, it is averred, being death. Since the time of Augustine, mainstream Christianity has held that without Adam's sin, there would be no death.[13] But because Adam sinned and left us prey to the power of death, we need a saviour, Christ. The 'anthropo-logic' implies, indeed states, that we human beings were distinguished from all others by being created by God to live forever. Our salvation by Christ means that God's purpose stands, and that we alone, out of all species, are to be exempt from death.

However, our bodies die. So a further logical move is necessary. It is our souls which Christ rescues from death. They are the 'immortal' element in the human being, the element which distinguishes us absolutely from every other species. Our souls, reunited with our bodies, will live forever with God in an unearthly realm we call heaven. In this Platonic universe Christ saves us, ultimately, from being what we are: members of the whole Earth household.

Those other members who do not (according to us) share the distinction of having souls are nevertheless, we say, inextricably, and negatively bound by our history. They are condemned to eternal death because of what one

---

13 See my discussion of this in Primavesi, A., *From Apocalypse to Genesis: Ecology, Feminism and Christianity*, London, Burns and Oates, 1991.

member of our species did. In a fundamentalist version of this traditional doctrine, their condemnation is shared by the majority of our own species, since Christ saves only those who believe in him. All those who lived before him and those who live after him and who, for reasons of space and time, have no opportunity to believe in him, are not saved either. They are condemned to living death in the unearthly realm called Hell.

This is the merest outline of a central Christian doctrine, and would, I know, be hotly disputed in regard to some of its features by representatives of different theological schools. But its centrality rests on an undisputed exclusive claim: that we are saved from death by Christ. The claim is validated by locking it into the claim to human dignity, one based on our being created in the image of God. That image, we are told, is centred in the human soul. As no other species is ensouled, we are distinguished from all others. These claims interlock with and are used to validate our claim to be the centre of creation.

However as I argued in *From Apocalypse to Genesis*, a close reading of the biblical texts on which this claim is based (the first three chapters of Genesis) reveals no apple, no 'Fall', no use of the word 'sin'.[14] The tradition of reading these last two concepts back into the text has become so much part of Christianity as to be apparently unassailable. It remains so because it appears to answer some of our deepest questions, and indeed fears, about the nature of life and death, about human weakness and evil-doing, about our experience of suffering and our role in inflicting it. We find answers which are summed up eventually in Christ as *the* answer, as the one who saves us from weakness, evildoing, suffering and above all, death.

Revelation and earth system science

There is another major change in western cultural perception of our origins which has, potentially at least, altered historical and ecological consciousness of the landscape within which Christian theology is set. Earth system science moves the timescale of our evolution back still further: beyond our species to the evolution of the first living organisms on the planet. There, ultimately, lie the days of our infancy, days so far removed from us in time and in emergent

14 Primavesi, A., *From Apocalypse to Genesis*, Chapters 11 and 12.

processes as to distance us almost completely from those life forms from which we originated. These processes continue to regulate the temperature and composition of the Earth's surface, keeping it comfortable for life. They are driven by free energy available from sunlight, and this fact, once intuited and now increasingly understood through modern scientific technologies, makes us all, whether we like it or not, heliocentric. We share and depend on this energy in all its forms, and constantly metabolise it for ourselves and for each other.[15]

The evolution of the planet over a vast timescale (ca. 4.6 billion years) presupposes theologically that God's relationship with those who emerged to form the Earth household is commensurate with the same period. God did not wait to form this relationship until we emerged, nor did we dictate the form it took. We relate to God from within and as part of the 'growing end' of an existing bond. It is continuous with the long, variegated lineages within the Earth household, and we share enough of our habits, needs and abilities with other species there to reveal our common life source, contemporary kinship and interdependence. Stardust we may be, but star-trekking is not for us. We cannot survive naturally outside the world-mothering air of our planetary home.

Refocusing our self-perception in this way realigns our focus on the concept of revelation. Franz Rozenzweig's insight into the Genesis text shows the sequence of revelation following this pattern:

God spoke. That came third.
It was not the first thing.
The first thing was: God created.
God created the earth and the skies. That was the first thing.

The breath of God moved over the face of the waters:
over the darkness covering the face of the deep.
That was the second thing.

15 See Primavesi, A., *The Recovery of Wisdom: Gaia Theory and Environmental Policy* in Cooper, D. and Palmer, J. (eds.), *Spirit of the Environment: Religion, Value and Environmental Concern*, London, Routledge, 1998.

Then came the third thing.
God spoke.[16]

Taking this sequence seriously, one common to the biblical and Gaian accounts, we realise that we have long understood that God was not first revealed through speech. From 'the beginning' God was and is revealed through the processes of creating, through the evolution of the planet, its atmosphere, its life, its species. Here, in Rozenzweig's phrase, 'the shell of the mystery breaks'. And as it breaks, God's self is expressed, revealed throughout the processes we call evolution.

To whom, or to what is God's self revealed? To every living creature which emerges through co-evolutionary process and which responds to God 'according to its kind'. But not with words. The morning stars sang together, the heavens recited the glory of God, but *no speech, no words, no voice was heard.*[17]

This humbling recognition of the nature of revelation and of every living being's response to it has been obscured if not totally discounted by theological traditions which elevate the human soul to the cosmic place of honour, as the only one capable of receiving God's self expression and responding to it. Furthermore, they presuppose that God's self is expressed only in human words, and that that self was not revealed until someone spoke in God's name; until there was a human voice to utter and a human ear to hear; until there was a human intelligence to interpret and a human hand to record; until there was a human response to the mystery of God's self-expression.

Jesus is credited with an alternative view:

If they tell you,
Look! This presence is in the skies!
remember,
the birds who fly the skies have known this all along.

If they say,
It is in the seas!

---

16 Rozenzweig, F., *The Star of Redemption*, translated by Hallo, W., Indiana, University of Notre Dame Press, 1985, p. 112 f.
17 Psalm 19[3] (my italics).

remember,

the dolphins and fish have always known it.

It is not apart from you.

It wells up within each and surrounds all.[18]

Revelation within Christianity, however, has been consistently limited to human speech in such categorical statements as: *in many and various ways God spoke of old to our fathers by the prophets; but in these last days he has spoken to us by a Son.*[19] In the eponymous text, *Revelation*, it becomes 'the revelation of Jesus Christ', in which Jesus, a man, is the 'full' revelation of God, a 'fullness' made problematic since it is in fact confined by time, place, species, race and gender and defined as and in human male presence and language.[20]

Earth system science, however, appeals to us to exercise our theological freedom responsibly by recognising God's continuous revelation to the whole Earth household and positing a response from each creature within it. This does not exclude revelation in Jesus, nor make it less precious to those to whom it is offered. But it does humble us, in the positive Mediæval sense of containing us within our limits (*virtus humilitatis in hoc consistit ut aliquis infra suos terminos se continet*).[21] So contained, we do not extend ourselves into those things beyond our capacity. The ultimate arrogance in traditional views of revelation consists in the fact that by placing no limits on our own capacity to receive the full revelation of God, not only do we place limits on others' capacities and responses, but we have also (in intent if not in effect) limited God's capacity to reveal to our capacity to receive. We have forgotten Job's instructions to Zophar:

But ask the beasts, and they will teach you;

the birds of the air, and they will tell you;

or the plants of the earth, and they will teach you;

and the fish of the sea will declare to you.

18 Gospel of Thomas, Chapter 3 (translated by Primavesi, M).

19 Hebrews 1[1-2] (my italics).

20 Primavesi, A., *The Spirit of Genesis* in Bergmann, S. and Eidevall, G. (eds.), *Upptäckter i Kontexten*, Sigurd Bergmann and Göran Eidevall (eds.), Lund, Institutet för kontextuell teologi, 1995.

21 Quoted in Oberman, H., *The Dawn of the Reformation*, Edinburgh, T & T Clark, 1986, p. 187, note 21.

Who among all these does not know
that the hand of the Lord has done this?
In God's hand is the life of every living thing
and the breath of all humankind.[22]

I am not saying that the mystery we call God has not been revealed to us through human language, nor that what has been revealed in and by the life of Jesus is not central for Christians. I am saying that we cannot reduce the whole of that revelation to what has been expressed to us, or by us; nor indeed can we reduce that to what has been said by or to a particular group of human beings at any particular time or place.

I am also saying that contemporary earth system science's appeal to us to develop the doctrine of revelation is at the same time an appeal to recognise the dignity of every living creature. All life forms which emerged, flourished and died in the billions of years before our emergence were worthy of knowing God according to their kind. Does recognising their dignity diminish ours? Is it not rather the case that by exercising our freedom to accord them their own dignity, the dignity of the whole Earth household is enhanced? By respecting the limits of our own freedom, we respect the freedom of other creatures to exist in dignity, without coercion or exploitation. And by learning the interdependence of our own and others' dignity, we develop our capacity to live with them in non-coercive relationships . . . which would be a positive contribution to the 'growing end' of scientific and theological tradition.

22 Job 12 [7].

Chapter Three

Justification by Gender:
Daphne Hampson's *After Christianity*

Angela West

Introduction

I received my baptism into the feminist faith sometime in the late seventies. But by the end of the 1980's I had begun to understand that this liberating new vision was not in fact 'self-evident' to all women as I had been taught, but rather an extension of the logic of modernist orthodoxy to those women who had been newly schooled in its doctrines. It became evident on the contrary that the radical feminism of those times, especially that which cast off with contempt the whole garment of patriarchal Christianity, was not quite as original or radical as it claimed. It was in fact a new edition of what one might call 'modernist scholasticism'; its newness consisted mainly in the fact that it was undertaken by educated women rather than educated men. Thus, I began to see myself as a kind of heretic in relation to the body of radical feminist opinion (whose own self-understanding was to a large extent defined by a consciously 'heretical' stance in relation to orthodox Christian faith). Nevertheless, heretical feminist as I had become, my next move could be clearly identified as orthodox feminist practice – I wrote a book of feminist theology which drew upon the data of my own experience![1]

The point of this little parable (or complicated conundrum if you prefer) is to demonstrate what may be a platitude – that those of us for whom theory (of one sort or another) is our profession are nearly always subject to a besetting sin, the secret lust for the Last Word. And as is the nature of sin, I believe, it is not so much different in every respect from the good, but rather it is similar in all respects bar one – thus, a kind of mirror image. And yet this one respect

---

1 West, A., *Deadly Innocence: Feminism and the Mythology of Sin*, London, Cassell, 1995.

makes the difference total as is the difference between the real and the reflected. To search continually for a truer seeing, and to refuse to be satisfied with conventional reasons and reassurances – this is, as I understand it, what both faith and the search for enlightenment enjoin us to. But in the act of so doing, the craving to have the last word may subtly insinuate itself; the desire to set ourselves apart by the superior quality of our own seeing/theory sets a fatal trap for us.

The publication of a book can be seen as an important way of contributing to a debate. But it can also become an act of staking out intellectual territory and thereafter defending it. In my own case, I observe that after publication I did not take much part in any feminist theological debate. Now if anyone were to suggest that this was my own particular brand of 'last wordism', I would of course leap to my own defence. I would point to the special circumstances, invoke the personal limitations that constrained me. Nevertheless, I think the charge would stand. For behind all these genuine 'reasons' there lies the fact that deep down I had concluded that there wasn't much more to be said on that subject. I was persuaded, however, to write a review (reprinted here) of Daphne Hampson's book *After Christianity* which, from an opposing angle, sought to clinch the debate.[2] What I wrote then I still stand by. But the distance that I have come is this: that I can see how it also represents a 'staking out of territory' – an activity which, if one persists, becomes futile and unfruitful.

Recently, two 'events' have helped to move me on. Susan Parsons' book *Feminism and Christian Ethics* made me realise that the debate from which I had dropped out had moved on in my absence, blossomed in new and interesting ways, and put down firmer roots in the soil this side of the Atlantic.[3] I felt that this was a book that did not give ground to 'last wordism', and I trust that this new collection will continue that. The second thing that assisted this new perception was when I attended the funeral of the husband of a dear friend – herself a contributor to the Christian feminist story in UK. It was a traditional funeral – those who had responded to feminism's challenge to the faith mingled with those whom it had hardly touched. But on this

---

2   Hampson, D., *After Christianity*, London, SCM Press, 1996. [EDITOR'S NOTE: There is a reply to the original review article by Hampson, D., *A Reply to Angela West* in the *Scottish Journal of Theology*, 1998, Vol. 15, No. 1.]

3   Parsons, S. F., *Feminism and Christian Ethics*, Cambridge, Cambridge University Press, 1996.

occasion, as mourners we shared the same sadness, with the same tea and sandwiches. And mourners, as I saw, always get the last word. They use it to speak about when and where and how they shared with you (the deceased) the journey that is now ended.

And so to a last word for Daphne, though she may not hear it. For a theologian to leave the faith in which she has been formed (for better or for worse) is I think tragic, like a premature dying – a kind of suicide. To recognise and expose all the ways that Christianity has carried within itself a negation of itself, the idolatry within the true faith, is a most necessary task and deepest obligation for theologians. But the claim for a superior seeing that totally invalidates the preceding revelation is a recipe for theological destruction. Paradoxically, to do this is to show yourself a product of the virulent (and largely dominant) deformation of the Christian faith you have rejected. For thus did the Church reject Judaism, the Protestant Reformation reject the Catholic church, the Enlightenment reject Christian faith, and now the genealogical thought of postmodernism undermines the Enlightenment. And yet the outcome of this supersessionist incubus, the lust for the Last Word, has not been a great new vision, but massacre, genocide and cultural destitution. Hope for us all, I believe, lies in the rediscovery of orthodoxy at a deeper level. We need to return to our Judaic roots, and to the true sources of enlightenment and reform, and to the gospel as the real and only challenge to father-rule. But this challenge is to women as much as to men. To condemn all faith as a product of male fantasy is to treat women of faith as the eternal dupes of men – to manifest once again the teaching of contempt. The strange beauty of the Gospel convinces me that our equality with men is founded on our equal capacity for error and sin; the ultimate self-realisation is to know that we do not need to have the Last Word, and the great freedom it offers is 'the joy of being wrong' (see James Alison's book by this name).[4] By this faith, I am called not to the perfection of theory but to the awesome responsibility of witness, a kind of seeing, that is with consequences but without control. And to this faith I invite you to return – to rejoin the sisters in the service of the Word that does not bring ultimate separation. There is still time.

---

4   Alison, J., *The Joy of Being Wrong: Original Sin through Easter Eyes*, London, Crossroads, 1998.

After Christianity

In her book *After Christianity* Daphne Hampson continues to re-work her familiar theme – the dangerous irrelevance of the Christian 'myth' for the modern feminist self. Christianity, she says, lays claim to a unique historical revelation of God in Christ, which cannot be verified according to a modern scientific understanding, nor can it be ethically justified since it fails to uphold the central value of gender equality, but instead symbolically legitimates the oppression of women by men under the patriarchal system. Thus modern women, in search of a spirituality that accords with their new sense of self, should eschew Christianity in all its forms (including liberal or feminist ones) and develop their own spirituality predicated on the self and its fundamental autonomy. It is such a spirituality, rooted in her own experience and congruent with that of other modern women, that Hampson believes her own feminist-theist position to be, and of which she gives a detailed exposition in this book.

Hampson claims to relate her theology to the "social situatedness of women", and in assessing the success of her endeavour I think it would be helpful to refine it. Thus, it could be said that the book represents in particular the social situation of women entering the academic world of theology which has been closed to women in previous generations. This situation, I suggest, also represents a dilemma which is replicated in other areas of feminist advance. On the one hand women in this situation are subject to a desire to prove themselves to be expert players on equal terms and by the same rules as their male colleagues. On the other, suspecting that these very terms and rules may be subtly or not so subtly weighted against them, they are tempted to undermine the game and start again with a new set of rules – reversing if possible the bias.

As a feminist (though not an academic) I find this sociological dilemma a relevant one, and I also believe it has significant theological implications. However, I do not find Hampson's answer to it either appealing or true. This disagreement is threefold: it is partly with her own intellectual strategies and style, partly with the particular feminist doctrines she adopts to resolve it, and partly with the nature of the whole modernist myth to which these belong.

Fundamental to her project is a belief in the equality of women, which she regards as one of those 'self-evident truths' of modernity the meaning of which it is unnecessary to expound since everyone already understands it. Thus she makes no philosophical enquiry into her central value, in the light of which Christianity is found to be sadly inadequate. She refers us to no doctrines of equality since she is not a believer in doctrines, these being all part of the patriarchal past which she declares to be superseded. Thus she can confidently assert that: "Half of humanity, throughout the ages and in all cultures, has effectively been prevented from expressing its spiritual aspirations or its understanding of that which is God. Culture and religion have been male: formed by men with a 'place' for women".[5] But woman must resist this 'place' that has been prepared for her by men and seek instead self-actualisation, and mutual self-realisation.

What is ethical for women is to ground their religious understanding in their own experience, and to resist and expose the claims of the Christianity, whose scriptures serve to establish the worship of the paternal God and legitimate patriarchal authority.[6] For a woman's new "duty" is to have a sense of herself as independent agent, owing no allegiance to "heteronomous" male authority, and having her own subjectivity as the equal of man.[7] She considers the concept of complementarity between men and women as part of the male plot to structure women into the role of subordinate Other as is the celebration of "female" virtues like gentleness, receptivity, humility, nurturative abilities and, worst of all, obedience.[8] Women should not be deceived by patriarchy's attempt to make these an ideal for men also, or to project "female" roles and qualities on to the Godhead; this is all part of man's attempt to deny woman her own subjectivity, to cope with the male fear and envy of women, and to displace women by usurping their roles.

But if these roles (of feeding and nurturing, for example) 'belong' to woman, how is it that they are also part of the plot to subordinate her? Contradictions begin to emerge. Hampson castigates men for re-creating a "gendered social reality" in their theological speculations (as in the theology of the Trinity). Yet her own presentation of social reality is relentlessly and deliberately gendered, and it is difficult to avoid the suspicion of a double standard. If men's theology reflects their experience, it is to be exposed as merely the concerns of the male psyche, and the paradigms of Christian

5   Hampson, D., *After Christianity*, p. 65.
6   Hampson, D., *After Christianity*, p. 137.
7   Hampson, D., *After Christianity*, p. 200; see also p. 193.
8   Hampson, D., *After Christianity*, p. 192.

theology can be dismissed as merely the projection of the hopes and fears of men.[9] But if women reflect their experience in their theology, it is to be applauded as ethical and true.

Her illustration drawn from the history of Western art does indeed illustrate the nature of Hampson's perspective – perhaps rather more revealingly than she intended. Considering the sculpture in the Piazza della Signoria in Florence, she observes how most of the major statues portray murder, rape or the celebration of war and concludes that violence is normative in the construction of masculinity under patriarchy.[10] Thus, the scene of the near slaughter of Isaac by his father on the baptistery doors is appropriate for 'baptism' into the world of male religion, the securing of God-Father-Son genealogy. Yet she is satisfied to observe that Donatello's statue of Judith after the beheading of Holofernes is also present in this prestigious art parade, and its presence is somehow "subversive" – for it is now a woman who perpetrates the violence. Hampson applauds Donatello for "his unique capacity to depict women in their strength, the equals of men". In her pleasure at the inclusion of a female figure here, she temporarily forgets her feminist ethical distaste for the religion of violence.

Thus, it begins to seem that feminist ethics are not superior because they are better ethics but because women have them! Both sides must have as their goal the becoming of an autonomous individual, but it just so happens, according to Hampson, that women are much better at it than men. The chapter on Feminist Ethics is designed to demonstrate this. Thus, the male self is constituted by "difference" and "separation", the father-son relationship is angst-ridden and problematical. The male imagination is riveted by individual achievement, and he is fearful of both intimacy and isolation. Thus men have constructed human relations in a hierarchical mode, which is deeply competitive and fosters aggression. Women on the other hand have a self constituted by connection, are a self-in-relation, seek interdependent relations, are less violent, have permeable ego boundaries, have very well-integrated brains, do not want to master the other but create themselves, and seem painlessly and naturally to differentiate themselves from the mother (and presumably the father) without angst.[11] Or, as playground feminism has it:

9   Hampson, D., *After Christianity*, p. 119.
10 Hampson, D., *After Christianity*, pp. 85 f.
11 Hampson, D., *After Christianity*, p. 97.

What are little boys made of?
Slugs and snails and puppy dogs tails.
What are little girls made of?
Sugar and spice and all things nice.

The only slight snag is that because women have been so persistently and relentlessly 'nice' throughout the ages, men, it seems, have always been able to take advantage of them and been the dominant sex for as long as recorded history.

All feminist theory that relies on woman-as-perennial-victim suffers from a certain fatal flaw which could be expressed by a question from the uninitiated: why, if women have these superb brains and both the natural capacity and desire to co-operate with each other – why did they not just go ahead and get men off their backs and express their spiritual aspirations for perfect equality long ago? Surely, by the law of averages if nothing else, there would have been some epochs when the war of the sexes would have gone in women's favour? Why was this universally desired consummation delayed until modern times? Hampson is at pains to present the superior quality of women's ethical and psychological make-up yet at a loss (since she never attempts it) to explain why women have failed to achieve their goals until now; why, as she puts it, career women have no ancestors. Was it that there was something about female psychological make-up that made them unfitted for the rational functions of the ruling gender? An unacceptable suggestion. Or was there some new understanding of the nature of equality linked to the phenomenon of modernity that made women understand and seek their equality in new ways? This would raise difficult questions about doctrine vis-à-vis self-evident truth. Moreover, it would create the embarrassing suspicion that women (or at least some women) in order to by-pass the historical handicap of being female had decided to adopt the 'values of the male'. And this in turn might raise another awkward question: Is it the case that women of all ages have understood their spiritual aspirations to equality as being unimpeded access to the top jobs? From here it is a short step to believing that women can only 'prove' their equality when they get the top jobs. Thus being top equals being 'most equal'. But from the naive point of view, it might seem that the opposite is the case – those at the top are the least equal mainly because there are relatively few of them, male or female. It is not the minority but the majority, with their relative poverty and unfulfilled ambitions, that have the most 'equality' with their fellows. Could it be that it is the opportunity to prove quality rather than equality that Hampson's feminism requires? But this would of course imply a hierarchy of values, and such hierarchies, as she frequently reminds us, are part of the "masculinist perspective".

I think perhaps it is time to reconsider the standard feminist analysis of patriarchy as a system of male domination universally imposed on women without their consent. As Hampson herself observes, it is not part of women's nature to desire to suffer – like all humans she seeks to protect herself from suffering, and to seek material security. Given women's role as child bearer – inescapable until this century – her role was bound up with the fate of children, weaker and more vulnerable due to their undeveloped brains and bodies. In all societies it is 'natural' for the weaker to seek protection from the stronger, and not unique to women. Thus, patriarchy and its gender hierarchy could also be regarded as a traditional 'contract' between men and women by which a structure of reciprocal obligations between the sexes was endorsed.

As Hampson herself suggests, women do in fact desire reciprocity in their relations with men and it is clear that the nature of child-rearing absolutely requires a certain co-operation between the sexes. This of course is not to deny that the patriarchal compact has been very restrictive and indeed oppressive to women over the ages in many of the ways that feminists have already exhaustively catalogued. But it is to deny that women universally see the patriarchal contract as inimical to their interests or as that which simply renders them victims. History (as well as contemporary society) abounds with examples of women demonstrating their loyalty to this patriarchal structure of gender relations, and on occasions rising fiercely to its defence. It is hardly possible to demonstrate that women in all cases favour relations with their own sex, or that they 'naturally' prefer non-hierarchical, non-violent and egalitarian relations. Women have indeed seen themselves as 'selves-in-relation' – the ideal so ardently espoused by Hampson. But for a majority of women over the ages it has been herself in relation to her children and her menfolk, rather than to other women (who, needing protection themselves, could not offer the protection and material support a woman needed). Even if women identified with other women in their own community, they did not necessarily 'privilege' these relations, and as to identification with women outside their own community/culture/class, I would suspect that evidence for this is very sparse indeed. Women, like all human beings, prefer not to be the recipients of violence, but like other members of the species they are very often not at all averse to being part of a group that directs its violence away from itself to conveniently defined 'outsiders', even when these are in fact within the same society. It has been part of the 'role' of women not to be personal perpetrators of this 'necessary' violence, but to endorse it, sometimes even to manipulate it, but above all to embody the 'value' of the community in the name of which the violence is undertaken. It is clear (to me at least) that women have frequently fulfilled this role without any sense of that frustrated spiritual aspiration that Hampson points to, nor shown a deep resentment of the hierarchical relations in which they are located, for this hierarchy has been seen by them as the guarantee of reciprocal relations with men that they desire and the material support and protection from violence that they need. One way of regarding this state of affairs (if we can pardon its non-inclusive language) is expressed by the old cracker joke:

Question: Why has the war of the sexes never been won?
Answer: Because there is always too much fraternisation with the other side!

If one challenges the view that all women experience themselves as victims of patriarchy, since they have an 'interest' in the system, one still needs to explain why some women (and indeed some men) are much more victimised by it than others. It is evident from her writing that Hampson considers the situation and consciousness of modern women to be in some sense unique and unprecedented, and here I would agree with her. But I find her account of what it is that makes us specifically 'modern' to be seriously defective. Her understanding of her own relation to the past is, it seems, extraordinarily 'optional'. Thus although she recognises that as human beings we stand in some already constituted relation to the past, she appears to believe that we are not in any way defined, conditioned or constituted by that past; we can raid our past for 'gold nuggets' of truth if we wish, but equally we can turn away from the dross of the past and make a leap into the unconditioned future.[12] The idea that the very structure of our perception, the way we see the 'facts' of the natural and social world, is heavily determined by our particular social and cultural past, and our location in the economic system is one that she does

---

12 Hampson, D., *After Christianity*, see p. 53.

not appear to accept. Yet, her writing, it seems to me, provides rather compelling evidence that this is the case.

From the seventeenth century onwards, our view of the world has been shaped by a cumulative rejection of the Aristotelian perspective of the character of the natural and social world. It is this, in many respects, which characterises modern consciousness. Thus, the first thinkers of the Enlightenment proclaimed themselves 'modern' in relation to the unenlightened Middle Ages, because they believed they had "stripped away interpretation and theory and confronted fact and experience just as they are".[13] Thus, they could see goodness and truth for themselves and had no more need of the Christian claim to 'revelation' with the hierarchy of patriarchal priesthood as its apparently unalterable accompaniment. On the political front, this revolutionary perception was played out in the cataclysmic events of the French Revolution, with its associated ideals of liberty, equality and fraternity, and in the founding of the USA as a republic proclaiming these 'self-evident' truths.

Thus, in the intellectual revolution and founding historical events of modernity, the challenge to father-rule (patriarchy) was begun by the sons. Symbolically speaking it was a band of brothers who proclaimed the identity of interest of all the enslaved, calling them to rise up and overthrow their masters and establish the republic – the state of the common good. Yet, when the dust had settled it was clear that this new state of liberal democracy that celebrated the rights and freedom of the individual in fact represented the triumph of a particular class of men. And feminism initiated by Wollstonecraft, which Hampson is heir to, could be seen as the sisters getting in on the act. To castigate the mystifications of theology and the crimes of priestcraft is to pay one's dues and receive the password into the New Mysteries of the Enlightened Ones. The marks of Hampson's intellectual paternity are clear to see in her dedication to the self-evident truth of equality – and also identity, women identifying with women. As Alasdair MacIntyre says of the revolution of the brothers, the belief that they could *see* the facts of the natural and social world without any need for interpretation (such as Aristotle had provided) was a kind of necessary fiction. This myth was "the sign of an unacknowledged and unrecognised transition from one stance of

---

13 MacIntyre, A., *After Virtue: a Study in Moral Theory*, London, Duckworth, 1981, p. 78.

theoretical interpretation to another".[14] Thus, the Enlightenment, as he goes on to say, "is consequently the period par excellence in which most intellectuals lack self-knowledge" and in which "the blind acclaim their own vision".

Hampson considers herself to be a dab hand at dating old churches and cathedrals from their architectural styles.[15] But the idea that the self might also be a kind of 'construction', dateable from the form and nature of its utterances, clearly does not appeal to her. Yet, could it be that she embodies this distinctive feature of the Enlightenment intellectual: the lack of self-knowledge, a self-ignorance that is necessitated by the nature of the intellectual project that she has set herself? For her aim is to show decisively that Christianity can no longer be accepted as the foundation for moral discourse or dictate ethical imperatives for (thinking) women. Thus, like a whole series of Enlightenment philosophers before her, she sets out to produce a new basis for ethics. Hampson is aware of MacIntyre's contention in his book *After Virtue* that the project of providing a rational vindication of morality has decisively failed.[16] But she feels that his conclusions are inapplicable to her project because these previous attempts were undertaken by men, and therefore, according to her reasoning, fatally flawed by their patriarchal presumptions.

Thus she can proceed, justified by her own creed of the equality of women. But what this 'equality' of women appears to mean in this context is that women are in fact not equal but morally – if not mentally – superior. Thus, she implies that women are capable of making common cause with all other women and promoting the 'interests' of women (in general) as opposed to those of their particular class, race, nation, family etc. Since it is very evident that men do not do this, why should we believe that women are collectively capable of it? There is something very arbitrary about grounding one's ethics in an implicit doctrine of the superior morality of women. It is tantamount to a faith in justification by gender. Thus her project becomes a classic example of the theory of ideology – that is the disguised expression of arbitrary prefer-ence – and exemplifies the problem that Nietzsche identified, i.e. that if there is nothing to morality but expressions of will, then my morality can only be

14 MacIntyre, A., *After Virtue*, p. 78.
15 Hampson, D., *After Christianity*, p. 82.
16 MacIntyre, A., *After Virtue*, p. 48.

what my will creates.[17] Hampson describes her feminism as "legislative".[18] But she does not consider the problem of what happens, for example, when two feminists want to 'legislate' different feminist ethics. If morality is just the (disguised) expression of my will, then the whole idea of the rationally justified moral subject, on which Hampson bases her ethics, is also a fiction.

The implicit arbitrary ascription of greater virtue to women is redolent of the structure of the eighteenth and nineteenth century bourgeois concept of male-female relations, whereby men were licensed to be active (and risk moral contamination) in the 'real' world of politics etc, while women were largely confined to the domestic sphere, where their role was to be the innocent guardians of certain altruistic values that it was difficult or inconvenient to apply to the male sphere. This ideal of feminine virtue has been remorselessly (and rightly) critiqued by feminists, but there has been insufficient attention to the class and racial basis of this ideal, and an unwillingness to recognise that women of the bourgeois class for the most part willingly colluded in the myth. This was not because they were specially sinful, but because they were normally so and showed a normal instinct to look after their own interests. Many women may have resented or suffered under the constraints of their position, especially those who were not so rich or good-looking, not heterosexually inclined, or on the contrary, those who were particularly intelligent or had an intellectual bent. But there isn't a lot of evidence to suggest that the average Lady Jane was full of frustrated aspirations to a spiritual equality with Mary Jane, with whom she might make common cause against the men who imposed on them a 'male' God.

Thus, as we look behind the grand Enlightenment façade of the universal equality of women that motivates Hampson's feminism, it becomes clear that this is in fact rather a particular story – quite as particular in its way as the scandalous particularity of the Christian gospel which she finds so offensive. It is, at least in part, the story of the attempt by bourgeois women intellectuals to scale the academic citadel and to take their rightful place within its foundational myth. The exaltation of a feminist 'spiritual' perspective and the 'shaming' critique of masculinist modes should not be taken at their face value, but rather as a kind of smokescreen which obscures the deal that is being struck behind the ideal. To appreciate its precise nature we have to

17 MacIntyre, A., *After Virtue*, p. 104; p. 107.
18 Hampson, D., *After Christianity*, p. 84.

penetrate a little further. One of the consequences of the Enlightenment's failure to offer what religion had previously provided, a shared foundation for moral discourse and action, has been that philosophy has lost its central cultural role and become a marginal, narrowly academic subject.[19] The feminism of the 1970's and 1980's, however, gave the impression of being a return of popular interest in 'philosophical' questions such as equality. Thus, to bourgeois women, whose changing social position allowed them for the first time to contemplate seriously entry into academic and intellectual life, it was an opportunity to bring something of value to the negotiating table at which they might otherwise seem rather disadvantaged. So what feminists engaging in theology and philosophy had to offer academia was the prospect of reawakened 'popular' interest in a rather shrunken academic discipline (hence new students) and what academia had to offer feminists was the opportunity for selected individuals to find a secure niche in the higher echelons of the academic hierarchy.

This analysis may seem at first rather cynical. But I think it is necessary to understand why much of the form of feminism in the last twenty years could be seen as the product of a 'Brainy Women's Charter' and why this is not necessarily the only form of feminism, or the only way to understand gender equality or our fundamental equality before God. It also helps to explain,I think, why Hampson shows no inclination to explore the negative side of the ideal of equality she so enthusiastically presents. She seems to be unaware that her much-prized sense of subjectivity could be seen as part of the process by which the class relations of the capitalist market are legitimised, and the notion of equality as a cloak for that fearful 'dumbing down' by the mechanism of the market of all those who fail to make it to 'equality'. As Terry Eagleton says in his critique of certain anti-elitist critics, they "fail to notice that the most formidably anti-elitist force in modern capitalist societies is known as the market place which levels all distinctions, garbles all grada- tions, and buries all distinctions of use-value beneath the abstract equality of exchange value".[20] In experiential terms, one could say that the God of Equality which Hampson worships rewards a favoured few of its devotees and leaves the rest harried, bullied and stressed, at the bottom of the heap, whether the heap is McDonalds or an academic institution. Since there is now no

---

19 MacIntyre, A., *After Virtue*, p. 48.
20 Eagleton, T., *The Illusions of Postmodernism*, Oxford, Blackwell, 1996, pp. 95 f.

legitimation of a hierarchy in which even the lowest place has *some* value, relative poverty or lowliness has no dignity, and everybody is forced to maintain the illusion of striving for 'equality' thus keeping up the oppressive pressure on everybody else. Hampson herself admits that she has witnessed fierce academic wrangling among feminists, but concludes that it is only among Christian feminists who are "more prone to insecurity because of their minority position"![21] But this would apply to feminist or female academics of all sorts, and I suspect that there is evidence to suggest that these, like male colleagues, are not immune to wrangling. A more credible explanation for the fierce bitterness between 'seekers of equality' in academia and elsewhere, I think, lies in precisely that culture of self-actualisation that Hampson so fervently espouses.

Though, like Hampson, I deeply value the greater intellectual freedom available to women, and the increased opportunity for them to participate in all areas of national life, I do not assume that the mere fact of their increased presence is a force for good. For women are not 'justified' by their gender. If it is true that more women than ever before are gaining access to positions of relative power and influence, it is also true that they are just as capable as men of abusing it. My quarrel is with a type of feminism which makes an implicit identification with the modes and privileges of ruling-class males, while maintaining an explicit identification with the disadvantaged female majority. The failure to acknowledge 'equality of ambition' with class brothers is as dishonest as the co-option of the suffering of sisters whose burden of disadvantage most feminists do not share.

Hampson believes that she has refuted the outmoded and irredeemably compromised claims of the Christian gospel. I suggest rather that she has interpreted the gospel according to her own narrow ideological focus, and echoed a polemic against it that has already been well-established for generations. She believes herself to be part of the 'revolutionary' movement of feminism, but her 'radical' rhetoric masks a profound accommodation with the status quo. She is indeed part of the successful revolt against the patriarchy of Aristotle whereby Enlightenment intellectuals believed that they could read off the 'facts' of reality, and the self-evident truths of experience. Those who commanded this revolt established the narrative of the autonomous rational self, and this became the orthodoxy of the class who masterminded

21 Hampson, D., *After Christianity*, p. 258.

the revolution. In place of the authority of scripture and spiritual traditions of wisdom, they asserted a discourse in which only knowledge derived from the work of the mind on the evidence of the senses was counted as real.

But what these intellectuals counted as truth can also be interpreted as a one-eyed vision, with its own particular blind-spots. The fearful consequences of its instrumentalist world view have only now in the twentieth century become fully apparent, as the rampant monoculture of profit lays waste the earth, and the anarchic play of market forces reduces the majority of its inhabitants to the slavery of debt. It was part of the understanding of Christian Scriptures that, mystified as we are by the structures of power, we do not see truth clearly but 'through a glass darkly'. Revelation can be understood as the 'blessed vision' of those rare souls who were able to penetrate the barrier of mystification, and the encoding of their wisdom through the generations to correct the flawed perception of our mystified senses. Thus, true vision is a seeing with two eyes – the eye of the mind and the senses, and the eye of wisdom we derive from our spiritual tradition.

Hampson rejects the conclusions of theologians as being the mere projections of the male mind; but ignores the fact that until very recently science was also the work of a largely male confraternity. Unlike Mary Midgley, she would not presume to detect any residue of male fantasy lurking in the ambitions of scientific knowledge. Nor apparently does she see it as part of the role of a radical intellectual to keep a critical watch over the pronouncements of these latest denizens of the authoritative claims department, whose power over the public imagination far exceeds that of theologians these days. Scientists have articulated the laws of the universe, and no breach of them can be entertained not even by God, indeed specially not by Him! – this is her reason for rejecting the Resurrection. The causal nexus is paramount and all such mysteries are to be disallowed. And yet, as science explores the workings of the universe under ever more extreme conditions, and reveals even space and time to be only the 'surface' of reality, it seems that science may not be able to play the role she assigns it – as guarantor of ultimate common sense and ordinary logic. Its conclusions may be as strange or as mysterious as the Resurrection appears to us now, and capable of inspiring us with a renewed sense of wonder and humility. But Hampson has made clear that she has no time for the virtue of humility, which is all part of the Christian patriarchal plot to deny the subjectivity of women.

Yet, perhaps humility may turn out to be the key ingredient of all intellectual endeavour without which we are in danger of producing a mirror-image of those whose spiritual arrogance we criticise, and in whose absence we can only impose the narrow vision of our own self-image and the class, race and gender mythology that have produced it.

Thus, Hampson has modernised the classic myth of women's superior moral sensibility, which emerged in tandem with the discourse of the autonomous rational self. But ironically, she has done it just at that time when this orthodoxy of the autonomous self is itself under threat. As she nails her colours to the mast of modernity, she may be boarding the Titanic. For the radically subjective approach to values which she favours has left the state as arbiter of value, and contributed to the emergence of the postmodern self of late consumer capitalism, where faith in the grand narratives of justifying reason (to which feminism belongs) is undermined. The new generation of women at the top, or aspiring to it, may well agree with her that the old-style patriarchal covenant between the sexes is no longer applicable for them. Yet as the novelty of being the 'bright girls in the boys' world' begins to wear off a bit, they still face the old question of how to collaborate (as well as compete) with male counterparts successfully. The evidence suggests that the feminism of the gender-damage-claim variety which Hampson advocates is losing its appeal, and a majority of women do not, on the whole, want to have an imaginary purity or moral superiority imputed to them. They want rather to be judged according to some sort of commonly agreed standards, which nevertheless do not privilege the male. And for many other women whose goal is not necessarily to reach the top, I suspect, her feminist ethics may seem inappropriate to their needs. As for those who long for God, they may well decide that God-as-a-dimension of the Hampson self does not answer their hunger for spiritual ecstasy and consolation.

Yet, Hampson might with some reason claim that her God-as-a-dimension-of–the–Self religion is well suited to the needs of the postmodern identity that shops around for a suitable personal spirituality; and her dismissal of all Christian theology as 'therapy for men' accords with its anti-authoritarian mood. But as she musters considerable scholarly erudition to 'see off' the Christian myth as irrelevant to modern woman, she could be in danger of sinking the very ship she sails on. In a rather revealing jest, she fantasises herself in heavenly conversations with her beloved Schleiermacher, or envisages Barth's posthumous conversion to her own version of religious truth. Yet it doesn't seem to occur to her, that if theology is an irrelevant activity, so are all these kind of conversations, and we shall have no need of that sort of theological erudition that she has laboriously acquired and proudly displays. We shall only need the occasional ideological entrepreneur to spice up people's personal spirituality – and these can exist as well or better outside the academic citadel.

Hence, the whole basis of the deal that feminist theology struck with academic philosophy is seriously under threat in the long run, as equally doomed to irrelevance as its predecessor.

And in the sober morning-after of the Enlightenment, we may be forced to realise that we have jettisoned those theological traditions of interpretation which contain the only key with the power to release us from the hermetically sealed ignorance of the modernist (and postmodernist) self.

In the New Testament, Christ instructs his disciples not to adopt the values of 'the world' – that system of kinship, patronage and status that resembles what feminists have termed patriarchy. Cutting across the assumptions and basis of this system, he calls for a community where no man is to be called father; and no woman to be valued for her childbearing role or the performance of kinship or gender obligations, but judged solely on the extent to which she has done the will of God. The poor are to be considered as God's own favourites, and capable of giving more to God than all the contributions of the rich. Those who hold power and authority are instructed not to lord it over each other but to wash the feet of those they serve. And the fate of the abusers of spiritual power is portrayed by the terrifying metaphor of drowning by millstone. The icon of God that the Christian drama reveals is not that of the divine ruler, but as the victim of violence, condemned by the mob and judicially murdered by the religious and political authorities. Could it be that the critique of patriarchy that we find in the gospels is far more radical than the one Hampson proposes?

It has been part of the radical potential of feminist thinking to summon women from out of the complex pattern of their allegiance to 'the world' based on class, race, generation and kinship and to re-evaluate the bond of gender with other women regardless of these factors. Feminism of the sort that Hampson advocates trades on this identification but ultimately betrays it. Her response to the biblical story of Ruth and Naomi seems to me to encapsulate the one-eyed nature of her vision. She does not see what might be 'evident' to some feminists – the bonding of two women in spite of patriarchal norms that prescribe their natural rivalry – their love, collaboration and courage as Ruth returns with her mother-in-law to a foreign country where she risks rape, destitution and death, rather than returning to the relative security of her own kin. Hampson sees only that Ruth is an unsuitable role model for feminists with a career to uphold, since she might be used by men to suggest that the work of caring for elderly relatives (and other such unworthy toil) is the duty only of women.

By proclaiming a false absolution of women from any collusion with the sinful structures of the world, Hampson returns feminist thought to a new version of class captivity. For our equality before God signifies more than a change of style and the balance of gender among the academic and other Western élites. As self-appointed priest of the religion of autonomy, she dismisses the discourse of previous theologians and presents instead herself as model of emancipated womanhood who can 'legislate' for us with her own newly-minted theism and ethics. But this is no gospel of freedom for women like Ruth and Naomi, the gleaners and trashpickers of history, now doubly enslaved by the fearful burden of global debt. It is a baleful heresy whose legacy has mortgaged the ultimate future of all women and their children, and crippled and confined our theological imagination. Only when we rediscover that in Christ such debts of sin are paid and must be remitted, shall we be free to re-image and proclaim the gospel of redemption. Then too will we understand that Resurrection is not merely a mega-miracle to confound the scientists and rival their achievements. Rather it is the down-payment of God on the promise that the torturer will not have the final triumph over his victim, and death by oppression will not be the last word.

Chapter Four

The Rehabilitation of Eve:
British 'Christian Women's' Theology
1972–1990

Jenny Daggers

This paper concerns the emergence of distinctive theological writings from a British Christian women's movement, which was active during the 1970's and 1980's, and which is documented in the Christian Women's Information and Resources (CWIRES) archive. The archive was collected by the CWIRES project in Oxford, between 1979 and 1991.[1] In this article I refer to the years 1979 to 1990 as 'the CWIRES period', and to the years 1972 to 1978 as 'the pre-CWIRES period'.[2] My analysis concerns Christian women who chose to associate themselves with this 'Christian Women's Movement' [hereafter abbreviated CWM – Editor], or who sympathised with its aims.

The context of 'Christian women's' theology

The significance of the CWM's context is that its theology reflects the central concern of the movement – namely change in the position of women in the churches. This concern is evident in the initial publicity leaflet issued by the

---

1 The CWIRES archive is now housed in the John Rylands University Library, in central Manchester. References made in this article to unpublished material held in the CWIRES archive include CWIRES accession information.
2 The time period of my research is determined by the end date of the CWIRES project, finishing at the neat cut-off point of 1990. My analysis therefore does not extend to developments in 'Christian Women's' theology after this date.

CWIRES project, which commented on "the number of people working for change in the position of women in the church".[3]

During the pre-CWIRES years, this concern with the position of women grew within four distinct currents in the churches: post-Vatican II Catholic renewal; the World Council of Churches, Community of Women and Men in the Church programme (WCC CWMC); Catholic and Anglican women's ordination debates; and radical Christianity. During 1978, groups active within the four currents came to see themselves as part of a wider common project. With the launch of CWIRES a single CWM became evident, comprised of groups which had emerged within the four currents.

The Anglican women's ordination debate became a significant focal point around which the CWM cohered. The 1978 tour of British churches by Canon Sr Mary Michael of the American Episcopal Church and the July 1978 vigil outside the Lambeth Conference were occasions where groups across the four currents in the churches acted in solidarity with Anglican campaigners.[4]

In the pre-CWIRES years, reinvigorated 'first-wave' Church feminism provided the major impetus within the first three currents – post-Vatican II Catholic renewal, the WCC CWMC programme, and the women's ordination debate; while 'second-wave' Christian feminism developed in pre-CWIRES radical Christianity and later spread throughout the CWM.[5] By 1984, when

---

3   CWIRS [subsequently CWIRES] Trustees and Working Group, publicity leaflet [CW unlisted], 1979. This widespread concern prompted Sara Maitland's research, later published as Maitland, S., *Map of the New Country: Women and Christianity*, London, Routledge, 1983.

4   See for evidence of widespread ecumenical involvement in Canon Sr. Mary Michael's tour: Champion, F. and Kroll, U. (eds.), *Churchwomanship in a Man's World*, in *Christian Action Journal* (Supplement), Spring 1978; *Christian Parity Group Newsletter*, 1978, Nos. 1-2 and 4-6; Burn, C. *et al.*, Christian Parity Group, *Celebrate a Whole Priesthood: information sheet concerning the July 1978 Lambeth Conference Vigil*; *Women Speaking*, 1978, No. 10. For documentation of ecumenical support for the vigil see Christian Parity Group, *Celebrate*.

5   'First-wave' feminism refers to the rise of a modern feminist movement in Britain and North America, frequently seen as originating with the publication of *A Vindication of the Rights of Women* by Mary Wollstonecraft in 1792, and culminating with the granting of the vote to women in 1918. 'Second-wave' feminism refers to the twentieth century women's movement, which rose during the 1960's and crested during the early 1980's. Heeney coined the term 'Church feminism', to refer to demands for the involvement of women in the government and ministry of the Church of England arising from the 'first-wave' women's movement. Heeney, B., *The Women's Movement in the Church of England,*

the Catholic Women's Network and the (Anglican) Women in Theology network were formed, 'second-wave' Christian feminist consciousness was widely diffused within the CWM.

Two features of 'first-wave' Church feminism are significant for analysis of the CWM of the 1970's and 1980's. Firstly, 'first-wave' Church feminism argued for a full inclusion of women in the life of the churches. Secondly, this case was argued in terms of 'spiritual womanhood', a term that refers to the Victorian reshaping of eighteenth century cultural constructions of femininity, which attributed superior spiritual qualities and therefore moral responsibilities to women, as opposed to men. Victorian women used spiritual womanhood to subvert women's domestic confinement by creating the Victorian female civilising mission within wider society. Church feminism was, in effect, an attempt to direct the female mission within the institutional churches, by arguing that women would bring particular spiritual and moral qualities to the ministry. Both features recurred in, and persisted throughout, the CWM of the 1970's and 1980's.

However, 'second-wave' feminism added new elements to reinvigorated 'first-wave' claims that obstacles blocking women's access to educational institutions be removed and that women be fully included in the professions – a claim that extended to church ministry. A new 'second-wave' focus on women's autonomy, mutuality and sexuality made a decisive challenge to lingering effects of spiritual womanhood, as perpetuated in the association of women with purity and in the attribution of principal responsibility for nurture and caring to women. This focus on women's autonomy, mutuality and sexuality was a common characteristic of feminist consciousness within the British 'second-wave' women's movement, including 'second-wave' Christian feminism.

In sum, in the British CWM, old 'first-wave' and new 'second-wave' Christian feminisms co-existed. 'Second-wave' Christian feminism infused

---

1850–1930, Oxford, Clarendon, 1988, pp. 101 f. There is also evidence of an equivalent 'first-wave' Catholic Church feminism in the publication in 1915 of *Ecce Mater* by Mildred Tuker and of *Christian Feminism: a Charter of Rights and Duties* by Margaret Fletcher (see for full references Inkpin, J. D. F., *Combatting the 'Sin of Self-Sacrifice?': Christian Feminism in the Women's Suffrage Struggle, 1903-1918*, unpublished Ph D thesis for the University of Durham, 1996: pp. 242 f.; p. 252); and in the 1911 formation of the Catholic Women's Suffrage Society, from which the St. Joan's International Alliance was to develop.

the central project of the CWM that women be fully included in the institutional churches, and influenced the way in which that project was articulated, while never displacing the central direction of that project which was towards change in the institutional churches.[6] By the CWIRES period, the Catholic Women's Network and Women in Theology combined a commitment to reformist activism within the institutional churches with a 'second-wave' Christian feminist consciousness. 'Second-wave' consciousness found expression in the liturgical life and feminist theological education of each network, both individually and in co-operation.

The CWM's project as a "rehabilitation of Eve"

Writing in a pamphlet published during Canon Sr Mary Michael's visit, Diana Collins argued for "the rehabilitation of Eve".[7] Collins' purpose was to argue that the Anglican ordination of women would infuse the church with a new creativity.[8] She portrayed the Eve of the Genesis myth as an instrument of a new consciousness, in which sexuality and spirituality are associated.[9] Collins was the first to link Eve with contemporary women, and with a positive assertion of women's sexuality. This theme was developed in subsequent writings arising in the context of the Anglican ordination debate.

Further, the figure of Eve as emblem of contemporary 'Christian women', who made a positive assertion of women's sexuality, became current throughout the CWM, being increasingly linked with assertions of women's capacity for autonomy within community where mutuality is practised, as opposed to women's subordination within male-controlled hierarchy. Women's autonomy, mutuality and sexuality were connected, and the reconfigured 'Christian women's' Eve epitomised this three-fold focus of 'second-wave' feminist consciousness.

---

6 See my *The Emergence of Feminist Theology from Christian Feminism in Britain*, in Methuen, C. (ed.), *European Society of Women in Theological Research Yearbook 1999*, Leuven, Peeters, for a brief analysis of the component groups constituting the CWM.
7 Collins, D., *The Rehabilitation of Eve*, in Champion, F. and Kroll, U. (eds.), *Churchwomanship*, pp. 4 f.
8 Collins, D., *Eve*, p. 5.
9 Collins, D., *Eve*, p. 5.

There is also a sense in which 'Christian women's' explorations of women's positive sexuality, autonomy and mutuality imply the figure of Eve, even where no explicit reference appears. I will briefly illustrate the Anglican development of the Eve theme, both explicit and implicit, and its echoing elsewhere in the CWM, before moving on to discuss the expression of the Eve theme in 'Christian women's' theology.

Susan Dowell and Linda Hurcombe, in naming their book about women and Christianity *Dispossessed Daughters of Eve*, stress the link between the current dispossession of contemporary women within the Church of England, and traditional Christian identification of women as "daughters of Eve".[10] In contrast, Susan Ashbrook Harvey argues that Eve/Mary images simultaneously confine women by defining them, and empower women as "'dispossessed daughters of Eve' to battle against or with" these images.[11] Harvey thus suggests an empowering potential for women in images of Eve and Mary.

However, Anglican women, such as Monica Furlong, made a decisive repudiation of Mary in favour of a chosen identification with Eve. When members of the Movement for the Ordination of Women (MOW) dramatic group, following their production entitled *After Eve*, named themselves *Eve's Lot*, their chosen identification expressed Anglican women's decisive rejection of what Furlong perceived as the continuing "stigma of Eve".[12]

It is clear that negative male perceptions of women's sexuality, which became evident in the course of the ordination debate, affected Furlong's option for Eve.[13] Also in response to the Anglican ordination debate, Gillian Court urged that the time had now come for men and women to face questions of the use and abuse of sexual power, and for women to declare a positive sexuality.[14] Furlong emphasises the constriction imposed on women by the male-defined duality in which women are depicted as either depraved or

10 Dowell, S. and Hurcombe, L., *Dispossessed Daughters of Eve: Faith and Feminism* (Second Edition), London, SPCK, 1987 [1981].
11 Harvey, S. A., *Eve and Mary: Images of Women*, paper to 1981 Modern Churchman's Union Conference, Birmingham, unpublished, 1981[CW G5 Acc 399].
12 Furlong, M. (ed.), *Mirror to the Church*, London, SPCK, 1988, p. 1. Concerning *Eve's Lot*, see *Movement for the Ordination of Women Newsletter*: 1982, No. 8, pp. 20 f.; 1982, No9, p. 16.
13 Furlong, M. (ed.), *Feminine in the Church*, London, SPCK, 1984, pp. 1 f. See also Furlong, M. (ed.), *Mirror*, pp. 7 ff.
14 Court, G., *Women and Ordination*, London, unpublished, 1979 [CW F110 Acc 1453], p.5.

pure.[15] Her key insight is that the placing of 'pure' woman on a pedestal conceals a 'profound hostility' to women.[16] Inherent in Furlong's argument is the conviction that women, now coming to voice and protesting against their prior silence and invisibility, cannot avoid repudiating purity in favour of the declaration of a positive sexuality as advocated by Court: the limited potential of the pedestal has by now been fully exploited.[17]

The declaration of a positive sexuality, with its repudiation of women's superior purity, signals the infusion of 'second-wave' Christian feminist consciousness within reinvigorated 'first-wave' Church feminism. Furlong makes a decisive challenge to lingering notions of spiritual womanhood as the grounds on which women request their full inclusion within the life of the Anglican Church. The choice of Eve, rather than Mary, as figure of the priorities and passions of contemporary 'Christian women', signals the emergence of 'second-wave' Christian feminism.

Although Janet Morley makes no explicit reference to Eve, she develops the (Genesis-derived) theme of women as in the image of God in her liturgical writings. When Morley moves from women as image of God to recovery of the neglected tradition of imaging God through the feminine, viewing sexuality as suggestive of language for addressing God, she writes in full awareness of the link between Eve and exploration of sexuality within the Anglican ordination debate.[18] Morley contributed to both of Furlong's collections, was present when Harvey gave her conference address, and would be aware of Dowell and Hurcombe's book. I suggest, therefore, that the Anglican identification between contemporary women and Eve is implied in Morley's notion of women in the image of God, and that there is an implied reconfiguration of Eve as positive model for contemporary women in Morley's treatment of women in the image of God.

Given the pivotal role played by the Anglican ordination campaign in the formation of a single CWM, the identification between Eve and contemporary 'Christian women' gained currency outside the Anglican debate. Thus, in an early editorial to the *Catholic Women's Network Newsletter*, Pat Pinsent comments that "Eve is re-examining her role!", so identifying Eve with

---

15 Furlong, M. (ed.), *Mirror*, p. 5.
16 Furlong, M. (ed.), *Feminine*, pp. 1 f.
17 Furlong, M. (ed.), *Feminine*, pp. 1 f.; *Mirror*.
18 Morley, J., *All Desires Known*, London, WIT and MOW, 1988, p. 5.

contemporary women active in the Catholic Women's Network.[19] Pinsent reconfigures Eve as a figure of the Catholic 'Christian women' who are re-examining their role in the church. Pinsent thus reiterates, in Catholic form, the Anglican Eve, figure of women's positive sexuality.

Other references linking Eve and contemporary 'Christian women' are made by Ruth Windle, the first woman to be ordained as a Methodist minister, and in papers for the Oxford Women's Theology Seminar, *The Mask of Eve* and *On Eve*.[20] The Quaker Women's Group included *Encountering Eve* as a piece in its Swarthmore presentation and text.[21] Eve figures in the article entitled *Genesis and Patriarchy*, written by Angela West of the Oxford Christian feminist network.[22] Eve makes her final appearance in the CWIRES period in the title of a collection edited by the Cambridge theologian, Janet Martin Soskice.[23]

References to Eve also occur prior to Collins' article and thus before the emergence of a single CWM.[24] I will look in more detail at these pre-CWIRES references to Eve in the following section, where I argue that the authors' concerns, while reflective of 'second-wave' feminist consciousness, are distinct from the dominant preoccupations of the British CWM.

Collins stands alone in her reference to the "rehabilitation" of Eve. However, in my view, her phrase epitomises the spirit of the wider CWM, which sought a rehabilitation of Eve/woman within the institutional churches. The distinctive ethos of the British CWM was fashioned by the fusion of

19 Pinsent, P., *Catholic Women's Network Newsletter*, 1985, No. 2, p. 1.

20 Windle, R., *The Feminine in the Pattern of Redemption*, in Pickard, J. and Windle, R. (eds.), *Sisters to Susannah*, special edition, *Alliance of Radical Methodists Reporter* 1978, No. 11, p. 9; Mertes, K., *The Mask of Eve*, unpublished paper, 1984 [CW D25 Acc 1034]; Smith, C., *On Eve*, unpublished paper to the Oxford Women's Theology Seminar, 1985 [CW WTG Acc 1169].

21 Quaker Women's Group, *Bringing the Invisible into the Light: Some Quaker Feminists Speak of their Experience*, Ashford, Headley, 1986.

22 West, A., *Genesis and Patriarchy, Part I: What has Feminist Discourse got in Common with the Language of Biblical Theology?* in New Blackfriars, 1981, Vol. 62, No. 727.

23 Soskice, J. M. (ed.), *After Eve: Women, Theology and the Christian Tradition* (Women in Religion Series), London, Marshall Pickering-Collins, 1990.

24 Nielson, M. L., *Eve Got the First Bite!* in *Theology and Sexual Politics*, London, SCM Publications, 1972; Condren, M., *For the Banished Children of Eve*, in Condren, M. (ed.), *For the Banished Children of Eve: an Introduction to Feminist Theology*, London, SCM Publications, 1976; Briggs, S., *Feminist Critique of Natural Law*, in Condren, M. (ed.), *For the Banished Children of Eve*, pp. 2 f.

'first-wave' Church feminism with new 'second-wave' feminist consciousness. The Anglican campaign for the ordination of women, which remained active throughout the CWIRES period, acted as a focus around which the various component groups cohered as a single movement. Collins' term "the rehabilitation of Eve" encapsulates the common rehabilitative ethos of the movement, and distinguishes this dominant project from radical Christian critique which eschewed the ('first-wave' Church feminist derived) project of full inclusion of women within the life of the institutional churches.

The rehabilitation of Eve in 'Christian women's' theology

Una Kroll writes as follows in the 1976 SCM pamphlet, *For the Banished Children of Eve: an Introduction to Feminist Theology*:

> Feminist theology challenges the distorted pictures of God, Christ and the Holy Spirit which have been transmitted through the historical process of patriarchy. It suggests that there is a hitherto unrevealed truth about the nature of God, the person of Christ and the work of the Holy Spirit which has been missed, suppressed and ignored because male theologians have predominated in the institutions of the Churches. We need to transcend our differences and discover that "in Christ there is neither male nor female, for you are all one in Christ Jesus".[25]

Kroll's early definition of 'feminist theology', as corrective to patriarchal distortions of Christian truth, was to prove sufficiently expansive to encompass the core writings of the 'Christian women's' theology which developed during the ensuing CWIRES period. However, where Kroll emphasises "neither male nor female" in Christ, the predominant genre of 'Christian women's' theology effects a theological rehabilitation of the female, a rehabilitation of Eve.

---

25 Kroll, U., *God According to a Woman* in Condren M. (ed.), *For the Banished Children*, pp. 19 f.

The breadth of 'Christian women's' theology

Before analysing developments within the predominant genre of 'Christian women's' theology, I will give brief consideration to 'Christian women's' writings expressive of differing concerns to those of the majority project. With one significant exception, the work of Angela West, these writings fall into two broad groups: writers in the first group express continuing 'first-wave' Church feminist concerns, whereas those in the second group give expression to 'second-wave' feminist consciousness. Both groups resist the infusion of 'second-wave' feminist consciousness within the reinvigorated 'first-wave' Church feminism which sought women's full inclusion within the institutional churches. It is precisely this infusion which is the distinctive mark of the British CWM of the 1970's and 1980's, as encapsulated in Collins' phrase "the rehabilitation of Eve".

The first group includes Joan Morris, who argues for women's inclusion in the Catholic hierarchy on grounds of historical precedent, Una Kroll in her advocacy of 'sexual parity', and those who wrote theological reflections on motherhood and God which explore women's sexuality in terms of maternity alone.[26] In my view, writers in this group would accept Kroll's definition of feminist theology, without seeking any expansion of her terms. Writers in this group make no reference to Eve.

The second group includes pre-CWIRES radical Christian writings and Jacqueline Field-Bibb's doctoral study analysing institutional resistance to women's inclusion in the priesthood, *Women Towards Priesthood*.[27] Writers

---

26 Morris, J., *Against Nature, Against God: the History of Women with Clerical Ordination and the Jurisdiction of Bishops*, London, Mowbrays, 1973; Morris, J., *The Lady Was a Bishop* in Condren, M., *For the Banished Children*; Kroll, U., *Flesh of My Flesh*, London, Darton, Longmann and Todd, 1975; Hebblethwaite, M., *Motherhood and God*, London, Chapman, 1984; Kroll, U., *A Womb-Centred Life*, in Hurcombe, L.(ed.), *Sex and God: Some Varieties of Religious Experience*, London, Routledge, 1987; Robson, J., *Reflecting on Pregnant Images*, paper to the First Hartlebury weekend, unpublished, 1982 [CW M9 Acc 508]; Robson, J., *Labouring in Hope*, in *MOW Newsletter*, 1982, No. 8.

27 Nielson, M. L., *The First Bite!*; Condren, M., *The Celibacy Syndrome*, in *Theology and Sexual Politics*; Condren, M., *For the Banished Children of Eve*; Condren, M., *Churchwomanship in a Man's World*, editorial article, in Champion, F. and Kroll, U. (eds.), *Churchwomanship* pp.1 ff.; Briggs, S., *Feminist Critique*; Jenner, J., *An Introduction to Feminist Theology* in Pickard, J. and Windle, R. (eds.), *Sisters to Susannah*, 1978, p. 8; Jenner, J., *Male-Female Issues*, in *Community*, 1980, No. 26, p. 19; Field-Bibb, J., *Women*

in this second group conceive of feminist theology as critique of women's oppression by institutional Christianity, and as envisaging better alternatives for women outside the institutional churches. Thus Judith Jenner writes of feminist theology as "a new creation".[28]   Both Jenner and Condren demonstrate a commitment to women's autonomy, mutuality and sexuality in their writings. In contrast to Kroll's "neither male nor female", Condren is concerned with the feminisation of Church and society and with the creation of a feminised "beatitudinal community".[29] It is clear from her discussion that feminisation means extending the influence of women's autonomy, mutuality and sexuality, not feminine servitude to men.

Field-Bibb shows a similar critical consciousness in using Elisabeth Schüssler Fiorenza's critical feminist theology as interpretative tool to elucidate "the theologising of dominant trends to impede the liberating impulses of women".[30] Field-Bibb's study begins with the encounter between Jesus and the Samaritan woman, where Jesus states that the hour will come when she will worship neither on this mountain nor in Jerusalem.[31] Significantly, she interprets Jesus' statement as meaning that "Religion and its liturgical celebration are de-localised and *de-institutionalised*".[32] For Field-Bibb, this Johannine exchange contradicts the Christian institution and its roles acting as "focus and locus" of the praxis of Jesus in the lives of women. Clearly her intention is not the rehabilitation of women within the institutional churches. Rather, her study traces the movement of women towards ministry under the Enlightenment "banner of equality", analysing male resistance to this move.[33]

Radical Catholic critique, which reiterated themes in Condren's early writings, was to emerge in the latter CWIRES years.[34] However, in my

Towards Priesthood: Ministerial Politics and Feminist Praxis, Cambridge, Cambridge University Press, 1991.

28 See Feminist Theology Project, *Our Stories: Feminist Theology Project 1980–1982*, Coventry, FTP, N. d., p. 7, note 2.

29 Condren, M., *Churchwomanship*, p. 1.

30 Field-Bibb, J., *Towards Priesthood*, p. 247.

31 Field-Bibb, J., *Towards Priesthood*, p. 1; John 4 [4-28].

32 Field-Bibb, J., *Towards Priesthood*, p. 1 (my italics).

33 Field-Bibb, J., *Towards Priesthood*, p. 1.

34 Fedouloff, K. (ed.), *The Wisdom of Christian Feminism: Papers on Wisdom and Human Sexuality*, London, Fedouloff, 1988; Fedouloff, K. (ed.), *The Wisdom of Christian Feminism: Papers on Violence and Peace and Women We Learn From*, London, Fedouloff, 1989; Walsh, K., McEwan, D. and Brewster, D. M., *Celibacy in Control: Three Papers on*

judgement, this later critique was harnessed to the 'Christian women's' rehabilitative project as given shape in the Catholic Women's Network, so contrasting with the critical distance from the institutional church maintained by Condren and Field-Bibb.

I will conclude this section with a discussion of the work of Angela West, who made a substantial contribution to the Oxford Christian feminist network and who was a prolific author of feminist theology.[35] West's is a distinctive and original voice, her theology informed both by her experience of the Oxford Christian feminists and Greenham, and by theological education with the Dominican order at Blackfriars, Oxford.[36] I argue that West's feminist theology is more a distinctive and individual woman's voice within Blackfriars theology and Pax Christi than a representative feminist theological expression of the CWM.[37] In this respect West differs from Morley, who both pursued her individual theological interests and spoke as representative of the wider CWM.

Three stages are evident in West's theology. Early writings stress the theological value of feminist critical consciousness acting from the margins upon Christianity. Eve figures in her *Genesis and Patriarchy*, where West returns to the Judæo-Christian myth and detects patriarchal origins in the post-lapsarian assignment to Eve of responsibility for reproduction, so placing her on the boundary of patriarchal culture.[38] Despite sharing the concerns of common humanity, contemporary women, like Eve, are marginalised.[39] The twist in West's argument appears when she asserts the potential of the "radical ambiguity" of women's marginality to patriarchal culture: thus marginalised, women are "well placed to become [culture's] critics".[40]

Sexuality and Power in the Roman Catholic Church, London, Fedouloff, 1987; McEwan, D. (ed.), *Women Experiencing Church: a Document of Alienation*, Leominster, Gracewing, 1991.

35 The Oxford Christian feminist network was a powerful presence within the CWM, from early pre-CWIRES activity, through its strong links with the CWIRES project, the development of the Oxford Women's Liturgy and its role in the Greenham Peace Vigil.

36 The Dominican order through their Priory at Blackfriars, Oxford, played a significant role in the development of the CWM by providing premises for the CWIRES project.

37 By 'Blackfriars theology', I mean the theological debate stimulated by the Dominican community in Oxford and reflected in articles published in their journal, *New Blackfriars*.

38 West, A., *Genesis and Patriarchy*, pp. 21 f.

39 West, A., *Genesis and Patriarchy*, p. 21.

40 West, A., *Genesis and Patriarchy*, p. 2.

For West, Christian theology, rather than women themselves, will be the principal beneficiary of women's critical consciousness. The essential integrity of theology requires feminist subversion of patriarchal misappropriation of the Word which is the object of theological discourse, thereby revealing the undistorted Word.[41] In contrast with the Anglican Eve, or with Morley's women in the image of God, West is little interested in Eve's specific identity. Eve's subversive work results in her reinstatement as equal to Adam, but this equality is within the vocational marginality of discipleship: West urges women to transform women's structural marginality into such vocational marginality. When she states that "It is only as Christians that women can be authoritative because the foundation of Christian truth is not patriarchy; it is a truth that originates . . . with God", she speaks of an authority associated with 'discipleship', rather than of women assuming authoritative roles within the institutional church.[42]

In West's second stage, feminist consciousness moves from margin to centre through her equation of the Oxford Women's Liturgy with the Body of Christ. Here West locates women as central within, rather than as marginal to, the Church's mission to the world, emphasising at first the Church's vocation of social justice, and later preaching the gospel of love in Christ. Her article *Sex and Salvation* is representative of a central strand of West's thinking during this second stage.[43] Here West, speaking from her grounding within the Oxford Women's Liturgy as one manifestation of the Body of Christ, effectively rehabilitates Pauline writings from their patriarchal misappropriation: West hears the Pauline good news and, as a member 'in Christ', preaches the 'love of Christ'.[44] West concludes *Sex and Salvation* by claiming that the Pauline good news enables her to critique "recent experiences within the women's liberation movement".[45]

In West's third stage, this critique takes precedence. In her criticism of the Womanspirit movement, *A Faith for Feminists*, she rejects the feminist turn

---

41 West, A., *Genesis and Patriarchy*, p. 19.

42 West, A., *Bodiliness and the Good News: the Story of the Holy Spirit and the Oxford Catholic Women's Group*, unpublished, 1982 [CW E78 Acc 585], p.15.

43 West, A., *Sex and Salvation: a Christian Feminist Bible Study on I Corinthians 6 ^{1}-7^{39}*, unpublished, 1984 [CW D28 Acc 1380]. A later and different version appears in *Modern Churchman*, Vol. 29, No. 3 (1987), and is reprinted in Loades, A. (ed.), *Feminist Theology: a Reader*, London, SPCK, 1990.

44 Loades, A., *Feminist Theology*: pp. 74 f.,p. 80.

45 Loades, A., *Feminist Theology*, p. 80.

to the Goddess on the grounds that feminists necessarily belong within the Judæo-Christian Western tradition, which superseded a-historical matriarchal Goddess religion.[46] Goddess religion is a misguided attempt to replace the incarnational Christian tradition with "a new mythology based on women's experience", reflective of women's new spiritual consciousness.[47] During the latter part of the CWIRES period, critique of the women's movement predominates in West's writings. Thus, speaking in the Wisdom of Christian Feminism lecture series, she warns that the new wisdom of feminism does not necessarily coincide with the wisdom of God.[48]

My argument that West's is primarily a distinctive voice of Blackfriars theology, rather than of the CWM, is supported by West's claim that traditional women's experience is subverted in the Oxford Christian feminists by the correctives, to members' liberal bourgeois conditioning, of Marxism and Christianity.[49] For most women in the CWM involved in emergent 'second-wave' Christian feminism, the major corrective was feminism, rather than Marxism and Christianity.

West was always more interested in theology than in the position of women in the churches. Her relationship to the CWM, and her particular 'second-wave' Christian feminist consciousness, are thus distinct from the central rehabilitative project and ethos of the wider CWM. West's contribution is also distinct from the radical Christian variants within the CWM, represented in differing forms in Jenner, Condren and Field-Bibb.

Eve in radical Christian critique

When Eve appears in this second group of writings, she is distinct from the 'Christian women's' Eve, who is a positive figure of contemporary 'Christian women' as they seek rehabilitation to a full inclusion in the life of the churches. Rather, the radical feminist analysis of the Genesis myth as

---

46 West, A., *A Faith For Feminists?* in Garcia, J. and Maitland, S. (eds.), *Walking on the Water: Women Talk About Spirituality*, London, Virago, 1983, p. 84.

47 West, A., *A Faith*, p. 71.

48 West, A., *Wisdom in the Faith of our First Century Sisters*, in Fedouloff, K. (ed.), *The Wisdom of Christian Feminism*, London, Fedouloff, 1988, p.15.

49 West, A., *A Faith*, pp. 73 ff; p. 85.

foundation myth of patriarchy is implied.[50] Thus Martha Lynne Nielson, in *Eve Got the First Bite!* exhorts churchmen, theologians, and scions of Adam "to restore to the daughters of Eve their rightful authority to speak up in church: to become Priestesses of the Divine".[51] Though clearly linked to the issue of women's ordination, Nielson's tone is hardly rehabilitative. Her brief article implies the radical feminist view that women's lack of authority derives from male control exerted through the image of Eve.

Sheila Briggs criticises the "Eve–Mary syndrome" in her contribution to *For The Banished Children of Eve*.[52] For Briggs, Eve symbolises woman as both "submissive body in the order of nature and 'revolting' body in the disorder of sin": Eve is an aspect of the use of natural law to sanction women's inferiority and subjection.[53] Though Mary acts as a counter-balance to Eve, Briggs finds Mary wanting as a liberating symbol, as women cannot emulate the immaculately conceived Virgin Mother of God, and therefore remain associated with Eve.[54]   For Briggs, Catholic Mariology is a conservative anti-feminist attempt to restrict women to motherhood, and the Genesis myth, and Eve within it, is read as a foundational myth of patriarchy.[55]   Briggs' argument thus runs directly counter to Harvey's proffering of Eve/Mary images as potentially empowering for women.

Similarly, when Condren offers her "introduction to feminist theology" to "the banished children of Eve", her radical critique exposes the function of the Genesis myth in the banishing of women from humankind and the world of thought, as well as from the altar.[56] Condren fronts her pamphlet, captioned "for the banished children of Eve", with a graphic portraying an enlarged woman's face barred by an iron grille from the altar, superimposed upon a

---

50 Stone, M., *The Paradise Papers: the Suppression of Women's Rites*, London, Virago Quartet, 1976; Daly, M., *Beyond God the Father: Towards a Philosophy of Women's Liberation*, Boston, Beacon Press, 1973. In this radical feminist critique, Eve is viewed with suspicion as a patriarchal creation encouraging women's subservience to men, and as a tool in the suppression of the Goddess, a positive symbol of female power and divinity, by the Judæo-Christian tradition.
51 Nielson, M. L., *The First Bite!*, p. 23.
52 Briggs, S., *Feminist Critique*, p. 5.
53 Briggs, S., *Feminist Critique*, p. 2.
54 Briggs, S., *Feminist Critique*, p. 5.
55 Briggs, S., *Feminist Critique*, p. 5.
56 Condren, M., *For the Banished Children*.

picture of bishops gathered to celebrate the mass. It is clear from the cover image that the banished children of Eve are her daughters.

Condren identifies notions of original sin (associated with Eve/woman) and atoning sacrifice (of Jesus) as the main elements in "the theological underpinning of the social and ecclesiastical subjugation of women".[57] As I will show, this insight was central also to the predominant group of 'Christian women's' writings, where it is subject to a contrasting development to that of Condren. Crucial to Condren's critique of the Eve/Mary pair is her analysis of how the unrealisable ideal of the Virgin Mother has facilitated male control of women, following the demise of the powerful Mother Goddess.[58] Condren thus analyses Eve/Mary in relation to the Goddess. Eve, the Goddess and Mary represent three ages in the religious history of Ireland in her subsequent doctoral research at Harvard.[59] Her interests thus overlap with those of members of the British Womanspirit movement, for example, Asphodel Long.[60]

The core of 'Christian women's' theology

I now turn to the core of 'Christian women's' theology, written from the mainstream of the movement. Eve figures large. Condren's evocative cover image to *For the Banished Children of Eve*, of woman barred from the altar, invited identification with Eve on the part of contemporary women who sought women's access to the altar as priests. Her chosen image and phrase inaugurated a theological rehabilitation of Eve in support of the project of the

---

57 Condren, M., *For the Banished Children*, p. 21.
58 Condren, M., *For the Banished Children*, pp. 22–3. Textual similarities suggest that Mary Daly's *Beyond God the Father* was a strong influence on Condren's title article.
59 Condren, M., *The Serpent and the Goddess: Women, Religion and Power in Celtic Ireland*, New York, Harper, 1989.
60 Long, A., *In a Chariot Drawn By Lions: the Search for the Female in Deity*, London, Women's Press, 1992. The Quaker Women's Group portrays a positive Eve who partakes in divine Wisdom and thus comes close to Long's exploration of the female divine, *Bringing the Invisible into the Light*. See also Hurcombe, L. (ed.), *Sex and God: Some Varieties of Women's Religious Experience*, London, Routledge, 1987, for theological explorations on the boundary between the CWM and Womanspirit.

rehabilitation of 'Christian women' within the churches, beginning with Collins' assertion that "the rehabilitation of Eve" was timely.[61]

I have already noted the positive potential in the Eve/Mary pair discerned by both Windle and Harvey. Both assert a redemptive role for Mary. Harvey claims that in the doctrine of Mary as Virgin, Mother and Second Eve is found an image of equivalent power to that of Christ as Second Adam, while Windle recommends Eve be recognised as sister of Mary, in the redemption of humanity.[62] Windle thus goes beyond Harvey in her rehabilitation of Eve, by also restoring Eve to a redemptive role, equivalent to that of Mary. However, Windle and Harvey alone pay attention to Mary; 'Christian women's' priority was to explore Eve in relation to either Adam or Christ.

Collins' unproblematic association of sexuality with spirituality in her portrayal of Eve is a benign strategy for the rehabilitation of Eve, which proved inadequate to deal with the evident misogyny and tension concerning women's sexuality, manifested in the Anglican ordination debate. In contrast, Dowell and Hurcombe show an appreciation of the continuing power of traditional readings of the Genesis myth and its effects within Christian churches and theology, when they emphasise the importance of contemporary women's connection with Eve, for their continuing "dispossession".[63] Yet, while Dowell and Hurcombe reiterate Nielson's radical insight, regarding women's status as daughters of Eve and their lack of rightful authority, and while their chosen title echoes Condren's "banished children of Eve", their book contributes to the core group of writings which support 'Christian women's' rehabilitation within the churches.

Theologically, Dowell and Hurcombe perceive women's dispossession in terms of the contrast between the baptismal promise of sexual equality in Galatians and biblical portrayal of women's silence and subordination.[64] Their strategy, in support of the 'Christian women's' rehabilitative project, is to claim women's rightful Christian heritage, already promised in the Christian baptismal statement. Dowell and Hurcombe's claim thus provides an example of the theology advocated by Kroll, who also invokes the baptismal statement. But Dowell and Hurcombe also begin the move beyond the terms in which Kroll argues: a move which is associated with the Anglican Eve. For they are

---

61   Collins, D., *Eve*, p. 5.
62   Harvey, S. A., *Eve and Mary*, pp. 9-10; Windle, R., *The Feminine*, p. 9.
63   Dowell, S. and Hurcombe, L., *Dispossessed Daughters*.
64   Galatians 3 [28]; Dowell, S. and Hurcombe, L., *Dispossessed Daughters*.

clear that women's dispossession results from women's association with the traditional reading of Eve, and their book is a response to the outworking of this association, as revealed within the Anglican ordination debate. Dowell and Hurcombe effectively declare that Eve, as well as Adam, is fully included in the salvation wrought in Christ, wherein the effects of the Fall are cancelled. Their case is tantamount to a claim that the rehabilitation of Eve is already achieved in Christ.

At first sight, Dowell and Hurcombe do not appear to follow Collins in reconfiguring the Eve of Genesis. Yet, when they argue that women's inclusion in the salvation of Christ necessarily challenges the longstanding exclusion of women in silence and subordination, they employ classical Christian orthodoxy to challenge traditional readings of the Genesis myth and their outworking. Though never stated, their argument implies the notion of a new Eve in Christ, in whom women's enforced exclusion in silence and subordination is contradicted. Implied also is a link between this new redeemed Eve and women's ordination: if Eve is included in the redemption of Christ, then women may be included in the priesthood.

Carol Smith and Kate Mertes make explicit the relations of Eve to, respectively, Adam and Christ, as implied by Dowell and Hurcombe. Thus Smith makes a similar challenge to biblical portrayals of women's silence and subordination by exegesis of the Genesis texts alone.[65] Mertes develops more fully the embryonic argument concerning Eve's relationship with the salvation of Christ, which appears in Dowell and Hurcombe, by taking issue with traditional readings of the Genesis myth which portray Eve as sexually corrupt sinner.[66] She argues that what people think of Eve, they think of women, so that a Church which accepts "the masks of Eve" will have difficulty over the full membership of women.[67]

Mertes' theological argument is that these masks lead to Eve's exclusion from salvation history, as women's salvation following the Fall depends on her fulfilling her domestic role rather than on the action of Christ.[68] Elsewhere she describes women as being in the tradition of Eve, and thus in ambiguous relationship to Christ, and defines feminist theology as emerging from "a distinctive school of Christian feminism" which seeks to "restructure

---

65 Smith, C., *On Eve*.
66 Mertes, K., *The Mask of Eve*, pp. 1 f.
67 Mertes, K., *The Mask of Eve*, pp. 9 f.
68 Mertes, K., *The Mask of Eve*, p. 7.

traditional images of women in . . . Church and . . . world" according to their faith that women are fully included in the salvation of Christ.[69]

Thus Mertes gives a fuller statement of 'Christian women's' development of classical Christology, from Kroll's reiteration of "neither male nor female", to an argument that Eve, and therefore contemporary 'Christian woman', is specifically included in the salvation of Christ. The orthodoxy of this position is well illustrated by Mary Hayter's *The New Eve in Christ*.[70] As an Anglican deaconess, Hayter sets out to make a scholarly evaluation of, in the words of her subtitle, "the use and abuse of the Bible in the debate about women in the Church". Her stated aim is to steer a middle course between respective conservative and feminist "misappropriations" of biblical material.[71] Hayter affirms the new Eve in Christ as in the image of God, while her closing words attest her "liberty" in Christ.[72] When Hayter concludes that New Testament teaching indicates that "Christ is the pattern for all creatures, woman included, so that in Christ there is a new Eve as well as a new Adam", she speaks in terms of classical and orthodox Christology.[73]

Conclusion

I have shown that arguments for the inclusion of Eve in the salvation of Christ lie at the heart of the theology emerging from the British CWM the 1970's and 1980's. This move represents a "rehabilitation of Eve" in terms of classical Christology, as expressed in Chalcedonian orthodoxy. Writings by Condren, Briggs, Jenner and Field-Bibb pursued a different trajectory, and were responsive to the critique of Christianity by Mary Daly or Elisabeth Schüssler Fiorenza. Their various projects differed to the mainstream impetus towards 'change in the position of women in the churches', which I have analysed as an attempted "rehabilitation of Eve" within the institutional churches.

---

69 Mertes, K., *Women and Salvation*, paper given at Oscott Diocesan Seminary, unpublished, 1984 [CW S13 Acc 1049], p.2; *Tensions between Theologians and the Women's Movement*, paper to St James' Piccadilly, unpublished, 1984 [CW E120 Acc 1113], p. 1.
70 Hayter, M., *The New Eve in Christ: the Use and Abuse of the Bible in the Debate about Women in the Church*, London, SPCK, 1987.
71 Hayter, M., *The New Eve*, p. 2.
72 Hayter, M., *The New Eve*, pp. 171; 153.
73 Colossians 1^{15-19}; Hayter, M., *The New Eve*, p. 153.

Janet Morley's liturgical writing and collections of 'Christian women's' liturgies demonstrate the infusion of 'second-wave' feminist consciousness with 'Christian women's' rehabilitation of Eve in institutional churches and in orthodox theology.[74] In my view these writings express the core ethos of the CWM.

---

74 Morley, J., *All Desires Known*; Morley, J. and Ward, H. (eds.), *Celebrating Women*, London, WIT and MOW, 1986; St Hilda Community, *Women Included: A Book of Services and Prayers*, London, SPCK, 1991.

Chapter Five

When God Beheld God:
Notes Towards a Jewish Feminist
Theology of the Holocaust

Melissa Raphael

No sustained Jewish feminist theological reading either of Jewish women's experience in the camps and ghettos or of post-Holocaust theological discourse has yet been undertaken.[1] Not only is there a scholarly lacuna but also, in the years to come, as a Jewish mother, I will have to tell my child about the Holocaust. And for this, I am unwilling to enlist the assistance of the Holocaust theologians of my parents' generation. Most of their writing on the Holocaust seems to me to be not only spiritually and morally unsatisfactory, but, skewed by its androcentrism and patriarchal models of God, perhaps even part of its problem. I suggest that it was a patriarchal model of God, not God-in-God's self, that failed Israel during the Holocaust. Drawing on the historical records of women's experience during this period, as well as a number of Jewish theological sources, I want to offer a post-Holocaust feminist theology of relation which both affirms the redemptive presence of God in Auschwitz (without which contemporary Jewish faith would struggle to survive) and also seeks to change our conception of that presence in ways which do not entail divine or theological complicity with evil.[2]

---

1   Among other reasons, this is partly because there is still very little Jewish feminist theology *per se*. Plaskow, J., *Standing Again at Sinai*, New York, Harper San Francisco, 1990, and Adler, R., *Engendering Judaism*, Philadelphia, Jewish Publication Society, 1998, remain the only full-length works of Jewish feminist theology to my knowledge. Neither book discusses the Holocaust.
2   As is customary among many commentators on the Holocaust, I am using the name of this death camp both as a symbol and summary of all Nazi death and concentration camps and also to refer to the death camp Auschwitz (*Oswiecim*) itself. The sense in which the word

I begin by suggesting that the feminist historiography of women's experience in the death and concentration camps provides a methodological and substantive groundwork on which a feminist theology might build. Not ultimately dependent, however, on the historical record, I use a traditional Jewish mystical understanding of the processes of exile and restoration within God as a structuring redemptive metaphor by which to interpret the record of (some) women's resistance to the Nazis' profanisation of their female personhood by those sacralising means available to them *as* (Jewish) women in conditions of absolute physical and spiritual deprivation. I suggest that by means of mutual care, these women summoned *Shekhinah* (the traditional female image of the holy presence of God) into the very abyss of profanity. Because women are made in the image of God, *Shekhinah* suffered in the suffering of women. So that what has been called the 'gender wounding' of Jewish women in the death and concentration camps was also a wounding of God. But conversely, that mutual care by which women restored the divine image to each other also restored God to God. For the erasure of the femaleness of God has divided God from God's-self over millennia of patriarchal theological and religious domination. In this sense, the redemption of both women and God from patriarchy was occurring at the same time as their fall into a pit of total darkness: a crisis of such urgency and intensity as to render the former process at least a prefiguration of eschatological judgement on the latter.

The historiographical context of the project

It is not that no one has documented what women went through in the Holocaust. Books have been published about Jewish women and children's experiences during the Holocaust since 1945. Much of this early post-war material describes conditions for women in ghettos and camps or is in the form of personal memoirs.[3] Studies of Jewish women's experience during the Holocaust were not, however, common in the 1950's and 1960's and it was

is being used should be clear in context. However, because not all Jews suffered and died in Auschwitz, this use is not uncontroversial.

3   Baumel, J. T., *Gender and Family Studies of the Holocaust* in *Women: A Cultural Review*, 1996, No. 7.

only from the late 1970's, and since the first conference on women and the Holocaust at Stern College in 1983, that a relatively small number of feminist historians have addressed the significant differences in the ways in which women – as "subjects and not just marginal objects of history" – died in and survived the Holocaust.[4]

In undertaking this historiographical project, feminist historians are *not* wanting to say that men's suffering does not count. Rather they wish to point out (in Myrna Goldenberg's phrase) that women suffered different horrors in the same hell. And the significance of women's gender-specific experiences is erased where these are simply absorbed into those of men – as if the experience of male victims of the Nazis and their collaborators was the experience of all.[5] Women died for different reasons, and were at many stages of the Holocaust more vulnerable to the Nazis' genocidal intentions than men. Nazi Germany would not countenance the survival of Jewish women to breed a new generation of Jewish children who would grow up to take revenge on Germany. So a woman arriving at Auschwitz holding a baby or a child's hand – even happening to be standing next to a child – would be automatically condemned to an immediate death.[6] Raul Hilberg has estimated that only a third of the Jews who survived Auschwitz were women.[7]

Androcentric studies of the Holocaust are oblivious to what Sara Horowitz calls the "gender wounding" of Jewish women: namely "a shattering of something innate and important to her sense of her own womanhood" which was distinct from the gender wounding of men.[8] This kind of 'female wounding' occurred especially where women suffered forced gynaecological experiments (torture) under camp 'doctors' like Josef Mengele and where they

---

4 Baumel, J. T., *Gender and Family Studies of the Holocaust*, p. 122.

5 Goldenberg, M., *Different Horrors, Same Hell: Women Remembering the Holocaust* in Gottlieb, R. S. (ed.), *Thinking the Unthinkable: Meanings of the Holocaust*, New York, Paulist Press, 1991. See also Lipstadt, D., *Introduction* to Adelsberger, L., *Auschwitz: A Doctor's Story*, London, Robson Books, 1996; Rittner, C. and Roth, J. K., *Prologue: Women and the Holocaust*, in Rittner, C. and Roth, J. K. (eds.), *Different Voices: Women and the Holocaust*, New York, Paragon House, 1993.

6 Adelsberger, L., *Auschwitz*, p. 100; Ringelheim, J., *Women and the Holocaust: A Reconsideration of Research* in Rittner, C. and Roth, J. K. (eds.), *Different Voices*, p. 378.

7 See Hilberg, R., *Perpetrators, Victims, Bystanders: The Jewish Catastrophe 1933–1945*, New York, Harper Collins, 1992.

8 Horowitz S. R., *Mengele, the Gynaecologist, and Other Stories of Women's Survival*, in Peskowitz, M. and Levitt, L., *Judaism Since Gender*, London, Routledge, 1997, p. 201.

suffered the particular terror and grief of abortion, pregnancy and childbirth in camps and ghettos whose purpose and product was death.

At the same time, it is not difficult to find moving testimonies of women in the camps and in hiding who were helped by the compassion and practical assistance of other women, often, but not always, their actual mothers and sisters.[9] And it is common for women's memoirs and testimonies to stress that mutual assistance or the forging of quasi-familial bonds with other victims was a significant factor in their physical and emotional survival. Some feminist historians of the Holocaust – notably Joan Ringelheim and Judith Tydor Baumel – have wanted to say that women's experiences were often shaped by these characteristically female patterns of relationship and that these could increase women's chance of survival or extend their lives beyond what might otherwise have been the case.[10]

There were thousands of mutual assistance groups active during the Holocaust at any one time.[11] But one that seems to me, from a post-Holocaust, feminist theological perspective, particularly to suggest a theology of relation is the group of ten 'camp sisters' researched by Judith Tydor Baumel which was known as the *Zehnnerschaft* ('group of ten'). This camp sisterhood was formed in the Spring of 1943 in the Plaszow labour camp in Poland by women between the ages of sixteen and twenty-six. All but one of the women were

---

9   See, for instance, Hart, K., *Return to Auschwitz*, London, Granada, 1983, *passim*; Isaacman, C. (as told to Grossman, J. A.), *Clara's Story*, Philadelphia, The Jewish Publication Society of America, 1984, *passim*; Nomberg-Prztyck, S., *The Camp Blanket* in Rittner, C. and Roth, J. K. (eds.), *Different Voices*.

10   Joan Ringelheim later revised her own earlier historical reading of sisterhood in the camps, regarding it as only one *aspect* of women's experience, her reading of which had been filtered through the ideals of what she now sees as the apolitical cultural feminism of the 1970's and early 1980's. Claims about women's mutual assistance – whether made by victims or scholars – may constitute a self-deceptive mythologisation of the Holocaust that may effectively valorise and de-politicise oppression, and suggest that oppression is merely physical or external, rather than, and perhaps most significantly, internal or psychological as well. See Ringelheim, J.: *The Unethical and the Unspeakable: Women and the Holocaust* in *Simon Wiesenthal Annual*, 1984, No. 1; *Women and the Holocaust: A Reconsideration of Research* in Rittner, C. and Roth, J. K. (eds.), *Different Voices*, first published in *Signs: Journal of Women and Culture*, 1985, No. 10.

11   Lucie Adelsberger, for example, describes being 'adopted' as mother by two girls in the children's infirmary in the women's camp at Auschwitz who at the same time styled themselves as Adelsberger's 'mother' and 'grandmother'. Adelsberger, L., *Auschwitz*, pp. 98 ff.

of common educational and orthodox religious background. The *Zehnnerschaft* was sustained at great risk for two years through three camps (Plaszow, Auschwitz, and Bergen-Belsen). Unlike many other mutual assistance groups in the camps, these women did not limit their assistance to those members of their group with whom they enjoyed 'mother-daughter' relations, but endangered their own lives to help women outside their circle. For example, they would share scraps of food and a precious lice comb with other women, regardless of whether these other women were observant of Jewish law.[12]

Both Baumel and Ringelheim find that although such groups were not unknown among men in the camps, men did not usually form the mutually dependent, protective, ersatz parent-child relationships that were found in camp sisterhoods. The practical, domestic nature of women's reactions to extreme physical and emotional deprivation allowed these groups to develop more quickly and to be more stable than men's.[13] The distinctively 'female' character of relationship among 'camp sisters' was, according to Baumel, characteristic of cultural patterns of nurture among women's extended families in the pre-war Jewish communities in Eastern and central Europe.[14] That is, these relationships were a product of nineteenth-century European ideologies of motherhood – proto-feminist as well as traditional – permeated by the characteristically Jewish sense that the whole people of Israel bears responsibility for one another.[15]

Apologists for Orthodox Judaism have always claimed that women have a sufficiently immediate spiritual relationship with God as to obviate the imposition of time-bound religious obligations upon them. Perhaps, ironically, in the camps, this compensatory rhetoric served Jewish women well. They may have perceived themselves as in no need of the mediation of

---

12 Baumel, J. T., *Social Interaction among Jewish Women in Crisis during the Holocaust* in *Gender and History*, 1995, No. 7.
13 Ringelheim, J., *Women and the Holocaust*, pp. 378 f. Baumel, J. T., *Social Interaction among Jewish Women*, p. 78.
14 Baumel, J. T., *Social Interaction among Jewish Women*, pp. 70; 74; 78.
15 However, no one could claim that the behaviour of all women was, or could have been, morally exemplary. Violently oppressive hierarchies of status and privilege existed among the women inmates of Auschwitz and other such camps. See Lengyel, O., *Five Chimneys*, New York, Howard Fertig, 1983, pp. 42 ff.; Nomberg-Prztyk, S., *Auschwitz: True Tales from a Grotesque Land*, North Carolina, The University of North Carolina Press, 1985:p.13; pp. 20 f.; pp. 75 f.

a now doubly prohibited legal apparatus in order to remain close to God. Female victims' quasi-maternal care for one another could remain a service not only to human beings, but through them, to God. For Rivka Englard, an Orthodox member of the *Zehnnerschaft*, "life in Plaszow and Auschwitz was a test of our willingness to 'sanctify God' by adhering to our faith, by assisting as many Jews as possible and by remaining decent human beings".[16]

Both Reform and modern Orthodox Jews accepted the moral imperative of ethical relation as a minimal definition of Judaism.[17] It is true that assimilated Jewish women such as Etty Hillesum and Anne Frank (who died in Auschwitz and Belsen respectively) gave an ethico–spiritual response to oppression and suffering which was coloured more by Christianity and liberal Enlightenment notions of human dignity and decency than by *halakhic* Judaism.[18] When Rega Laub was asked how she (a secular Zionist) came to join the *Zehnnerschaft* she replied: "Because of their devotion to morality in an amoral camp universe".[19] But even where Judaism informed the care of women for one another it was often of a broad theistic type. (From their youth, the women of the *Zehnnerschaft* had internalised very general ethical precepts such as the well-known Talmudic dictum: "He who saves a life, it is as if he saves the whole world".[20]) Their resistance to degradation by adherence to the moral and religious imperative of preserving their (Jewish) humanity may have included but also transcended formalised obedience to the patriarchal God of law (alone).[21]

Traditional religious means of resisting the Nazis' gross profanisation of Jewish personhood would have been differently available to women than they were to men (or not at all). For example, the possibility of martyrdom

---

16 Cited in Baumel, J. T., *Jewish Women in Crisis*, p. 79.
17 Mendes-Flohr, P., *Law and Sacrament: Ritual Observance in Twentieth-Century Jewish Thought* in Green, A. (ed.), *Jewish Spirituality: from the Bible Through the Middle Ages*, London, SCM Press, 1989, p. 323.
18 See Brenner, R. F., *Writing as Resistance: Four Women Confronting the Holocaust: Edith Stein; Simone Weil; Anne Frank; Etty Hillesum*, Pennsylvania, Pennsylvania State University Press, 1997.
19 Cited in Baumel, J. T., *Jewish Women in Crisis*, p. 74.
20 Baumel, J. T., *Jewish Women in Crisis*, p. 79; Sanhedrin 37a.
21 It is not that the commandments (*mitzvot*) were simply forgotten. For example, some religious Jewish women went to great lengths to make a Sabbath blessing over any available source of light. See Milton, S., *Women and the Holocaust: The Case of German and German-Jewish Women* in Rittner, C. and Roth, J. K. (eds.), *Different Voices*, p. 230.

(*kiddush hashem*) during the Holocaust was surely a gendered one. *Kiddush hashem* is an act of self-offering in calm and dignified acceptance of one's imminent death. Hasidic commentators regard it as a privilege requiring spiritual preparation, concentration (*kavanah*) and ecstatic song, prayer and dance.[22] Dan Cohn-Sherbok writes of the Holocaust martyrs that "when their last moments arrived they died without fear . . . With love and trust they awaited the death sentence. As they prepared to surrender themselves to God, they thought only of the purity of their souls".[23] But this could not often have been a religious possibility for, say, a mother trying to hold on to and look after several sick and terrified children in a vast crowd of people on their way to the gas chambers, surrounded by guards with whips and clubs. And nor would the joyous gift of her life to God have been a meaningful choice for a woman whose obligations to the covenant and Jewish sacred history had always been mediated through her care and nurture of others as a living wife and mother. In short, the different meaning of a Jewish woman's survival or death would have been established from her birth.

It is more probable that, for a woman who was not with young children and who had been selected to be worked to death, the preservation or restoration of Jewish holiness in Auschwitz would have been grounded in the traditional, though less heroic, notion of *kiddush hahayim* – the sanctification of God's name in life. The vocation of *kiddush hahayim* is consistent with the Hasidic emphasis on *avodah begashmiut* or the worship of God through the everyday conditions of life in community.

Many women's actions in the anti-community of the camp were 'ordinary' acts of friendship and giving such as those performed by the *Zehnnerschaft*. And if everyday acts of care or kindness (*hesed*) sanctified God's name outside the camps, then *a forteriori* they must have done so inside them. For there, radical loss, physical debility and sadistic terrorisation and cruelty by camp guards and *Kapos* (supervisors) rendered even the most ordinary act of

---

22 Hasidism is a Jewish mystical movement emphasising the joyousness of worship and the sanctity of its spiritual leaders. It arose in eighteenth-century Eastern Europe and remains a highly influential branch of contemporary 'ultra'-Orthodox Judaism. It is patriarchal in all aspects of its religious philosophy and practice and in its social organisation. See Schindler, P., *Hasidic Responses to the Holocaust in the Light of Hasidic Thought*, New Jersey, Ktav, 1990. For his account of some of the *Rebbes'* (necessarily masculine) acts of martyrdom see pp. 61 ff.

23 Cohn-Sherbok, D., *Issues in Contemporary Judaism*, Basingstoke, Macmillan, 1991, p. 17.

human decency an extraordinary moral and physical feat or quite simply impossible.

The camp regime deliberately failed to provide the most basic facilities for bodily hygiene.[24] And yet practical attempts of care maintained the dignity of the divinely created, embodied person against what Terrence Des Pres has called the Nazis "excremental assault" upon the Jews.[25] It is his term which encapsulates not only the modus operandi of the Final Solution but also the means by which patriarchal systems make all things available (that is, profane) for their own use. The profane is, it seems to me, both the quality and product of patriarchy which colonises, breaks, spoils, wastes or uses up what it appropriates for the expansion of its own power and sphere of operation. Nazism represented a demonic, but logical, conclusion of the patriarchal world view which objectifies all things as disposable means to power.

Nazism was a racist rather than a religious ideology. Nonetheless, its means to power were not entirely secular and nor were their consequences. Nazism sought to extinguish European Jewry (and so, in every sense, expand its own *Lebensraum*) by its systematic isolation and, in effect, though not specific religious intention, its profanisation. Once the divine image of the Jewish person had been defaced, it would no longer reflect the face of God. Literally covered in filth and sores, Jewish bodies would be (as the word 'cover' once implied) possessed or owned by a power other than God. These contagious bodies would have been deported geographically and ontologically: to the East, and into the realm of the profane. Here, the soiled, irredeemably material Jew would have become, or so the Nazis might have intended, repellent even to their own, Jewish, God. Voided of the divine, the Jewish 'shape' (as Jews were referred to by Nazis) could be processed into a corpse – the primary product of the Final Solution – and then, secondarily, into soap and fertiliser.

Different forms of patriarchy had deprived women of any means to hallow the world besides love. And yet in the camps and ghettos it was an ethic informed by love which protected some women from this destruction of their

---

24 See, for example, Pelagia Lewinska's important record of the Nazis' deliberate profanisation of the women in Auschwitz, and of her attempts to resist it. Lewinska, P., *Twenty Months at Auschwitz*, in Rittner, C. and Roth, J. K. (eds.), *Different Voices*, esp. p. 87.

25 Des Pres, T., *The Survivor: An Anatomy of Life in the Death Camps*, Oxford, Oxford University Press, 1976, passim.

integral relation to God. Nazism imposed radical, systemic obstructions on the free flow of love. Camp sisters and those like them lifted up the greatest possible patriarchal obstructions to love and invited God into a world apparently voided of God as real indwelling presence: as *Shekhinah*.

For a contemporary religious feminist to sanctify God's name is to name the profanity of patriarchy. A Jewish feminist may, then, interpret the relations of care between women in the camps as being 'ordinary' in the natural, practical sense, but in another, as 'non-ordinary' because their cleaning or restoration of the (female) divine image pointed towards a meta-patriarchal, dimension of divine being. An open circle was traced out within the closed circle of their perimeter walls and fences. Within the open circle the world was sanctified for the coming of the *Shekhinah*, while at the same time *Shekhinah*'s presence held open the circle.

The role of Jewish mystical theology

Jewish mysticism is helpful to a feminist theology of relation (and therefore of its opposite – alienation) because it is premised on two basic notions. First, the Mediæval kabbalistic notion that the catastrophes that befall the Jews are also catastrophes for God, tearing God apart from God's-self. And second, that the *tikkun* (restoration, reconciliation, healing, completion) in God and in the world can be brought about by human activity. This concept of *tikkun* is grounded in the Lurianic doctrine of the 'holy sparks'.[26] In this kabbalistic scheme, when God emerged from concealment in order to create the universe, the vessels of the seven lower *sefirot* (or emanations of God) shattered because they could not contain the divine light or holiness that filled them. This stream of spilled light ran down from world to world until, catastrophically, it reached the 'Other Side'. Here, the 'shells' (*kelipot*) or forces of impurity spilled the light, and the holy sparks were scattered all about, falling into the impure material world. The redemption of the world is brought about when Jews consecrate the world by their goodness, if necessary by descending into the very abyss of impurity to rescue the hidden or imprisoned sparks, and, by their elevation, return them to God.[27] Human efforts to reunite God with God

---

26 Rabbi Isaac Luria was a leading sixteenth-century Jewish mystic.
27 Schindler, P., *Hasidic Responses to the Holocaust*, p. 53.

by the elevation of the sparks have cosmic repercussions. They enable the female *Shekhinah* (also known as *Sefirah Malkhut* – the emanation of God closest to humanity) to be reunited with the male *Sefirah Tiferet* (beauty). This is a sacred marriage bringing peace and harmony to the sefirot and enabling the free flow of divine grace to the world.[28]

Much of the kabbalistic scheme is too gnostic, esoteric, and dualistically inclined to be of interest to a feminist theology of relation. Also, kabbalists have traditionally taught that redemption or the restoration of divine unity can be achieved by highly focused prayer, study, the observance of the 613 *mitzvot*, and a number of technical ritual practices. Here, though, I argue that *tikkun* cannot be contingent upon orthopraxis because Orthodoxy is profaned by its patriarchal nature. Nonetheless, the basic kabbalistic redemptive myth can serve as a structuring metaphor for the feminist theology of the Holocaust suggested here. That is, each act of 'female' *hesed* can be likened to lighting the Sabbath candles which traditionally invite the Shekhinah into the home. Each act of *hesed* elevated the profaned spark of the divine image in each woman they supported. That meant the redemptory process was going in a manner all the more mysterious and powerful to contemplate *because* it happened there, in a place precisely organised for the profane to overwhelm and extinguish the holiness of human life.

And in different times and places this process continues wherever religious feminist resistance rescues the sparks from the 'shells' of patriarchal oppression by invoking *Shekhinah* and other (subordinated or denied) Jewish female images of the divine. When women identify themselves as manifestations or reflections of *Shekhinah* then the femaleness of God is restored to God because she can behold herself in her creation. The oral tradition of the Kabbalah claims that God brought the world into existence because "God wished to behold God".[29] Now if Auschwitz meant that God could no longer behold God on earth, then her being and her reason for creation were close to destruction. She would become blind to herself. This was the case when God seemed so dispersed by absolute atrocity as to have disappeared altogether. But if God could behold her image even in the smoke-blackened mirror of Auschwitz, then God's original creative purpose was not

---

28 Jacobs, L., *Hasidic Prayer*, London, The Littman Foundation, 1993, p. 106.
29 ben Shimon Halevi, Z., *Kabbalah: Tradition of Hidden Knowledge*, London, Thames & Hudson, 1979, p. 5.

utterly thwarted. In those moments when God *could* behold God in the midst of Auschwitz, through the thick scale of our profanisation, these were moments of *tikkun*; they were not the destruction of its possibility.

A different theology of the Holocaust

We have seen that feminist historiography of the Holocaust has challenged the customary assumption that the normative 'Jew' of religious and social discourse (who is in fact a male Jew unless specified otherwise) also represents all victims of the Nazis. So, too, it should be readily apparent that masculinist religious responses to the Holocaust cannot be considered normative or inclusive of women's experience and response.

A post-Holocaust theology grounded in the concept and symbol *Shekhinah* rather than the sovereignty of God as *Rebono shel olam* ('Master of the Universe') will travel a different moral and spiritual trajectory, though one largely provided by the tradition itself. After all, in the earliest *midrashim* the *Shekhinah* was an image of the female aspect of God caring for her people in exile.[30] During the twelfth and thirteenth centuries, kabbalistic literature rendered her a separate feminine hypostasis in the manifestation of God in the world.[31] In Hasidic theology she suffers not only with the whole Jewish people, but with each Jewish soul. Without her sharing their suffering, humanity could not endure.[32] The word *shekhinah* comes from the root *shakhan*, to be present, or dwell as in a tabernacle, sanctuary or tent.[33] Rabbinic literature has an "unshakeable belief" in the indwelling presence of God among the daily life of the people of Israel and there is, according to the Talmud, no place without *Shekhinah*.[34] In the mystical tradition, after the destruction of the second Temple in Jerusalem, the Shekhinah (also referred to in the tradition as a mother, a daughter and as the Sabbath Bride), no longer indicated God's presence in a particular place. Instead she went into exile, an

---

30 *Midrashim* are Jewish biblical commentaries in narrative form.
31 Smith, C., *The Symbol of the Shekhinah: the Feminine Side of God* in Pirani, A. (ed.), *The Absent Mother: Restoring the Goddess to Judaism and Christianity*, London, Mandala, 1991, p. 6.
32 Schindler, P., *Hasidic Responses to the Holocaust*, p. 26.
33 See Exodus 25 [8].
34 Jacobs, L., *A Jewish Theology*, p. 63. (Midrash Exodus ii, 9.)

accompanying God, wandering with the Children of Israel.[35]   By the seventeenth century *Shekhinah* had been figured as a woman mourning for and comforting her people.[36] *Shekhinah*, then, represents a God who sets up her tent in our midst wherever that might be. In diaspora Judaism the synagogue and home replaced the Temple as the chief loci of the *Shekhinah*. And when the Nazis had destroyed the synagogues and homes of European Jewry, *Shekhinah* may be said to have gone yet deeper into exile with her children – into the hiding places, ghettos and camps of Nazi-occupied Europe.

A feminist reading of the *Shekhinah* tradition makes it clear that God-She in Auschwitz, manifest as *Shekhinah*, could not be that imagined by patriarchal, androcentric post-Holocaust theology. A God whose presence is a mothering one is not that of Emil Fackenheim, whose God is the "Commanding Voice of Auschwitz" pronouncing a 614th commandment: that Jews must deny victory to Hitler by enduring as Jews.[37] The Jewish people were surely subject to enough deafening commands in that place. God-She is not the God of the Reform rabbi-theologian Ignaz Maybaum who uses Hitler as the servant of his will just as he once used Nebuchadnezzar (in the destruction of the first Temple) to bring about a *churban* – an event of such awesome, catastrophic proportions as to bring about a new and revitalised form of Jewish existence.[38] God-She is not the God of the Orthodox theologian Bernard Maza who countenances and executes unlimited suffering on his people in order to ensure the future of his own glorification through a resurgence of learning and observance of Torah.[39] And a Mother-God in Auschwitz is not like Arthur Cohen's almost deistic, withdrawn God who, in the name of freedom, lets the *tremendum* of human Godlessness take its most terrifying course.[40] Nor is God-She the God of the Orthodox theologian

---

35 See Smith, C., *The Symbol of the Shekhinah*, p. 6.
36 Freeman, H., *Chochmah and Wholeness: Retrieving the Feminine in Judaism* in Sheridan, S. (ed.), *Hear Our Voice: Women rabbis tell their stories*, London, SCM Press, 1994, p. 187.
37 Fackenheim, E., *God's Presence in History: Jewish Affirmations and Philosophical Reflections*, New York, Harper and Row, 1970, p. 84.
38 Maybaum, I., *The Face of God After Auschwitz*, Amsterdam, Polak and Van Gennep, 1965, pp. 66 ff.
39 Maza, B., *With Fury Poured Out: The Power of the Powerless During the Holocaust*, New York, Sure Seller, 1988.
40 Cohen, A., *The Tremendum: a Theological Interpretation of the Holocaust*, New York, Crossroad, 1981.

Eliezer Berkovits, the God who, in order to protect human free will, must hide his face; must turn away. As Berkovits puts it, "while He shows forbearance with the wicked, He must turn a deaf ear to the anguished cries of the violated".[41] The *Shekhinah* is a manifestation of God *defined* by her presentness. She may be so ordinarily present that she is imperceptible, but that is not to say that she has hidden *herself*. If she seems hidden it is by virtue of the ordinariness of medium of her presence. Yet Berkovits' God, by a cruel paradox well-known to rabbinic Judaism, is present in the very fact of his absence.

I am not saying that every word and thought of androcentric post-Holocaust theology is simply worthless. Although most patriarchal Holocaust theology is premised on the divine recompense of territory in the establishment of the Jewish nation state in Israel in 1948, the best of it calls God's purposes during the Holocaust to moral account and refrains from any facile claim that the Holocaust was a punishment for Jewish sins.[42] There is much in this body of theology that can be transposed into a feminist context and which moves by its scale and grandeur of conception. But it would make little sense for a feminist to attempt to reconcile the patriarchal God's supposed moral perfection with the facts of the Holocaust when, with other religious feminists, I consider that model of God to be morally imperfect from the outset, and irrespective of the Holocaust. Rather, I wish to propose that were divine power to assume a different (female) face it would no longer make sense to ask God to stretch out his hand and do the sorts of interventionary jobs that the patriarchal model of God failed to do in the Holocaust (or could not do precisely because this *was* a patriarchal model of God and therefore defined in such a way as to be incapable of surrendering certain divine rights, privileges and instrumentalist habits).

Indeed, I would argue that theological analyses of the Holocaust that persist in using patriarchal categories of understanding are not identical with, but are continuous with, the ideological conditions that produced the Holocaust and therefore cannot move beyond them. These theologies are not a solution to the problem; they are often themselves, to use Phyllis Trible's

---

41 Berkovits, E., *Faith After the Holocaust*, New York, Ktav, 1973, p. 106.
42 Berkovits, for example, writes that in the creation of the state of Israel "we have seen a smile on the face of God. It is enough". Berkovits, E., *Faith After the Holocaust*, p. 156.

phrase, "texts of terror": they are part of the problem.[43] For patriarchal post-Holocaust theology shares with all patriarchal ideologies the view that supposed creative ends (whether those of the biblical God or the Nazis) may deploy absolutely destructive means. Although the biblical God is *also* a God of justice and liberation, both this God and the Nazis are prepared to produce conditions of numinous horror to achieve their own will. Moreover, patriarchal post-Holocaust theology shares with all oppressors the assumption that some human beings (whether women or, in the Nazis' case, Jews) are not entitled to the dignity of full subjecthood and free religious agency. In other words, patriarchal theological discourse on the Holocaust may fail to signal redemption when it is predicated upon a model of God whose will and character shares significant elements of the alienated patriarchal world view of its perpetrators. It does not and cannot mount a significant moral critique on the world that produced and inherited Auschwitz because it enjoys discursive and religious privileges within that world.

And yet Marc Ellis' early contribution to Jewish liberation theology rightly insists that the Holocaust should have sensitised Jewry to our own oppressiveness.[44] The post-Holocaust era has demanded not only the repentance of all those complicit with Nazism, but, differently, calls Jewry to a repentance or *teshuvah* of its own sexism.[45] So too, it has demanded that women try to imagine how the unknowable, eternal, transcendent, limitless

---

43 Trible, P., *Texts of Terror: Literary-Feminist Readings of Biblical Narratives*, Philadelphia, Fortress Press, 1984.

44 Ellis, M. H., *Towards a Jewish Theology of Liberation*, London, SCM Press, 1988, passim.

45 As Cynthia Ozick has pointed out, Jews rightly grieve for the tragic losses of the Holocaust but are indifferent to, or simply have not noticed, the cultural and intellectual debilitations that Judaism's sexism has produced. There has been a "wholesale excision", "deportation" and isolation of women – half of world Jewry – "from the creative centre" of "Jewish communal achievement" for centuries upon centuries. And yet of this catastrophic loss of "thousands upon thousands" of poets, artists, writers, scientists, doctors and discoverers, "Jewish literature and history report not one wail, not one tear". Ozick, C., *Notes Towards Finding the Right Question* in Heschel, S. (ed.), *On Being a Jewish Feminist: A Reader*, New York, Schocken Books, 1983, pp. 133 ff.

God (*En Sof*) might at the same time have been present within the conditions of an agonised finitude in Auschwitz and who is still at the side of those Jewish women who mourn for a God twice ruptured by the profanisation of her people and by her people's profanisation of the femaleness of the divine.[46]

---

46 Excerpts from *When God Beheld God: Towards a Jewish Feminist Theology of the Holocaust* in *Feminist Theology*, 1999, No. 21. Some very minor amendments have been made to these excerpts to improve flow or clarity.

Chapter Six

Harmony in Africa: Healing the Divided Continental Self – Mercy Amba Oduyoye, Feminist and Theologian

Carrie Pemberton

For an appropriate understanding of a contextual theologian it behoves any commentator to afford some time to the history of her subject. This can in no way be seen as comprehensive, but does delineate some of the seismic changes which Mercy Oduyoye has lived through in the change from colonial Ghana under British 'tutelage', the heady days of independence and the contemporary struggle with economic and cultural bondage which informs so much of her production. Mercy Amba Oduyoye is not an easy theologian to encounter from the comfortable study chair of a western professional. Her work is often abrasive and challenging, particularly to those who inherit the fair hair, light pigment and generous coffers of the colonial victors. It is important to note our own context as we engage with her work. What are our expectations of 'theology' as we face the enormous range of essays, addresses and monographs which she has published over the last thirty years?

If we are looking for a philosophical engagement with the systematic giants of the western tradition, detailed exegesis of biblical texts, or linguistic finessing with the problems of truth, meaning and coherence, then we will be disappointed. You do not go to Oduyoye to hear the approach of the western classical tradition. Some students who have listened to the voice of Oduyoye through reading some of her more popular articles have claimed that they cannot find any theology in it whatsoever. This is in itself to pose an important question at our discipline and praxis. What is theology and who is it for? For Oduyoye the answer is simple. Theology is to be concerned with the restoration of dignity for those who go hungry, who are held in contempt or whose basic needs are neglected; "*practising* the Christian faith has become a cardinal orientation in doing theology . . . (for theology in Africa) is the outcome of the Black struggle . . . it is challenging the various expressions of the capitalist ideology, the racism that dismisses things African, and the sexism that depersonalises women. Women's active participation in the unmasking of the ideological base to the dominant theology" is thus critical to the development of theology in Africa.[1] It is for Oduyoye a praxis-orientated theology which is being spoken and lived out by women theologians committed to "mutuality, equality, freedom, differentiation and sharing which characterises the Triune God" of orthodox Christian faith, but she claims neglected by "the western missionary orientation which counted souls instead of whole human beings".[2] Her applied and occasionally acerbic approach to the nature of the theological task and its importance for contemporary Africa and African women has its origin in her formation at the cusp of inter-continental change in a denomination committed to building societal vision and reinvesting in national esteem. Her indefatigable accompanying of women through some of the worst alienations of ecclesial and societal discrimination, and her outrage at all manifestations of violation and violence, a deeply attractive weft of her *Asante* weave, has the cultural power of the *Fantse* matrilineal matrix to inform and inspire.[3] She places this practice of resistance and solidarity as one which is central to the liberating message and woman-friendly practice of Jesus.[4]

    The same *Asante* and gospel waters have inspired the Circle of African Women Theologians, a women's solidarity movement which has developed from a tantalising dream of Oduyoye's to a membership base of over five

---

1   Oduyoye, M. A., *Liberation and the Development of Theology in Africa* in *The Ecumenical Movement Tomorrow*, Reuver, M., Solms, F. and Huizer, G. (eds.), Kampen, Kok Publishing House, 1993, p. 208.

2   Oduyoye, M. A., *Liberation and the Development of Theology in Africa*, p. 207.

3   Akan is a generic term used to refer to a large number of linguistically related peoples who live in southern Ghana and southeastern Côte d'Ivoire. It incorporates a cluster of Twi languages and at present accounts for over 4 million people. The Fante peoples, along with Asante, comprise two of the largest and best known ethnic groups that make up the Akan. Visit http://www.uiowa.edu/~africart/ for further information.

4   Oduyoye, M. A., *The Christ for African Women* in Fabella, V. and Oduyoye, M. A. (eds.), *With Passion and Compassion: Third World Women Doing Theology*, New York, Orbis Books, 1993.

hundred and fifty over the last twenty years. A pan-African, largely sub-Saharan network of women theologians, pastors and engaged women of faith, the Circle is substantially Christian in its orientation; but there are importantly members who are members of Moslem, Hindu and African Traditional Religion faith communities, a significant recognition that the plural nature of faith in the continent must be recognised and addressed by women gathering on common ground. These African women share Oduyoye's conviction that to partake in theology and explore their holy scriptures and religious rituals is not an act of passivity. Rather it is an engagement with the past and the present for the purposes of challenge and transformation. As contextual feminist theologians they gather the 'experiences' of their own lives, their families, sisters, aunts, mothers, and grandmothers, and see disclosed patterns of "belief systems which continue to dehumanise women".[5] Fundamental, then, to the contemporary African woman is the pervasive power of religion and ritual in the way in which her place is described and prescribed. Yet it is at this very point of alienation, both in imagination and ritual performance, that alternative visions emerge. Oduyoye invokes suppressed narratives and practices which are redolent with power for human liberation and gender justice, within and beyond Africa's national boundaries. It is a call which involves her own story, to which we now turn.

The theologian

Elected in December 1997 as General Secretary of the Ecumenical Association of Third World Theologians (EATWOT) at their fourth international conference in the Philippines, Mercy Amba Oduyoye has well fulfilled the promise of the eldest daughter of the Akan household into which she was born in 1934. Her father, the Rev'd Charles Kwaw Yamoah, was President of the Wesley Methodist Church of Ghana. Like other daughters of an African manse, the young Yamoah was sent away to a Methodist boarding school, Mmofraturo, in the heart of the Ashanti nation of Kumasi. Amba Yamoah regularly read from the Authorised Version of the Bible for morning prayers, and particularly valued the Old Testament books of Ecclesiastes,

---

5   Kanyoro, M. R. A. and Oduyoye, M. R. A. (eds.), *The Will to Arise: Women, Tradition and the Church in Africa*, New York, Orbis Books, 1992, p. 5.

Proverbs and the Sermon on the Mount.[6] She went for her sixth form studies to Achimota School, a government school dedicated to retaining Ghanaian cultural pride whilst imparting an English curriculum.

It was at Achimota that Oduyoye learnt some of the songs which were to shape her future. Her music teacher was a Ghanaian nationalist *Owura* (Master), Ephraim Amu, who proudly wore the *Ntama* (the great-cloth, woven for leading men in the community) in the days before independence.[7] Three of these songs merit note: *Yen ara Asase ni*, meaning 'this land is ours'; *Okofo Kwasi Barima*, a song encouraging the subject to return and pick up weapons which have been neglected and forgotten, the weapons of knowledge, peace and wealth; and *Ewarade no nim na obehwe ara*, a song based on the words of Jesus on the cross to his mother and the beloved disciple.[8] The themes of national pride, neglected reserves of African wisdom and the compassion of Christ in the midst of suffering are integral to an understanding of Oduyoye's work. Like the great-cloth of the elders, the warp of national pride is interleaved by the weft of compassion for and by women in Christian scripture and personal history. Her indebtedness to her matrilocal upbringing, with the inspiration of *Asante* foremothers and churchwomen who surrounded her in oral tradition and practical solidarity, is the unbroken thread which pervades her work. As Oduyoye herself has written:

> The women of the Christian community, symbolised by my grandmother and my mother, are not only an inspiration, they are a guide, and sometimes they function as monitors of what I write. I feel accountable to them as someone expected to carry on a tradition of ensuring life-centredness in the community. I have sought to articulate what my grandmother acted out in her lyrics . . . to this I have added my mother's quiet insistence that a person owes her community nothing less than her best, but she cannot give of her best if she is not empowered to do so. Luckily for me, my father shared this view of human development.[9]

6   Oduyoye, M. A., *Daughters of Anowa: African Women and Patriarchy*, New York, Orbis Books, 1996, p. 174.
7   Oduyoye, M. A., *Hearing and Knowing: Theological Reflections on Christianity in Africa*, New York, Orbis Books, 1986, p. 71. The great-cloth, the *Kente* cloth, woven on behalf of royalty, has come to symbolise African power throughout the world.
8   John 19 [26-27].
9   Oduyoye, M. A., *Be a Woman and Africa Will Be Strong* in Russell, L. M. (ed.), *Inheriting Our Mother's Gardens: Feminist Theology in Third World Perspective*, Philadelphia, Westminster Press, 1988, p. 50.

Amba Yamoah went to Legon University where she took courses under Professor Kwesi Dickson and Dr John S. Pobee, leading Ghanaian theologians from the protestant wing of the churches, both interested in developing the idea of inculturation and skenosis of Christian theology. Dickson had embarked on his development of a *Theologia Africana*. This would involve the rehabilitation of African Ancestors by Christian theology, proposing African histories and genealogies as an alternative Old Testament for the reception of Christ in Africa.[10] Pobee, soon to become a member of the World Council of Churches (WCC) team in Geneva, with a particular brief for the provision of theological education in Africa, was hard at work on his idea of *skenosis* and the 'communion of the community'. *Skenosis* works with the idea of releasing the person and message of Jesus Christ afresh into a culture, and allowing an engagement to take place relatively unencumbered by the trappings of history, privileged across space and time by virtue of their proximity to the processes of Christian mission and alignment to Imperial power. Pobee's parallel commitment to the "communion of the community", with his desire to see the mission of the church as one of gathering in the plurality of religious aspirations on the continent rather than generating further subdivisions, was also underway.[11]

From Legon, Yamoah proceeded to Osei-Tutu Teacher Training College at Akropong from whence she came as a mature student to Newnham College, Cambridge, to read theology at the University in 1963. In 1965 she returned to Ghana and taught at Wesley Girls High School for two years before being recruited for the post of Education Secretary in the Youth department of the World Council of Churches. In 1970 she returned to Nairobi to work as the Secretary for the newly created Youth department in the reorganised secretariat of the All Africa Conference of Churches (AACC) following the Abidjan Conference of 1969. Participants at Abidjan had issued a clear call for acculturation, Christian-Islamic dialogue, ecumenical co-operation, the

---

10 Dickson, K.: *Towards a Theologia Africana* in Fasholé-Luke, E. and Glasswell, M. (eds.), *New Testament Christianity for Africa and the World*, London, 1974; *Theology in Africa*, London, Darton Longman and Todd, 1984; Dickson, K. and Ellingworth, P., *Biblical Revelation and African Beliefs*, London, Lutterworth Press, 1969.

11 Pobee, J. S.: *Toward an African Theology*, Abingdon, Nashville, 1979; *Skenosis: Christian Faith in an African Context*, Gweru, Mambo, 1992; *An African Anglican's View of Salvation* in Wingate, A., Ward, K. and Pemberton, C. (eds.), *Anglicanism: A Global Communion*, London, Cassell, 1998.

recognition of the previously shunned African Initiated Churches (AICs) and had begun the process which was to lead to the call for a missionary moratorium at Lusaka in 1974.[12] Mercy Yamoah, soon to marry the future editor of Daystar Press Ibadan, Nigerian theologian Modupe Oduyoye, was in the institutional centres of the maelstrom of change sweeping across the mission churches of Africa.

After marriage Mercy Oduyoye moved to Ibadan, a virilocal move which further extended her grammar of difference in the gendered distribution of political, ecclesial, educational and domestic power in 'other' African polities away from the *cantus firmus* of her own matrilineal *Fantse*. She became the first woman lecturer in the Religious Studies Department of the University of Ibadan, where she taught Church History and Christian Doctrine. Her concerns were at once inter-disciplinary and applied to the challenge of culture and ritual in the reconstitution of African identity in the post-colonial world the African churches were being forced to address as a matter of missiological priority. She felt compelled to communicate to both "church women and men" the "ideals" of the Christian faith and the riches of "the traditional view that the life-force . . . in us is that of God".[13] Feeling like "an Elijah in the midst of all the priests and prophets of the patriarchal Baal", she was urgent in her desire to release theology from "the past-time of an obscure and marginal group of eggheads".[14]

A pioneer who has never been minded to mince her theological words, Oduyoye is at once a stimulating and prophetic voice within the new theological literature emerging from West Africa, and an acerbic and frequently frustrating protagonist of women's societal entitlements and religious authority. The frustration which can ambush those who engage in an extended dialogue with her work is the lack of sustained attention to the theological and socio-anthropological domains she addresses. Her voice is one of the charismatic leader, a role which she has acquitted with energy and indomitable persistence. She has successfully stoked the imaginations of the next generation of African women theologians, teachers, ministers, community workers and academics who make up the body of the Circle of

---

12 Utuk, E., *Visions of Authenticity: The Assemblies of the All Africa Conference of Churches, 1963–1992*, Nairobi, AACC, 1997, pp. 82; 87; 118.

13 Oduyoye, M. A., *Doing Theology in Nigeria* in Oduyoye, M. A. (ed.), *The State of Christian Theology in Nigeria 1980–81*, Ibadan, Daystar Press, 1986, p. 7.

14 Oduyoye, M. A., *Doing Theology in Nigeria*, p. 6.

Concerned African Women Theologians, with the fuel of a world where women not only make up the majority of those in the pews of the churches, but also build their communities alongside men in positions of trained and authorised leadership.

Oduyoye had been part of the World Council of Churches' gender-awareness project, exploring relationship and participation in the member churches under the rubric of the 'Community of Women and Men in the Church', which culminated in the Sheffield report of 1981.[15] During her time as one of the three deputy general secretaries of the WCC, and moderator of the Education and Renewal unit, Oduyoye oversaw the delivery of the 'Churches' Decade in Solidarity with Women', and wrote *Who Will Roll the Stone Away?*.[16] These two initiatives within the WCC and their associated impact on the life of the women's desk where South African Brigalia Bam, later to become General Secretary of the South African Council of Churches, was at work, and the wider penumbra of church women's conscientisation, should not be underestimated. After Sheffield, Oduyoye would create a working group of Nigerian women theologians, academics and practitioners, to reflect on the situation of women in African Church and society.[17] Within a year of the start of the Churches' Decade in Solidarity with Women in 1988, the first convocation of the Circle of Concerned African Women Theologians took place in Legon, Accra. However, there were other movements shifting the balance of theological reflection from its former domination by the Northern hemisphere. This was the emergence of EATWOT, an association whose thirty-year congress of minds has been exceptionally fertile across the Southern hemisphere. Its impact on Oduyoye's life will be explored in the second dimension of her theological contribution.

15 Oduyoye, M. A., *Preface at Dresden to the Sheffield Recommendations* in Parvey, C. F. (ed.), *The Community of Women and Men in the Church: The Sheffield Report*, Geneva, World Council of Churches, 1983.

16 Oduyoye, M. A., *Who Will Roll the Stone Away?*, Geneva, World Council of Churches, Risk Series Book 47, 1990.

17 Pemberton, C., *Feminism, Inculturation, and the Search for a Global Christianity: An African Example. The Circle of Concerned African Women Theologians*, unpublished PhD thesis for the University of Cambridge, 1998.

The literature

With over eighty published articles to her name and eight monographs, much of Oduyoye's work has openly crusaded for Africa's self-confidence in future and past and her women's empowerment. She has written for North Atlantic collections including Ursula King's *Feminist Theology*, Letty Russell's *Inheriting our Mothers' Gardens*, and Susan Thistlethwaite's *Lift Every Voice*.[18] She has been the African women's 'voice' in numerous EATWOT conference papers, and an essayist for several WCC conference reports, particularly on Youth, the Lima process towards Unity, the Community of Women and Men in the Churches and theological education. She has edited both reports on the Circle's biennial conferences in 1989 and 1996: *The Will to Arise: Women, Tradition and the Church in Africa*, and *Transforming Power*. Her most recent monograph, *The Daughters of Anowa*, is a passionate call to discover an African theology rooted in the religious cultures of Africa which realise the dignity, leadership spirituality and autonomy of African women.

Theology in Africa

There are three themes of prevenient importance in the work of Mercy Oduyoye: the celebration of Africa's commitment to life, reproduction and human harmony; the cultural displacement of Africa's identity under pressure from the Northern economic order; and the imperative of peace and inclusivity in her mandate for Africa's future. These themes have resonance in the life of EATWOT, which has proved a productive matrix for the development of Oduyoye's theology and the creation of the Circle of Concerned African Women Theologians. From the first convocation in 1976 recorded in the *Emergent Gospel* through the landmarks of the *Irruption of the Third World*

---

18 Oduyoye, M. A., *Reflections from a Third World Woman's Perspective: Women's Experience and Liberation Theologies* in King, U. (ed.), *Feminist Theology from the Third World: A Reader*, London, SPCK, 1994; *Be a Woman and Africa will be Strong* in Russell, L. M. et al. (eds.), *Inheriting Our Mothers' Gardens: Feminist Theology in Third World Perspective*, Philadelphia, Westminster Press, 1988; *The Empowering Spirit of Religion* in Thistlethwaite, S. B. and Engel, M. P. (eds.), *Lift Every Voice: Constructing Christian Theologies from the Underside*, San Francisco, Harper & Row, 1990.

to the *Spirituality of the Third World*, Protestant, Catholic and African Independent Church theologians, initially predominantly male but now with an increasingly confident female representation, have explored theology from a particular location of alienation.[19] This alienation is made up by the specific perspective of poverty, colonial negation, dysfunctional resources of tradition and wealth, retrieved by a persistent cry throughout for justice and hope for societal well-being in the face of the 'death dealing of the West'. Over the last two decades EATWOT, particularly under the influence of Asian and African theologians, has broadened its theological production from the lens of its initial South American Marxist-liberation theology to one which sees the importance of first nation theology and spiritualities, and gives a fresh account of anthropological poverty and the importance of developing an inculturated theology sensitive to the religious plurality of one's context, in what Sri Lankan theologian Aloysius Pieris called the theopraxis of liberation.[20] This has led in turn to fresh acknowledgement of independent churches in Africa and areas of women's traditional empowerment as well as the less satisfactory and pervasive areas of women's ritual exclusions particularly associated with menstruation and childbirth. However, there have been important unresolved struggles within the network as to how the urgent issues of economic inequalities and political fascism within Africa can be addressed by developing what, to some, seem to be local cultural theologies without political teeth.[21]

19 *Emergent Gospel: Theology from the Developing World*, Papers from the Ecumenical dialogue of Third World Theologians 5–12 August 1976, Dar-es-Salaam, London, G. Chapman, 1978.

20 Pieris, A., *The Place of Non-Christian Religions and Cultures in the Evolution of Third World Theology* in Fabella, V. and Torres, S. (eds.), *Irruption of the Third World: Challenge to Theology*, Papers from the Fifth International Conference of the Ecumenical Association of Third World Theologians in New Delhi, 17–29 August 1981, New York, Orbis, 1983; Mveng, E., *Third World Theology – What Theology? What Third World? Evaluation of an African Delegate* in Fabella, V. and Torres, S. (eds.), *Irruption of the Third World*.

21 Cone, J. H., *Black Theology: Its Origin, Methodology, and Relationship to Third World Theologies* in Fabella, V. and Torres, S. (eds.), *Doing Theology in a Divided World*, New York, Orbis Books, 1985; Cone, J. H. and Wilmore, G. S., *Black Theology and African Theology: Considerations for Dialogue, Critique, and Integration* in Cone, J. H. and Wilmore, G. S. (eds.), *Black Theology: A Documentary History 1966-79*, Volume 1, New York, Orbis Books, 1993; Tutu, D., *Black Theology/African Theology: Soul Mates or Antagonists?* in Cone, J. H. and Wilmore, G. S. (eds.), *Black Theology: A Documentary*

Two-winged theology

In her opening address to the Circle of Concerned African Women
Theologians in 1989, Oduyoye advocated a 'two-winged' theology to be the
paradigmatic heart of how African women theologians should engage in
theological reflection and action – a theology which incorporated men as
colleagues in a common task to establish a humane Africa in the midst of
intra-continental conflict and societal injustice. Not surprisingly this two-
winged theology is buffeted both by her own analysis of the tasks ahead for
African women and by western feminism's analysis of patriarchy.[22] The lurid
warnings of the "suffocating grip of patriarchy", which Oduyoye notes, are
neutralised by her *Fantse* mother-centred perspective where "men are precious
as the male-aspect of life that we need to make us carriers of life and whose
responsibility is to be spirit-protectors of the lives we bring into being".[23] This
vision is bathed in maternal imagery as it binds women alongside men in the
promotion of human well-being in Africa. African women theologians are to
be "part of the team of midwives assisting at the rebirth of African women and
the resurrection of the human in Africa".[24] It is a process which eschews the
standpoint of "westernising Africa" as the path to liberation, affirms the
lessons of African-American womanism that power is given to those to whom
one grants it, and alerts her own African sisters to the importance of resisting
the "power African men think they must have over African women".[25] She
advocates traditional African 'woman-power' in protest against all attempts
at 'exclusion and marginalisation' of women in church and society from their
part in making Africa's present and future.

The sense of interdependence derived from the sphere of the bio-religious,
of the African *communitas*, is an interdependence generated by the
heterosexual necessity of reproduction and the multiple connections of life,
both in the world of the spirit, the ancestors, those yet to be born, and the
present domain of the living. This typology locks Oduyoye into an active
participation with African men in the goal of building human society despite

History 1966–79.
22 Oduyoye, M. A. and Kanyoro, M. R. A., *Talitha Qumi: Proceedings of the Convocation of
    African Women Theologians 1989*, Ibadan, Daystar Press, 1990, p. 27.
23 Oduyoye, M. A. and Kanyoro, M. R. A., *Talitha Qumi*, p. 44.
24 Oduyoye, M. A. and Kanyoro, M. R. A., *Talitha Qumi*, p. 47.
25 Oduyoye, M. A. and Kanyoro, M. R. A., *Talitha Qumi*, p. 48.

some of her more outraged statements against male bad behaviour.[26] For western-trained feminists some of her perspectives on woman and her ontic relation to motherhood can on first encounter seem hopelessly unreconstructed. In an article written for *Concilium* in 1989 Oduyoye states that: "Mothering is a religious duty. It is what a good socio-political and economic system should be about".[27] However, women are not to be denied their humanity apart from their work as mothers, and motherhood is not something only gifted by physical reproduction. In Oduyoye's *Asante* culture, a child belongs to the mother "until it is born" and then its welfare and well-being passes over to the whole community.[28] This is traditionally weighted towards women nurturance, but its nourishment in men is now advocated.[29]

What Oduyoye brings to western feminism is a re-articulation of the power and societal blessing which women, as biological mothers, bring to their societies, and in which all women can partake for the mutual enhancement of life. After all, she reflects "it is only women and biological mothers (who) continue to see . . . mothering of the human race as a sacred duty", a role otherwise neglected by the state and other institutions.[30] Only the "anti-baby economy of the North" denigrates the value of mothers, and indeed children, whereas for Oduyoye mothers should be "honoured" and "empowered".[31] It is at these moments when Oduyoye asserts the importance of children as "assets of the whole nation", motherhood as "a sacred duty", and the interdependence of men and women in the task which faces African church and society, that the cultural distance of her world from the orbit of radical western feminist reflection becomes apparent. However her theological mandate against the injustices of colonialism and the continued economic exploitation 'crystallised' in external debt, offers an alternative point of alignment, but one which has similar barbs for the over-confident.

26 Oduyoye, M. A., *Reflections from a Third World Woman's Experience and Liberation Theologies* in Fabella, V. and Torres, S. (eds.), *The Irruption of the Third World*.
27 Oduyoye, M. A., *Birth* in Pobee, J. S. and von Wartenberg-Potter, B. (eds.), *New Eyes for Reading: Biblical and Theological Reflections by Women from the Third World*, Geneva, World Council of Churches, 1986, p. 24.
28 Oduyoye, M. A., *Birth*, p. 28.
29 Oduyoye, M. A. and Kanyoro, M. R. A., *Talitha Qumi*, p. 43.
30 Oduyoye, M. A., *Birth*, p. 28.
31 Oduyoye, M. A., *Birth*, p. 29; p. 30.

The African crisis

At the Seventh Conference of the All African Council of Churches, in Addis Ababa in 1997, Oduyoye, as the newly elected General Secretary of EATWOT, challenged delegates in her keynote speech to consider their situation as citizens of Africa: *Den mmusu na yaabo?* "What has happened to us?" she asked:

> Why is it that culturally we have become what the Akan proverbs enjoin us not to be, "a people who takes out its own stomach and fills the void with straw"? We are alienated from our roots, but do not seem to have the means to become fully integrated into the Western world, which we so much yearn to be a part of. We do not lay the ground rules for the games in which we participate . . . We are ready to follow every advice of others whose real interest is to help their own people to sustain and enhance their own standard of living. We know of nations whose people are unemployed even while their gross national income rises and their production lags; they live on the interests we pay them. We are witnessing the sad paradox of an abortive economic development policy which induces an inversion of financial transfers . . . What has happened to us? We are unable to provide quality education for our children. Instead we engage in remedial adult education. *Den mmusu na yaabo?* Have you not heard? Have you not seen? Do you not experience it in your life encounters? That in being poor, we are making others rich.[32]

This is one of the clearest statements by Oduyoye of two central concerns which have helped inform her theological writings over the last twenty years: the cultural displacement of Africa's identity and the continued economic 'bondage' of Africa's post-independence reality. EATWOT has consistently united its disparate theological concerns and approaches through an outrage at the prevailing North/South division of wealth, using categories of dependency of the periphery to the metropole. The WCC through the eighties and nineties became used to the terms of theological engagement being established first of all on lines of wealth and poverty. When Oduyoye spoke in the AACC submission to the sixth General Assembly of the WCC at Vancouver in 1983, she called for the removal of "rags" and "beggary" and

---

32 Oduyoye, M. A., *Troubled but Not Destroyed*, an unpublished paper presented at the Seventh Assembly of the All Africa Conference of Churches, Addis Ababa, 1997.

a return to "wholeness of life", a blessing not simply of Christianity but present in the "dynamic" of African society.[33] That economic concerns should inform a modulated part of her theological reflection is consonant with the theological currents present in the AACC, WCC and EATWOT and the political atmosphere of contemporary Africa. However Oduyoye's roots in the Methodist tradition with its connection with the Wesleyan holiness movement so influential in nineteenth century mission in Ghana, and the specifically Ghanaian inculturation of Methodist class discipline in economic and political orientation is important to keep present in the welter of other interstices.[34]

This form of Methodism was committed, from its genesis, to the freeing of slaves, resistance to economic poverty and to a vision of community and individual wholeness through the salvific message of Christ in both the United States of America and England before it came to the Gold Coast.[35] These common roots present possible avenues of co-operation which transcend the national divisions of wealth and poverty which within the over-determined political discourse of EATWOT are frequently portrayed as irreducible as the *ipsissima verba* of the divine.

The call to life

For Oduyoye, the way forward out of the economic, military and civil dis-ease of Africa is to draw afresh from her own religious and cultural resources.[36] Her theology is a call to life from all that would deal death to Africa and her women.[37] Her world is one where the West is pariah, and Africa a suppliant

33 Oduyoye, M. A., *Wholeness of Life in Africa*, in Masamba, M. m., Stober, R. and Appiah, E. V. (eds.), *An African Call for Life*, a contribution to the World Council of Churches Sixth Assembly 'Jesus Christ – the Life of the World', Ibadan, Daystar Press, 1983: p. 118; p. 119.

34 Bartels, F. L., *The Roots of Ghana Methodism*, Cambridge, Cambridge University Press, 1965.

35 Hollenweger, W. J., *Pentecostalism, Origins and Developments Worldwide*, Massachusetts, Peabody Press, 1997.

36 Oduyoye, M. A., *Wholeness of Life in Africa*, pp. xix; 114.

37 Oduyoye, M. A., Kanyoro, M. R. A. and Njoroge, N., *Circular Introductory Communication*, to participants at Nairobi Pan-African Circle meeting, 4 April 1995, unpublished paper.

amnesiac who is returning to consciousness, re-discovering ancient resources of resistance, weapons which had been left behind but now invite wise warriors to return and collect them. Although her analysis is simple, her range of answers is more complex. In reply to her question, *Den mmusu na yaabo?* she develops a theology which is dependent on a number of factors. All of these are familiar to the EATWOT constituency: liberation theology committed to the underside of history, the voice of the poor and the privileging of contextual readings of the Bible. She deploys 'theologies' across her corpus, with the freedom of a postmodern critic: African inculturation theology, feminist theology, womanist theology, Minjung theology, black theology from South Africa and the United States and simple sermonic style assertions of the power or example of Christ are pressed together to form her theological call to arms. But when is theology disinterested and pure? I think Oduyoye would probably reply 'when it is irrelevant'. For what drives Oduyoye in her work is the production of speeches and papers which energise and transform horizons. Hers is undoubtedly a pragmatic theology which has as its horizon an Africa at peace with itself, and in peer relation to the North untrammelled by debt and post-colonial cultural neurosis.

The sources of alienation

There are consequently many paradoxes with which Oduyoye struggles in her theological writings. The most explicit is the failure of Africa to live up to her vision of west African *shalom*: how is it that an "Africa which thinks whole (and) preaches wholeness . . . is riddled with divisiveness and brokenness"? she asked in her deposition to the WCC conference in Vancouver.[38] Oduyoye's early work at Ibadan University posited the answer that Africa has forgotten herself, and that African Christians had allowed themselves to be detached from their roots in the pursuit of enrichment and "self-centeredness", under the "cloak of 'Westernisation'".[39] So if Africans returned to the ancient paths of communal accountability, with the whole of life viewed as sacred, and not the degenerate 'Western deviation' of Christianity, then Africa would

38 Oduyoye, M. A., *Wholeness of Life in Africa*, p. 114.
39 Oduyoye, M. A., *Wholeness of Life in Africa*, p. 122.

be able to heal itself. Western Christianity is fundamentally flawed and in many areas bankrupt, having lost the foundational unity of the vision of Christ's ministry of gender justice and societal well-being sundered in the Constantinian settlement, a theme she pursues in *Hearing and Knowing* and infers throughout her corpus.[40] Maybe a better title for *Hearing and Knowing* would be *Hearing and Accepting*. For in Oduyoye's mind many Africans have not accepted the package of 'mission Christianity' (indeed, in her mind, should not) and therefore live in an ambivalent relationship with their religious cultures. This is particularly the case, Oduyoye argues, with women, who have retained pre-Christian perspectives on life and spirituality, despite the transformation of Africa's public conceptual landscape. The early conversions of the nineteenth century were, she contends, based on the African commitment to hospitality and gratitude. It was the gratitude of freed slaves to their liberators, who then offered hospitality to the white religion, as part of the goods of trade and education.[41] But gratitude is different from negotiation and evaluation of all the new ways.

Oduyoye advocates both an acceptance of the transforming power of Christianity in the affirmation of Christ as a saviour figure, a particularly powerful and significant friend for women and an important healer for the marginalised and distressed, and at the same time she looks for African independence in working out how the particularity of Christ will sit within the religious plurality of contemporary Africa. She is a constant campaigner for advocating the cultural moments within African traditions where women are manifested as leaders, religious mediums, prophets and King-makers. As a *Fantse* princess herself, she has a rich tradition to draw on from Akan history.

However it is not a history which all African traditions share; hence the range of voices within the Circle constituency on the potential of their own particular gendered anthropologies in the reconstitution of African society and church.[42]

---

40 Oduyoye, M. A., *Wholeness of Life in Africa*, p. 117.
41 Oduyoye, M. A., *Hearing and Knowing*.
42 Edet, R.: *Men and Women Building the Church in Africa* in *Voices from the Third World*, 1985, Vol. 8, No. 3; *Christianity and African Women's Rituals* in Oduyoye, M. A. and Kanyoro, M. R. A. (eds), *The Will to Arise*; Getui, M., *The Status of Women in African Naming Systems* in Wamue, G. and Getui, M. (eds.), *Violence against Women*, Nairobi, Acton Publishers, 1996; Kanyoro, M. R. A., *Feminist Theology and African Culture* in Wamue, G. and Getui, M. (eds.), *Violence against Women*.

Theological method in religious plurality:
A life-protecting path for religious toleration

In the light of the last thirty years of Africa's history, in which the continent has been traumatised by ethnic and religious divisions in its search towards new socio-political equilibriums, Oduyoye's commitment to a theology of religious multiplicity, which does not privilege any one religion for the purposes of asserting African identity or nationhood, is laudable and urgent. Her reconciliation is mediated through recourse to ancient *Asante* practice and myth. Here clan, or ethnic difference, is not posited on the desire for power, but on affirming connectedness. The foundation and possibility of this connection, in a world saturated with difference and apparent discontinuity, is the biological location of a common womb, possessed by a common ancestress. This is the notion of *abusua*. In my view it represents one of Oduyoye's most original theological developments, and the theological vein which will be most richly mined in the future.

The idea of *abusua* appears in two articles, one written in honour of liberation theologian Gustavo Gutiérrez in 1989 and the other for the WCC's *Ecumenical Review* in 1991.[43] The *abusua* is a lineage, with a common female ancestor, made up of numerous households which are "ever-expanding, outward looking communit(ies)"; they are multi-generational, and are organised through bifocal systems of authority for men and women ensuring the full participation of all.[44] Although households within each *abusua* are chronologically diverse, including the living-dead and those yet to be born, as well as 'spatially dispersed', families in 'diaspora' (as African-Americans or in Europe or across the continent itself), the *abusua* consider themselves to be one blood because they have a common female ancestor. Wherever a member of the *abusua* finds herself, her responsibility is to seek out the head of the local family and make herself known. For, as Oduyoye insists, as an Akan no one is expected to operate "as an individual isolated from the *abusua*".[45]

---

43 Oduyoye, M. A.: *Christian Feminism and African Culture: The Hearth of the Matter* in Ellis, M. H . and Maduro, O. (eds.); *The Future of Liberation Theology*, New York, Orbis Books, 1989; *The African Family as a Symbol of Ecumenism* in *Ecumenical Review*, 1991, Vol. 43, No. 4.
44 Oduyoye, M. A., *The African Family as a Symbol of Ecumenism*, p. 446.
45 Oduyoye, M. A., *The African Family as a Symbol of Ecumenism*, p. 468.

The *abusua* is an indivisible unity from which one cannot separate oneself. There are no distinctions between siblings and cousins, mothers and aunts, fathers and uncles. In this way a childless woman, such as herself, is enabled to be respected as a mother within the *abusua*, for she is a member of a wider familial unit, a unit in which every member is committed to each other's welfare and carries the responsibilities of each age-set. This experience of being a member of a unit of mutual interdependence has furnished Oduyoye with a model of how the Circle could operate as a theological group committed to research, publication and mutual support. It also provides her with a powerful illustration of how the Church could outwork its vocation of catholicity and ecumenical solidarity. It is not enough, she argues, for the 'Christ clan' to honour the same mother, but at the same time act viciously and irresponsibly with one another. She calls denominations to understand themselves as different households within the same *abusua*, respecting one another as part of the same clan and blood inheritance.

Abusua and inter-faith relations

Typically, creative theologian that she is, Oduyoye plays with the idea of an 'other *abusua*' in an important extension of this symbol. Other *abusua* in this instance would be other religious communities, such as Islam, Hinduism, Buddhism and African Traditional Religions (ATR). The 'Christ family', the Christian *abusua,* demonstrates the hospitality of Africa with an 'open-door' approach to the outside world, with particular rules and regulations which structure the relationships with other *abusua,* households of other faiths. Oduyoye encourages her readers to consider the advantages of adopting a method of being in 'pro-existence', not simply co-existence, with other faiths, recognising that *abusua* with its network of household relationships engineers human goodness.[46]

Abusuas may be different in language, origin and cultures, but they share a world view which "rests on a religious interpretation of the universe".[47] In

---

46 Oduyoye, M. A., *The African Family as a Symbol of Ecumenism*, p. 471; Kanyoro, M. R. A. and Njoroge, N. (eds.), *Groaning in Faith: African Women in the Household of God,* Nairobi, Acton Publishers, 1996.
47 Oduyoye, M. A., *The African Family as a Symbol of Ecumenism*, p. 467.

this way the Akan experience of clan, household and family is offered by Oduyoye as a way of resolving the tensions raised by aggressive North Atlantic missionary activity.[48]   It becomes instead a means of creating harmony and co-operation with the two other major religions of the continent, Islam and ATR, whose presence, in varied percentages of dominance or minority, marks every country across Africa.[49]

The concern for inter-faith reconstruction in Africa is high on Mercy Oduyoye's agenda. The Circle's 1996 conference dedicated a full morning to explicating Muslim-Christian dialogue, facilitated by Dr Janice Nassibou, African-American director of the Programme for Christian/Muslim Relations in Africa (PROCMURA). One morning's worship was led by Muslim participants, another by traditionalists from South Africa. In the *Will to Arise*, Dr Rabiatu Ammah explicates the position of women within Islam for a mainly Christian audience, and concludes, "in reality, the picture might be bleak for Muslim women, but we must also aim at the ideal. So must women in all religions".[50] Circle women are asked to recognise the disadvantage at which Islamic approaches to education has placed women – and reflect on the asserted alienation the early Christian monopoly on educational provision in Africa has created for post-Independence Africa particularly north of the Equator. The hardening of Islamic fundamentalism in the north with the emergence of Taliban style movements is a very real challenge to the realisation of Oduyoye's vision, yet at the same time calls churches and theologians alike to a fresh examination of the 'common' in the constitution of Christian community and language of spirituality.

48 Oduyoye, M. A., *Teaching Authoritatively amidst Christian Pluralism in Africa* in Meeks, D. M. (ed.), *What Should Methodists Teach? Wesleyan Tradition and Modern Diversity*, Nashville, Kingswood Books, 1990; Gifford, P., *Christian Fundamentalism and Development in Africa* in *Review of African Political Economy*, 1991, No. 52.

49 Barrett, D. and Johnson, T., *Annual Statistical Table on Global Mission:2000* in *International Bulletin* (50th Anniversary edition), 2000, Vol. 40, No. 1, pp. 24 f.; Pobee, J. S., *Skenosis: Christian Faith in an African Context*, pp. 62; 132; 133.

50 Ammah, R., *Paradise Lies at the Feet of Muslim Women*, in Oduyoye, M. A. and Kanyoro, M. R. A., *The Will to Arise*, p. 84.

Conclusion

Whilst Mercy Amba Oduyoye has been at the forefront of pointing out to African male colleagues, and North Atlantic 'would be saviours', that the agenda of African women is distinct from both their strategies – both those of African males, and the neo-liberal ideologies of western feminists entrapped in the two-thirds world division of debt and post-colonial dependency – there have been theological motifs of reconciliation in her work. Alongside her overtures to co-operation in 'two-winged theology' where women work alongside their male peers in the restructuring of African hope, and her considerable work through the WCC in the Church's decade of solidarity with women across the hemispheres, her most original theological contribution to the urgent task of making peace across a troubled continent is that of *abusua*. Oduyoye proposes this motif as a way forward out of the politicised religious aggression unleashed within the continent. However, as a first world theologian I see the theme of a common ancestress as a helpful addition to the ideas developed by Carol Christ and Judith Plaskow in their collection of essays exploring the ideas of cosmogenic goddess figures and primal women-spirit visions emerging, yearning for integration and relationality across the created order.[51] Moreover I would suggest that extended beyond Africa, *abusua* offers a new road for the fractured discourse between theologians of the two-thirds world and the first world. If we are all part of *abusua,* then we know how to recognise one another, and offer each others' perspectives and contexts hospitality in a common dedication to the 'life' of the extended household . . . the household of a world-wide humanity.

Oduyoye's one-time colleague at the WCC's women's desk in Geneva, Brigalia Bam, offers something of this in her challenging contribution to *Anglicanism: A Global Communion* where she suggests that our Christian eponymous ancestor Eve, "the womb, the nurturing centre, the place of birth for humankind" is "Mother Africa" from whom all humanity is descended.[52] Common ancestry, runs the sub-text, is the basis for co-operation and mutual esteem. This is a shift from arguments generated by incarnational or salvific

---

51 Christ, C. and Plaskow, J. (eds.), *Woman Spirit Rising: A Feminist Reader in Religion*, New York, Harper and Row, 1979; Christ, C., *Laughter of Aphrodite: Reflections on a Journey*, New York, Harper and Row, 1987.
52 Bam, B., *All About Eve* in Wingate, A., Ward, K. and Pemberton, C. (eds.), *Anglicanism: A Global Communion*.

inclusion; they move from the assumption by God in some specific act in history, or in the future, to the commonality of earth, womb and generation. Oduyoye's proposal of common objectives for securing life and humanity in Africa echoes something of Habermas' idea of legitimate communication, possible only where common goals and aspirations are mutually understood.[53] Oduyoye's common goal is that of the well-being of Africa, her women, children and men. Particularity is inevitable and critical for action, but at present her theological and anthropological vision is too limited.

I propose that a genuinely global vision is required from both hemispheres, echoing and extending Oduyoye's argument that without two wings a bird cannot fly. Just as there are particular issues to be worked through in the skewing of power between men and women in Africa, which Oduyoye argues must be overcome in a spirit of co-operation and interdependence, so there is an urgent requirement to face the systemic economic malaise of debt, resource allocation and capital transfers in the arrangement of power between first-world and two-thirds world, from both sides of the divide. Although the particular impact of the history of colonial alienation and contemporary frustration in the failure of Independent Africa to soar with the young tigers of Asia and the economies of the northern hemisphere is sharp and discouraging, a theological discourse shaped around the optimism of 'two-winged theology' and the hospitality of *abusua* does offer Oduyoye and her sisters working in the sphere of western theology a way forward.

53 Habermas, J., *Legitimation Crisis*, London, Heinemann, 1976.

Chapter Seven

The Mute Cannot Keep Silent: Barth, von Balthasar, and Irigaray, on the Construction of Women's Silence

Rachel Muers

The provenance of this paper is somewhat complex. It arises out of work I have undertaken recently on theologies of gender difference in Karl Barth and Hans Urs von Balthasar, but I have re-examined that work in the light of my doctoral research, which is looking at 'silence' as a theological theme.[1] Feminist theology is one of the few theological areas in which silence is ever talked about; but readings of silence within feminist theology tend to be negative – they are critiques of the silencing of women.[2] My current work is an attempt to incorporate the insights of feminist theology into a more positive, or at least a more nuanced, reading of silence. That is the larger context out of which this paper arises.

Silence and muteness

I should, first, explain my title: The mute cannot keep silent. The act of keeping silent, as philosophers and literary theorists alike have noted, can have a multiplicity of meanings. A silence in conversation can be the avoidance of speech on a particular subject, a recognition that no words can be an adequate response to the situation, an affirmation of an intimacy that includes but is not exhausted by verbal exchange. Responding to a question with silence can

---

1 See Muers, R., *A Question of Two Answers: Difference and Determination in Barth and von Balthasar* in *Heythrop Journal*, 1999, Vol. 40, No. 3.
2 For a summary of these critiques see Dumais, M., *Le Sacre et l'autre parole selon une voix féministe* in Blodgett, E. D. and Coward, H. G. (eds.), *Silence, the Word and the Sacred*, Waterloo, Wilfred Laurier University Press, 1989.

indicate agreement, indifference, ignorance, deep thought, refusal to acknowledge the questioner. The keeping of silence is not equivalent to an utterance, but is equally a part of human communicative behaviour.[3]

In the Gospels and in Christian theological texts, appearing amid the polyphony of significant sayings, we find significant silences. Mary falls silent in the second chapter of Luke's Gospel, "treasuring" all the words of the birth narrative. Jesus' opponents are reduced to silence; the disciples at the transfiguration can find no words. The Gospel of Mark ends with a paradoxical silence. Jesus stands silent before Pilate.[4]

All of these acts of significant silence must be distinguished from the silence of Zechariah at the beginning of Luke's Gospel, when he disbelieves the angel's message and is deprived of speech. Zechariah is rendered mute.[5] Speech is impossible for the mute person, but so is keeping silent. As Heidegger puts it in *Sein und Zeit*: "If a man is dumb, he still has the tendency to speak. Such a person has not proved that he can keep silence; in fact he entirely lacks the possibility of proving anything of the sort".[6] The mute person's silence, in and of itself, communicates nothing.

In commentaries on Luke's Gospel, theologians from the patristic period onwards have linked the muteness of Zechariah with the 'silence of the prophets' before John the Baptist. Speech was impossible before, but now through the coming of the incarnate Word and through the Holy Spirit which gives the power of speech, creation has been given back its voice.[7] Muteness is a possibility that the coming of Christ negates. The dumb are among those healed by Christ; if the disciples become mute, the stones themselves will lose their muteness and cry out.[8]

---

3   See, for a lengthy consideration of this, Dauenhauer, B., *Silence: the Phenomenon and its Ontological Significance*, Bloomington, Indiana University Press, 1980.
4   Luke 2 [19]; Mark 3 [4]; Mark 9 [6]; Mark 16 [8]; Mark 15 [5].
5   Luke 1 [20].
6   "Der Summe hat umgekehrt die Tendenz zum 'Sprechen'. Ein Stummer hat nicht nur nicht bewiesen, daß er schweigen kann, es fehlt ihm sogar jede Möglichkeit, dergleichen zu beweisen." Heidegger, M., *Sein und Zeit*, Tübingen, Niemeyer, 1993 (1927), pp. 164 f. Translated as *Being and Time* by Macquarrie, J. and Robinson, E., Oxford, Blackwell, 1962, p. 208.
7   See on this Mortley, R., *From Word to Silence*, Volume II, *The Way of Negation*, Bonn, Hanstein, 1986, pp. 37; 63 ff.
8   Mark 9 [17] ff.; Luke 19 [40].

Christian feminist theology, from its earliest years, has belatedly claimed this promise of the Gospel for women. Attention has been drawn repeatedly to the muting of women within the churches and within academic theology. Women have been summoned to speech, exhorted to 'find a voice'. Criticism has been directed, not only at the institutional and cultural muting of women in the doing of theology, but also at the construction of women *as silent* within theological texts. Luce Irigaray's words concerning psychoanalysis could equally have been said of theology: "[Women's life] is assigned within a discourse that excludes, and by its very 'essence', the possibility that it might speak for itself".[9]

This paper will look at aspects of the construction and function of women's silence in the work of Karl Barth and Hans Urs von Balthasar. In the case of Barth I shall consider a specific text – the discussion of the creation of Eve. In the case of von Balthasar I shall make use of *Word and Silence* by Raymond Gawronski, a recent work that brings together various texts on women's silence in von Balthasar.[10] Both of these theologians develop readings of gender difference in which the silence of women, or woman, is both extremely important and a major point of weakness. After discussing their work I shall introduce, for contrast, a brief discussion of Luce Irigaray's treatment of woman's silence in her *Epistle to the last Christians*.

The central point to be made about the silence of woman in Barth and von Balthasar is that, to fulfil its role in their theological scheme, it needs to be an act of keeping silent. It needs to be a significant silence, not the result of muteness. However, in the process of constructing 'woman' as the bearer or embodiment of that silence, the theologians in question render it a meaningless silence, an imposed muteness; the mute cannot keep silence.

I hope to bring out three interconnected features of the construction of woman's silence, which relate to this central point. Firstly, there is a tension between woman as object-to-be-talked-about, by definition excluded from speech, and woman as fully human subject – the latter point being essential to the anthropologies of both Barth and von Balthasar. Secondly, there is a tension between inexplicability and explanation. Both Barth and von

9 Irigaray, L., *This Sex Which is Not One*, translated by Porter, C. and Burke, C., Ithaca, Cornell University Press, 1985, p. 91. For a discussion of this theme in Irigaray, see Walker, M., *Silence and Reason: Women's Voice in Philosophy* in *Australian Journal of Philosophy*, 1993, Vol. 71, No. 4.

10 Gawronski, R., *Word and Silence*, Edinburgh, T & T Clark, 1995.

Balthasar want to state that woman and her silence are in some way inexplicable, irreducibly 'other'; at the same time, both find it necessary for their theological systems to give a full explanation of woman's silence and its significance. Thirdly, in this explanation of silence, there is the tension between silence as a free act and silence as muteness.

Much of the first section of the paper might sound like purely negative criticism, fired off at what we all know are easy targets. I hope the later parts will bring out some more positive suggestions – but to some extent the paper is intended to open up discussion, rather than to provide complete answers to its own questions.

Barth's silent woman

In the first division of the third volume of Barth's *Church Dogmatics*, he develops a theological account of creation by following the Genesis narrative, introduces woman as the 'answer' to man. Man, the male, is said to constitute a 'question' to which woman provides, or crucially, *is*, the answer. Man is incomplete without woman, as the question is incomplete without its answer. In the words of Genesis 2^{18}, "It is not good for the man to be alone".[11]

'Question' and 'answer' is a model based on speech. But note that the woman is characterised as 'answer' rather than as the 'one who answers'; it is this feature of the presentation that allows Barth to portray woman's existence as essentially silent from the moment of her creation. Barth follows what he takes to be the logic of the Genesis text: the man acknowledges the woman ("This at last is bone of my bone . . . ") and the woman makes no response. Her silence is for Barth a sign that "She does not choose: she is chosen"; her acknowledgement of man is implied in his acknowledgement of her. As Barth develops from this a full account of the created interrelation between the sexes, "silence" and "quiet" are described as the "distinctive features of woman" revealed by the New Testament, features which, Barth assures us, are in no way to be regarded as "lack".[12]

The characterisation of woman as 'answer' brings out the first tension to

11 Barth, K., *Church Dogmatics* translated by Bromiley, G. W., Edinburgh, T&T Clark, 1948, Volume III, I, p. 290.
12 Barth, K., *Church Dogmatics*, Volume III, I, pp. 303; 327.

which I alluded earlier, and raises the question: How human is woman? It is essential for Barth's purposes that she should be fully human, because he uses the man-woman relation as the paradigm of human community and an 'image' of the Trinitarian God – that is his reading of Genesis 1 [27]: "In the image of God he created them, male and female he created them".[13] Gender difference is for him fundamental to human existence. In the discussion of Genesis 2, however, a male standpoint is tacitly assumed. It is the existence of *woman* that is a matter for theological reflection, not the existence of man, nor simply of sexual difference. Although the original Adam is in some sense sexless (Barth explicitly states, on the basis of biblical exegesis, that Adam is not 'male' before the creation of the 'female') it nonetheless becomes male in the discussion of sexual difference. The 'woman' is from the first a problem, an object of the text's enquiry, and it is the nature of an object of enquiry to be silent. On the one hand, then, woman is fully human. So if she is silent, her silence cannot simply be assumed; it must, to some extent, be explained as an action. On the other hand, woman is an object, and her silence is an inevitable consequence of her positioning within the text.

Barth describes woman as a "mystery" to man, and therefore able to meet him as an inalienable Other. He refers, for example, to "the reality and multi-dimensional depth of the unmistakable mystery of the existence of woman and the sex relationship".[14] Her mystery is, however, not allowed to remain multi-dimensional; her silences must be explained, until in the discussion of the New Testament passages her silent existence is fully transparent; "She cannot be mistaken, but can be recognised without any effort on her part".[15] The logic of rendering women mute requires from them not only silence, but unambiguous silence.

Michel de Certeau's comments on the logic of torture are instructive here.[16] The torture victim, for de Certeau, is required to speak a word of surrender and then fall silent, but, paradoxically, the speech must not be heard, for it simultaneously reveals the violence that produces the victim's silence. The woman in Barth's text is made to give an unheard consent to her own silencing. Of course, we hear from Barth, she accepted man's choice of her

13 Barth, K., *Church Dogmatics*, Volume III, I, p. 186 ff.
14 Barth, K., *Church Dogmatics*, Volume III, I, p. 297.
15 Barth, K., *Church Dogmatics*, Volume III, I, p. 327.
16 de Certeau, M., *Heterologies*, translated by Massumi, B., Manchester University Press, 1986, p. 40 f.

and the place she was thus allocated in the order of creation. Of course the women who keep silent in the churches do not perceive their own silence as lack.

What function is this silence of women made to serve within the text? In its context in Genesis, it provides the basis for a crucial comparison between sexual difference and the ontological difference. Woman's silence, which accepts man's election, is held in a precarious analogical relation to human acceptance of God's election. Barth writes: "Woman is as little asked about her attitude to man as was solitary man about his attitude to God when God animated him by His breath".[17] The silence of woman is the silence of one who hears and accepts the word of electing love.

What can we say of this specification of women's silence? If we ignore its association with 'woman', we can see its theological importance. It signals the perfect adequacy of the word of election to the one who hears it, so that nothing more needs to be said. It is the intimate silence of the disciples with Jesus at the end of John's Gospel: "No-one dared to ask, 'Who are you?'; they knew it was the Lord".[18] It is the silence of the disciples who, in the words of Whittier, in response to "the gracious calling", "without a word/Rise up and follow".[19]

The crucial point about this silence, however, is that it relies for its significance on its status as a free act. Muteness cannot keep silent. It cannot, therefore, keep silent as a sign of complete and joyful acceptance of God's call. Barth's interpretation of the silence of the woman in Genesis relies on her being paradoxically both free and unfree. She must be free, because she must signal by her silence her acceptance of her election. She must be unfree, because her silence is decreed from the beginning and by her nature; her creation out of man means she has no choice. Man, in the story as Barth tells it, has a choice: to speak or keep silent; woman is required to be silent in order to symbolise, for man, what his silence might mean.

17 Barth, K., *Church Dogmatics*, Volume III, I, p. 303.
18 John 21 [12].
19 Whittier, J. G., *Dear Lord and Father of Mankind* in *Quaker Faith and Practice*, London, Religious Society of Friends (Quakers), 1995, extract 20:03.

Von Balthasar's *Jawort*

A similar problem appears in von Balthasar's development of a theology of sexual difference. Like Barth, he uses the image of woman as 'answer' to man. In von Balthasar's discussion, however, the 'woman's answer' is from the start a "double answer". There is the personal answer which constitutes the completion of the I-Thou relationship, in terms already familiar from Barth; man "requires the existence of the other . . . in order to make his own perfection possible".[20] Beside this, and inseparable from it, however, is the answer which transcends that relationship, the answer expressed in terms of *Fruchtbarkeit*, fruitfulness or fertility. The female or the feminine principle does not carry and bring forth a form determined by the male, but "something new, in which his gift is indeed integrated, but which encounters him in an unexpected, renewed form".[21] In von Balthasar's Mariology and Ecclesiology this double answer is developed in terms of the 'bridal' and 'maternal' roles of Mary and the Church. Again, woman *is* the answer and does not *give* it; so again, despite the use of a 'conversational' image to depict sexual difference, woman is constructed as silent. In a later section of the *Theo-Drama*, Mary's relation to the life of Christ is portrayed as a silent one; she conceives and bears the child in silence and shares the silence of the crucifixion.[22]

Here, again, the characterisation of woman as answer, rather than as the one who answers, points to a tension between the need to render her a fully human subject and the tendency to objectify her. The immense significance of Mary in von Balthasar's *Theo-Drama* heightens this and the other tensions to which I have referred.

An utterance by Mary – the *Jawort*, the word that accepts what is promised in the annunciation – is central to von Balthasar's *Theo-Drama*. The whole possibility of that drama rests on the establishment of a position from which she can give that response. In terms of the 'theo-drama' of the male-female encounter, von Balthasar's insistence on the "double answer" and the requirement that woman's answer should be "something new" makes it even

---

20 Von Balthasar, H. U., *Man in History* translated by Glen-Doepel, W., London, SCM, 1968, p. 306.
21 Von Balthasar, H. U., *Theo-Drama*, translated by Harrison, G., San Francisco, Ignatius Press, 1988, Volume III, p. 286. [*Theo-Dramatik*, Einsiedeln, Johannes Verlag, 1978, Volume 2/2.]
22 Von Balthasar, H. U., *Theo-Drama*, III, p. 358 ff.

more important that she should be given an independent subject-position from which to respond. The inexplicability of woman, the irreducibility of her otherness, is the precondition of her "double answer". Yet Mary is characterised as pure "answer" – and as pure "femininity". She gives her consent, her *Jawort*, silently, and falls silent.[23]

Gawronski's discussion of "Word and silence" in von Balthasar's theology is illuminating partly for its portrayal of sexual difference in relation to silence and speech. Mary's silence before God, her listening obedience, is characterised as "feminine", and at the same time presented as the primary stance of the whole Church, indeed of the whole of redeemed creation. "Masculine" approaches to prayer – the use of prayer techniques, the attempt to take possession of God – are condemned as the spiritual equivalent of the "sin of Sodom".[24] Men within the Church, it seems, are enjoined to learn to keep silent; to discover, spiritually, their "feminine side", or to play a "feminine" role. We saw in Barth, also, that man by virtue of his positioning within the text has the ability both to speak and to keep silent.

But gender difference, Gawronski insists with von Balthasar, must be preserved; so women are not to play a "masculine" role, not to participate themselves in the interweaving of speech and significant silence which forms the Church's activity.[25] They are not to keep silent but to *be* silent, in a silence whose significance is known primarily to the male theologian who observes and speaks of it. They are to remain mute, speaking only to reaffirm their muteness. If this line of thought is taken much further, the inevitable conclusion is that women, in these theologies, are not and cannot be fully human or fully part of the redeemed relationship of humanity to God. If silence is their nature, it cannot be their act. It cannot be a vocation they accept or a role they play. Like Mary in the *Theo-Drama*, all women, in von Balthasar's vision of the Church, are defined by and confined to their "feminine" silence.

---

23 See on this Gardner, L. and Moss, M., *Something Like Time: Something Like the Sexes* in Ayres, L. et al. (eds.), *Balthasar at the End of Modernity*, Edinburgh, T&T Clark, 1998.

24 Von Balthasar, H. U., *Sponsa Verbi*, Einsiedeln, Johannes Verlag, 1961, p. 198. Published in English as *Spouse of the Word*, translated by Littledale, A.V. with Dru, A., San Francisco, Ignatius Press, 1991, quoted passage 188. Quoted in Gawronski, *Word and Silence*, p. 172.

25 See von Balthasar, H. U., *New Elucidations* translated by Skerry M., San Francisco, Ignatius Press, 1986, pp. 189 ff.

The explanation of the inexplicable

In both Barth's and von Balthasar's treatments of the silence of women, we see both a determination of woman as inherently silent and a determination of woman's silence as significant in a particular way for the observers – supposedly the whole Church, but often implicitly limited to men. Women are not just mute persons who might at some future time retain the possibility of speech; they become less than persons. They are symbols, images, 'answers'. An answer is spoken, read or interpreted; it does not speak, read or interpret itself. The construction of women's silence constructs necessary silences. It is necessary, within the theological systems of Barth and von Balthasar, that there should be silence in creation so that the Word of God can be heard and creation can respond obediently. It is necessary that there should be silence, in order for dialogue to take place. It is necessary to preserve the possibility of silence being kept within the Church. Woman is used to mark the place of this necessary silence.

It is also important to note, however – this is the second tension to which I referred – that von Balthasar, and Barth to a lesser extent, make a double demand of woman's silence. On the one hand, they require woman's silence to have a clear significance – the obedient hearing of God's Word. On the other hand, insofar as sexual *difference* is itself important to them, they require woman's silence to be in some way inexplicable. Woman's silence denotes her difference, her mysteriousness, the impossibility of assimilating her to the monologue of male discourse. For von Balthasar, this difference is what permits the 'double answer' of woman to man (and, within the *Theo-Drama*, of creation to God), the 'fruitful' answer, which brings about something 'new' and unexpected. For Barth, this difference is what makes human existence inescapably relational, constituted by 'I' and 'Thou'. Woman's silence marks this indispensable difference. But, at the same time, woman's silence is constructed, interpreted and controlled, assimilated to the monologue.

Irigaray's silent woman

It is worth noting that both Barth and von Balthasar derive woman's silence from biblical narratives, particular narrated silences of women, which are taken to reveal some essential aspect of the feminine nature, and are developed into explorations of aspects of the relation of God and humanity. The interpretation of narrated silences is rarely straightforward, as the diversity of opinion among biblical commentators regarding the silence of Christ before Pilate, for example, clearly shows. Is it possible to re-read the narrated silences of women, not as imposed muteness but as significant silence?

Luce Irigaray's *Epistle to the Last Christians* concludes with a tentative question: "Grace that speaks silently through and beyond the word?"[26] A recurring theme throughout the piece is the silence of Mary. The proclamation of Christianity makes her, as Irigaray describes it, the "dumb virgin, with her lips closed", not permitted to speak herself, but only to hear and reproduce the "Word of the Father". Irigaray identifies the paradoxical demand made by the theological tradition of Mary; that she should utter a "silent yes" to the divine will and, in doing so, establish her own silence. Christianity can be "saved" from the erasure of difference - and of embodiment - by ending Mary's muteness. She must be "unsealed" from her "silent yes" and "given the Word".[27] Irigaray's central question is: "Who listens to the annunciation Mary makes?"

What Irigaray offers, however, is not straightforwardly a critique but rather a reinterpretation of Mary's silence. The "annunciation Mary makes" is intimately connected with her keeping of silence. Irigaray re-describes Mary's silence as that of "the only one left who still has some understanding of the divine . . . who still listens silently".[28] Her silence both learns and expresses the "grace that speaks silently through and beyond the word"; it signals the revelation of God in what cannot be completely assimilated to one word, one discourse, or one philosophical system. It signals the unrecognised implications of incarnation – the "Word's faithfulness to the flesh" above and beyond the "redemptory submission of flesh to the Word".[29]

Asking "Who listens to the annunciation Mary makes?" points to a dramatic revaluation of Mary's silence. It becomes a communicative silence deliberately chosen. Like all communicative silences, it is not replaceable by speech, but makes sense only in the context of the possibility of speech.

26 Irigaray, L., *Epistle to the Last Christians*, in *Marine Lover of Friedrich Nietzsche* translated by Gill, G. C., New York, Columbia University Press, 1991.
27 Irigaray, L., *Epistle to the Last Christians*, p. 171.
28 Irigaray, L., *Epistle to the Last Christians*, p. 175.
29 Irigaray, L., *Epistle to the Last Christians*, p. 169.

In the introduction to this paper, I referred to the muteness of Zechariah. Luke's birth narrative contains a contrasting instance of silence in Luke's Gospel: "But Mary treasured all these words, and pondered them in her heart".[30] The verbs used, συντηρέω and συμβάλλω, both have the component συν . . . 'with', 'together with'. What seems to be indicated here is a 'gathering' of the words. Mary 'takes in' all that is said, in order to 'draw it together'. Commentaries often suggest that this verse is intended to identify Mary as a witness; she recounted the story faithfully to the evangelist or the disciples. If we accept that explanation, Mary becomes again a silent 'receptacle' for the words of others, for the Word of the Father. She can contribute nothing of her own, she can say nothing of her own. Her silence is fully transparent to the interpreter, its meaning and use fully within his control; and she herself means nothing by it.

We can, however, re-read this narrated silence. Mary's "treasuring" of the words is open-ended; she never speaks again in the Gospel narrative, except briefly to question the young Jesus in the Temple.[31] If her listening is described in order to identify her as a witness, it remains the case that her 'witness' itself is never mentioned within the confines of the text. The possibilities created by this listening are never stated. Is she acting only as a 'receptacle' for the words? Or is she gathering them actively, drawing them together in her thoughts, to allow new words or thoughts to emerge? Her silence contains the whole Gospel narrative, because it gathers together the words of prophecy spoken at the birth of Christ and carries them forward to their fulfilment; but it also points to the incompleteness, the openness to new speech, of this or any theological narrative. It points to and reveals the limitless, unassimilable and endlessly generative grace of God. Unless, of course, Mary never speaks again because she is forced to be silent, because nobody hears her, or because she has handed over her silence and its interpretation to the Gospel's author. The silence can only be revelatory if there is the possibility of Mary speaking and being heard.

Von Balthasar affirms the "second answer" given by woman to man; he wants to make Mary other than a silent and passive receptacle of the Word; he wants to affirm the centrality of difference to his theological scheme; he

---

30 ἡ δὲ Μαριὰμ πάντα συνετήρει τὰ ῥήματα ταῦτα συμβάλλουσα ἐν τῇ καρδίᾳ αὐτῆς.
    Luke 2 [19].
31 Luke 2 [48].

wants, it seems, to "listen to the annunciation Mary makes". Barth likewise wants to retain irreducible difference within his system as the basis for human community. They try to develop the 'silence of woman' in order to do precisely this, but by defining women as inherently silent, and by presenting their silence as something that can be fully explained and controlled, they lose its capacity to signify difference. The silence they are left with is a meaningless emptiness in which the monologue of their theological discourse resounds. Developing a theology that gives genuine value to sexual difference will involve analysing and critiquing women's muteness. But it may also involve attending to the possibilities signalled by the keeping of silence.

Chapter Eight

Losing One's Life for Others:
Self-sacrifice Revisited

Kerry Ramsay

The equation of love with self-sacrifice, self-denial and self-abnegation in Christian theology is dangerous to women's psychological, spiritual, and physical health, and it is contrary to the real aim of Christian love.[1]

Feminist theology finds itself in a new place. Whereas before it relied on the assumptions of the infallibility of experience, it now finds itself coping with the ubiquity of experience and technique. It seems that there is a breadth of methodological difference which divides present day feminist, womanist and *mujerista* theologies and so the challenge of women's experiences which do not 'fit' into generalised categories challenges the way women do theology together.[2] While some have attempted to map the differences, others have sought to make universalising statements about what it might mean to be or not to be a woman of faith. Indeed it seems that if the insights of the post Christian feminists have anything to offer us they suggest the development of a 'feminist orthodoxy', where to be feminist is to make totalising statements about what women can and cannot say. I find myself challenging this sort of orthodoxy and wanting to revisit some of the traditional sticking points. At risk of making my story too specific I want to begin with the particularity of my own experience in the belief that there are commonalties for other interest groups.

---

1 See Gill-Austern, B. L., *Love Understood as Self-denial: What Does it do to Women?* in *Through the Eyes of Women: Insights for Pastoral Care*, Moessner, J. S. (ed.), Minneapolis, Fortress Press, 1996, p. 304.

2 See Jones, S., *Women's Experience between a Rock and a Hard Place: Feminist, Womanist, and Mujerista Theologies in North America* in *Horizons in Feminist Theology: Identity, Tradition, and Norms*, Chopp, R. S. and Davaney, S. G. (eds.), Minneapolis, Fortress Press, 1997, p. 52.

Introduction

I live and work in Britain. It was not always so. I was raised in Africa and spent my most formative years in South Africa, a country where structural violence was instituted and legislated for 40 years, and where the response to a theology of the cross was not only part and parcel of what it meant to be a people of faith but, for many, an inspiration. This personal history has critically shaped and forged my response to the problems of suffering and redemption. There was and is no getting around the cross for the people of South Africa. It is this problem of paradox that confronts me as a feminist theologian and as a woman who is a priest in the Church of England. My work involves not only giving exposition to scripture in preaching but also making some sense of my own integrity at the altar. It is in response to these tensions that I suggest that feminists attempt a theology of the cross, but asking this might well be asking that they lose their life in order to find it. It is a risky undertaking.

This article is an attempt to explore the feasibility of reconsidering some of the stumbling blocks of traditional theology on the problem of suffering. All specifically Christian theology and spirituality is refracted, as it were, through the prism of the cross. In 1519, Luther gave a very precise meaning to the phrase *theologia crucis* in his Heidelberg disputation. For Luther the sole locus of our knowledge of God is the cross. God is seen only from the rear in the very things which human wisdom regards as the antithesis of deity – such as weakness, foolishness and humility. Theologians of glory, Luther argued, seek to know God by intellectual effort and to please God by moral and ethical striving. They contemplate the wonders of creation and the 'glory' of men and women made in the image and likeness of their creator. Theologians of the cross, on the other hand, seek to know God indirectly in the redemptive mystery where God is revealed in and through the hiddenness, obscurity and suffering of a crucified Christ. God is, in this reading, found in the opposite to where might be expected. Communal anguish is no stranger to those in any period of history and the suffering in the last century appears to have reached devastating proportions. Responding to the intense suffering of two world wars and an increasing bombardment of media coverage, from things as wide-ranging as domestic violence to the effects of floods, has challenged any attempt to either dismiss suffering as a fact of life or something 'out there'. In the light of such developments it is not hard to see why a theology of the cross was rewarded with renewed interest, respect and recognition. Moltmann's "Crucified God" is perhaps one of the seminal texts on the subject that have emerged out of this period.[3] Feminist theology too has occupied itself with the implications of some of this theology.

Feminists and the deconstruction of the Cross

Much of the work of Christian feminist theology has been to deconstruct theologies of the Cross. They have repudiated anything that has reinforced the all too familiar exhortation to live lives of humble obedience, subordination and self-giving and self-denial. This glorification of suffering has led to critiques of theories of atonement, doctrines of redemption, interpretations of the crucifixion and questions of theodicy. In naming the evil represented in the notion that it is both God-like to suffer and that suffering is inevitably the consequence of personal sin, Christian feminist theologians have called into question the very foundations of Christian tradition, all of which represent a view which sees self-denial and self-sacrifice as the defining attributes of Christian love. Stephen Post suggests that divine love is often understood as the perfect example to which humans must conform, and is mistakenly interpreted as containing no self-concern, an idealisation, he argues, that not only misleadingly exaggerates the valid principle of unselfishness, but also rests on an unsatisfactory concept of God.[4] The liturgical mysticism of the Middle Ages developed this theme in which devotion to the sacred humanity of Jesus produced an attention to the literal mimicry of the humanity of Christ. Popular in the late fourteenth and fifteenth centuries was the *Imitation of Christ*, a work commonly ascribed to Thomas à Kempis, who saw the whole of the life of Christ as a cross and martyrdom and enjoined Christians to take the "royal road of the holy Cross".[5]

The writings of the imitation of Christ are perhaps a good example of calling us to endure an evil that befalls us, to accept its blow and thereby

---

3   Moltmann, J., *The Crucified God*, New York, Harper & Row, 1974.
4   Post, S. G., *The Inadequacy of Selflessness – God's Suffering and the Theory of Love* in *Journal of the Academy of Religion*, 1994, Vol. 56, No. 2.
5   Tinsley, E. J., *Thomas à Kempis* in Wakefield, G., *A Dictionary of Christian Spirituality* SCM Press, London, 1983, p. 378., citing Book 2, Chapter 12 of *Imitation of Christ*.

imitate the Cross of Christ. As a Christian ideal, this has played an important role in both Christian ethics and spirituality, an ideal reinforced by the image of the suffering servant upheld in the writings of the prophet Isaiah in which suffering *per se* is good.[6] This is in turn fed by the higher value that Christianity has accorded to love which is agape, disinterested. Not only is this a misreading of Jesus' life but one with significant pastoral implications. When Jesus' passive victimisation is seen as necessary to salvation then it is a small step to the belief that to be of value is to sacrifice oneself for others.[7] This glorification of suffering can lead to abusive structure and relationships. From Mediæval times the message of the Cross has been preached particularly to Christian women to accept not only their condition of subjugation, but also the arbitrary violence visited upon them by their husbands. In Chaucer's *The Canterbury Tales* the story of the patient Griselda who endures without complaint the extreme suffering and arbitrary trial imposed on her by her husband is told as a model of wifely decorum.[8] In using Christ's sufferings as a model for women's suffering the question of whether Jesus' innocent suffering on the Cross is redemptive in itself is raised. The double bind of women's deserved suffering for guilt and the promise of becoming Christlike in the hope that an abusive husband may be influenced or even converted by the wife's sweet acceptance has been a difficult message for Christian women to challenge.[9]

Anger at these interpretations has been good and necessary. The virtues mediated by the traditional interpretations of a theology of the Cross, from humble obedience and giving of self, to serving and sacrificing love, only serve to stabilise the existing distribution of power in society and intensify the oppression of women. Put alongside the all too familiar exhortation to women to submit to lives of self-destructive subordination, it is no surprise that the themes of self- emptying, vulnerability and suffering are as muted as they are

6   See Isaiah 42 [1-4], 49 [1-6] and 50 [4-11] for an understanding of the mission of the Servant who will with all patience restore justice to the nations.
7   Daly, M., *Beyond God the Father: Toward a Philosophy of Women's Liberation*, Boston, Beacon Press, 1973, p. 77.
8   See reference to Chaucer's *The Clerk's Tale* cited by Ruether, R. R., *Suffering and Redemption: the Cross and Atonement in Feminist Theology* in *Introducing Redemption in Christian Feminism*, Sheffield, Sheffield Academic Press, 1998, p. 99.
9   This is the view particular to the consequences of Eve's sin as recorded in Genesis 3 [16], in which God "greatly increases (Eve's) pangs in childbearing".

in the western feminist debate. For too long women have been disempowered, kept outside the task of theology and silenced. Their sexuality has been crucified, vilified and blamed for all that is wrong with the world. As descendants of Eve, they have been charged with a pre-disposition to moral laxity and all that is unstable and irrational. Their only redemption is perceived to be in the impossible virtues of Mary as new Eve. All of which has aroused the anger of feminists with the result that there have been some devastating critiques on the patriarchal bias of traditional theology. There is then no doubt that women's experience over the centuries has been oppressive and often continues to be so. An important task of feminist theology has been in exposing how religion has colluded with and upheld some of these distortions. Indeed, the task of faith is perennially just this.

The view that the very theology that should be challenging violence, suffering and sacrifice instead glorifies and sanctifies them has come from a wide range of feminist writing. Strong challenges have come from Brown and Parker in their exploration of the difficulties surrounding the issue of redemptive suffering in their work on the victimisation of women.[10] They critique the 'satisfaction' theory of atonement as formulated by Anselm. Their primary criticism is that it is surely a wretched theology that conceives of God as a sadist who can achieve his ends or find his pleasure only in making human beings suffer. Sacrifice and the crucifixion in this instance are seen as the supreme act of love, and suffering love has since become identified with the Christian ideal. Their criticism is not new. The idea that justice is established through adequate punishment has been questioned by theologians over the centuries. Abelard's rejection of the satisfaction theory and founding of the 'moral influence' theory also invites its own potential for abuse. It too is rejected by Brown and Parker as one that condones suffering and death. That we could be morally persuaded by Jesus' willingness to die for us into believing in God's overwhelming mercy presents real problems for victims of violence and particularly for women suffering wife-abuse. That the Cross of Christ has been used as a tool to justify domestic violence and advise women to endure suffering without complaint is a strong warning to anyone attempting to retrieve value in suffering. Undertaking such a task could too easily be seen to condone victimisation, whereas justice occurs when

10 Brown, R. and Parker R., *God so Loved the World* in Carlson Brown, J. and Bohn, C. R. (eds.), *Christianity, Patriarchy and Abuse*, New York, Pilgrim Press, 1989.

terrorisation stops, not when the condition of the terrorised is lauded as a preventive influence.[11]

Indeed Brown and Parker join the American Womanist theologian, Delores Williams, in claiming that most of the history of atonement theory in Christian theology supports violence, victimisation and undeserved suffering. Williams uses the figure of Hagar to explore the abuses surrounding the issue of surrogacy.[12] The Egyptian slave women Hagar was forced into surrogate motherhood for the childless Sarai and Abraham and then cast into the wilderness into an encounter with God. She becomes for Williams a paradigm for African-American women's experiences – who like Hagar were made surrogate objects as well as oppressed labourers by the plantation masters and fled in order to find freedom. Williams sees their struggle for survival and 'quality of life' for themselves and their children in the wilderness as the way to redemption. To extend Jesus' suffering on the Cross as surrogacy for sinful humanity reinforces unjust suffering. She is clear in her call to recognise the Cross as a symbol of evil, not a means of redemption.

The European feminist Dorothée Sölle has focussed on the traditional interpretations of atonement as a message that we are powerless sinners who can only passively receive redemption from above. For Sölle, this reinforces a collaboration with the power of violence and oppression. Resurrection in this instance becomes a victory over the Cross but the Cross is not necessary and not in itself redemptive. Rita Nakashima Brock has suggested that the concept of Jesus' death as sacrificial presents us with an image of divine child abuse of the perfect child.[13] These are just some of the writings emerging out of difficulty of dealing with tradition in an attempt to find a way of speaking about the value of women's suffering. There are many more that have explored the themes of evil and suffering but it is beyond the scope of this article to do justice to them here.[14] Perhaps one of the most fruitful critiques

---

11 Brown, R. and Parker R., *God so Loved the World*, p. 13.
12 Williams, D. S., *Sisters in the Wilderness - the Challenge of Womanist God-Talk*, New York, Orbis, 1998, pp. 15 ff.
13 See Brock, R. N., *And a Little Child will Lead us: Christology and Child Abuse* in Carlson Brown, J. and Bohn, C. R. (eds.), *Christianity, Patriarchy and Abuse*, pp. 50 ff.
14 For an insightful analysis of modern feminist interpretations of atonement, evil and suffering see Rankka, K. M., *Women and The Value of Suffering: An Aw(e)ful Rowing Toward God*, Minnesota, Liturgical Press (Michael Glazier), 1998.

of traditional theologies of the Cross has come from the challenges of pastoral theology.

The pastoral lens

Attempting to retrieve a feminist theology of the Cross by revisiting themes of suffering and self-sacrifice with the assistance of the insights from pastoral theology reveals the very real problems facing such a move.[15] This is, not least, because women's experience of identity as essentially defined in connectivity and relation has acculturated them to see others' needs as more important than their own. Hence there is a real risk of sacrificing the 'I' for the 'we'. Part of this is reinforced by the tendency of western religious ethics frequently to depict the highest form of love as already discussed. This call to live lives utterly heedless of self is fuelled by the suggestion that their needs are somehow less and something to be sacrificed. The belief that they have less social worth plagues women with self-abnegation and self-doubt, and false guilt leads too easily to them attuning themselves to the needs of others. Low self-worth is endemic to those socialised in structures of domination and subordination so they seek to be needed.

Gill-Austern's analysis suggests that consistent patterns of self-sacrifice lead to women losing touch with their own needs and desires. Any stating of their own needs throws women into potential conflict with the needs of others and may even feel like a threat to the relationship. This devaluing of need and desire also silences the self and leads to a loss of voice which in itself is a major cause of depression in women. Too often the options are over-simplified and polarised in terms of mutually exclusive alternatives e.g. self-sacrifice vs. egoism, or showing too little interest in themselves and taking too much interest in the welfare of others. The result can be a reservoir of resentment, bitterness and anger as they come to feel more and more victimised. The stress of modern women who strive for self-development while continuing as self-sacrificing caretakers is revealed in the large number of women who suffer from a wide range of physical disorders: digestive

---

15 I am indebted here to the comprehensive treatment given to the psychological, cultural and theological issues that motivate self-sacrifice and self-denial in Gill-Austern, B. L., *Love Understood as Self-denial*, p. 304 ff.

problems, allergies, high blood pressure, strokes, nervous ticks, insomnia and sheer exhaustion. All of this is seen to be supported and endorsed by a view of Christian love. It is then, in the face of these alarming realities, no surprise that the themes of self-emptying, vulnerability and suffering are muted themes in the feminist debate. But has Christian feminism gone too far?

The challenge to reconsider

In protesting against patriarchy, the general misogyny in ethics, doctrine, biblical interpretation and anthropology, feminists have avoided some of the paradoxes of scripture. An increasing body of writers has challenged this neglect. Linda Woodhead has accused feminist theology of failing to be sufficiently theological, by which she refers to the failure of feminist theology to engage in any sustained way with the realities of Christian faith and tradition.[16] It risks, she suggests, turning itself into another variant of individualised modern spirituality which is exemplified in the New Age movements, and turning feminist theology into a synthesis of life-affirming strands. Pushing feminists to enter into "malestream" debate and to revisit traditional mainline theology becomes then a priority for feminist theology.

In speaking of feminism's inability to develop a Christian understanding of God and God's relation to the world she writes:

> They may indeed tell us new and important things about how religion has oppressed women, but their scattered attempts to tell us new and important things about God and about life lived in relation to God are rather less successful.[17]

Her charge that in favouring an alternative ideology feminist theology has abandoned the central tenets of faith as the revelation of God in Christ is a serious one. Any reconstruction will need to risk coming to terms with the paradoxes of faith. What are feminists to make of the hard sayings like: 'Those who lose their lives will save them'; 'We are made strong in our

---

16 See Woodhead, L., *Spiritualising the Sacred: A Critique of Feminist Theology* in *Modern Theology*, 1997, Vol. 13, No. 2, p. 193.
17 Woodhead, L., *Spiritualising the Sacred*, p. 205.

weakness'; and 'Take up your Cross and follow me'? Is Woodhead right in thinking feminist theology is at risk of idealising a life free of suffering?

A similar position can be found in Sarah Coakley's article on kenosis in *Swallowing a Fishbone*.[18] This is an essay in which she explores the sticking points associated with re-conceptualising the power of the Cross and resurrection. Coakley calls for distinctions to be made between abusive suffering on the one hand and a productive or empowering form of 'pain' on the other.[19] It is Coakley's contention that the central meaning of the Christian message has to be located where the paradox of glory and suffering, joy and sorrow find a place together.

In rejecting the outworn gender assumption that presumes power and the abuse of power to be a male problem, Coakley identifies the new task of feminist theology as one that is willing to construe forms of weakness or vulnerability as either normatively human or even revelatory of the divine. Jesus' vulnerability, when viewed as a primary narrative rather than a philosophical embarrassment, raises the question as to whether vulnerability need be seen as passivity and weakness and whether it is possible to locate a systematic alternative, both Christological and spiritual, which finds an appropriate place for human kenosis without merely reinforcing gender stereotypes. In challenging feminists to reconsider some of these traditional stumbling blocks, Woodhead and Coakley are challenging what has become feminist orthodoxy. Further challenges have come from Angela West in her book *Deadly Innocence*.[20] In a very readable analysis of feminism, West questions whether we are at risk of romanticising the myths of perpetual victimhood and innocence. She moots that feminist theology's pursuit of liberation from guilt and its claims of women's innocence are part of an ancient pattern of electing a scapegoat. Moreover she suggests that women can be and have been both accessories and perpetrators, victims and victimisers.[21] In cautioning feminist theology against spiritual pride and the

---

18 Coakley, S., *Kenosis and Subversion* in Hampson, D. (ed.), *Swallowing a Fishbone? Feminist Theologians Debate Christianity*, London, SPCK, 1996, pp. 82 ff.

19 See Townes, E. M., *Living in the New Jerusalem: The Rhetoric and Movement of Liberation in the House of Evil* in Townes, E. M. (ed.), *A Troubling in my Soul: Womanist Perspectives on Evil and Suffering*, New York, Orbis, 1993, esp. pp. 83 ff.

20 West, A., *Deadly Innocence: Feminist Theology and the Mythology of Sin*, London, Cassell, 1995.

21 West, A., *Deadly Innocence*, p. 35.

potential to be crushed under a burden of self-righteousness, she calls for a more honest identification of our sins rather than pursuing our ideals. Her own disaffection with an enterprise which she interprets as driven by an ideological purity is born of her need to see how the silenced aspects of tradition might actually help us in the quest for liberation. In her challenge to surrender the myth of 'women's special nature' and to come of age theologically, she too invites a reconsideration of aspects in the Christian tradition that have long been regarded as stumbling blocks for feminists. The challenges are clear, but where are we to go from there?[22]

Toward a political theology of survival

A way forward might be that these feminist critiques of the classical theology of the Cross should force theologians and liturgists to tell the Jesus story in a different way. Any understanding of the Cross needs to be seen as tragic. Jesus did not come to suffer and die – the Cross is never the goal of love, though it is the length to which God will go in order to restore broken community.[23] Claiming this for women is not without difficulties, but it reminds us of Jesus' lament over a city that stoned its prophets.[24] His cry from the Cross belies his willingness to accept death and a terrorising public execution. Acknowledging that it was the length to which he would go, or acknowledging that it was the cost of loving, is something quite different from conceiving of crucifixion as something to be sought after as a means of redemption.

Feminists who follow Christ need not only to continue to struggle for life against death and unjust suffering but also to try and re-identify the distinguishing characteristics of Christian love. While salvation through immolation is one way of considering the nature of love, it is neither the best nor the only way. Women need though to resist the increasingly widespread tendency to condemn all forms of self-giving. Self-sacrifice is not pernicious by definition; it is not always a manifestation of co-dependency. The feminist

22 West, A., *Deadly Innocence*, p. 85.
23 King, M. L. (Washington J. M. [ed..]), *A Testament of Hope: The Essential Writings of Martin Luther King, Jr.*, San Francisco, Harper & Row, 1986.
24 See Luke 19 [44] and John 5 [43].

principle of mutuality can and should critique the prevailing individualistic orientation of western culture that has contributed to an understanding of success, which is defined in terms that glorify the self through the worship of the idols of autonomy, independence and self-sufficiency. Being dictated to by this not only colludes with limited definitions of womanhood, but also with patriarchal ideals of adulthood.[25]

Imitating distorted images of power is something that still needs to be resisted. And yet love and vulnerability are at the heart of what we do. The oft-romanticised notions of women being instilled with nurturing of others and facilitating and empowering the growth of others is, on one level, very limiting. On another, it is one which is grounded in generosity, empathy, yielding, receptivity and, sometimes but not always, relinquishment. This can be a life-giving form of self-giving but needs of course to be weighed against all that is life-denying and unhealthy. The question we are left with is how women can hold the tension of those who, in losing their life, find it. How can women sacrifice in ways that fulfil rather than diminish their lives and the lives of those around them? How might women challenge the notion of placing the self at the centre of the world?

Is it possible for feminist theology to reconstruct some of these symbols? Are we ready to be part of a more self-critical feminist theology without losing the gains of the past? In visiting some of the traditional paradoxes of Christianity could we move beyond always being the victim and ask whether it is enough to define feminist theology purely by protest? The danger of creating universalisms is one to be taken on board, but beyond those critiques lies also the need to build community across differences. We need to learn from each other's stories of pain in order to build solidarity and find envisioning ways of relating with others that do not dismiss or trivialise another's pain. Rankka asks whether we might be able to identify areas of needed change and conversion in how we respond to experiences of suffering that might be quite different than our own or for which we might be partially responsible.[26]

Struggling for life against death will involve some commitment to wrestling with God and necessarily requires some "wading through sorrow",

25 Glaz, M. and Moessner, J. S., *Women in Travail and Transition: A New Pastoral Care*, Minneapolis, Fortress Press, 1991, p. 69.
26 Rankka, K. M., *Women and the Value of Suffering*, p. 211.

but such a struggle can empower, heal and transform women's lives and inform their political practice.[27] This will require some faithfulness to *remembering*. If forgetfulness is the order of the day, the dead are slain once more. Painful remembrance preserves hope; remembrance hastens redemption. In being willing to find their own meaning in suffering, women will redeem it from misuse. Willingness by feminists to re-construe some of the central issues of faith in a way that resists distortions and redefines caricatured virtues will take energy. The problem of evil is a vexing one, especially when it is a structural violence. However, could not the Cross be a 'yes', not to what is authorised by God, but to the darkness that surrounds the protest and *resistance*?

The contributions of feminist theology have concerned, and should continue to concern, themselves with what is damaging and destructive for women, but encountering and confronting suffering is not always co-terminous with passive acceptance. We need to see the possibilities of regaining a sense of choice with regard to alleviating it when possible, bearing it when necessary and transforming it for others and ourselves when feasible.[28] Anger might find a home here, for at best it is a signal that something is amiss in relation. Where that goes unchecked, the power of love, the power to act, to deepen relation dies. The question feminist theology faces in the task of this retrieval is whether we want a world with an essential incapacity for suffering or fateful subjection to suffering, or a willingness to open oneself to be touched, moved, affected by something other than oneself. Above all, we need to ask of ourselves if it is possible to *speak of suffering* without it leading to martyrdom, abuse, masochism, denigration or further justification for the trivialisation of the oppression of women.

Acknowledging that pain is always an experience embedded in a particular social, political, cultural and historical setting does not foreclose the debate, for the experience of suffering cuts across every ethnic, economic, social and cultural division. This is vital to the task, for inasmuch as the experiences of suffering will be particular, the experience of suffering is universal. Is it possible then to share across differences our knowledge of suffering, and try to locate a value in them while still remaining faithful to the work of

---

27   See Copeland, M. S., *Wading through Many Sorrow: Toward a Theology of Suffering in Womanist Perspective* in Townes, E. M. (ed.), *A Troubling in My Soul*, pp.109–130.

28   Rankka, K. M., *Women and the Value of Suffering*, p. 8.

emancipation and transformation, and while speaking of hope? In doing so, I want to end where I began, by reflecting on my experience of a black woman's response to a lifetime of suffering. I am still wrestling with the meaning of it and what reading of suffering and redemption it offers us.

I spent the summer of 1993 working in the Cathedral of the Holy Nativity Pietermaritzburg. The political scene was not promising and townships across the length and breadth of Natal were sites of violent political intimidation. The Cathedral staff received a message for the last rites to be administered to an old woman dying in the township outside the city. Together with an interpreter, a Mothers' Union worker and a clergyman, we drove twenty kilometres to the smouldering township and eventually abandoned the car on the unmanageable roads. Picking our way past burnt buildings and a police station hidden behind bullet-pierced sandbags, we found our way to the house – newly built. Blind, and in her nineties, the woman told of how she had rebuilt her home three times, buried all her sons and her husband in the struggle. On establishing that I was a white woman training to be a priest, her eyes filled with tears and she said in Zulu: "Now I know that my God and my Redeemer lives. He has saved me, for in my lifetime a white woman has come into my home to bring me healing".

Thinking about this experience and trying to come to terms with her willingness to conceive of herself as part of another generation's hope continues to challenge me. A victim of white racism greeted a perpetrator as a sign of hope, found hope at the end of a pain-filled life lived under the banner of structural violence, and, in it all, identified such an experience with a redeeming God.

Chapter Nine

Touching upon the Soul:
The Interiority of Transcendence after
Luce Irigaray

Lucy Gardner

Man is divided between two transcendencies: his mother's and his God's –
whatever kind of God that may be. These two transcendencies are doubtless
not unrelated but this is something which he has forgotten.[1]

For Irigaray, the question of transcendence is intimately bound with the
question of sexual difference which has so marked her work. She identifies
in the western tradition a "specular economy", which requires of woman
conformity to a biological identity. In this economy, the relations between
men and women are constructed in terms of woman being "a currency of
exchange", and "at the disposal of man".[2] Disturbed at this economy and its
subjugation of women, Irigaray is equally disturbed at the neutralising
tendencies of women's decisions to become men's equals. Her work thus
traces what may be termed a "Nuptial Quest" for an "amorous economy", in
which women and men will be loved by and loveable to themselves and each
other. This amorous economy will not be able simply to co-exist alongside
the specular economy and its paradigms of masculine transcendency, but will

1   Irigaray, L., *Passions élémentaires*, Paris, Les Éditions de Minuit, 1982. Translated by
    Collie, J. and Still, J. as *Elemental Passions*, London, Athlone, 1992, p. 1.
2   Irigaray, L., *Elemental Passions*, p. 2.

demand their modification.[3] The quest will insist upon a reworking of our notions of transcendence.

Irigaray's quest is neither simple nor easy: it is for her self; it is for love; it is for "new", more truthful ways of thinking, being, experiencing and relating; it is, therefore, also for an understanding of the inner logic of the present ways, and in particular their discord with more ancient ways (past, present and future), of thinking, being, experiencing and relating. The movement forward cannot be achieved except through the movement backward, just as the movement backward cannot be achieved except through the movement forward. Similarly, the search for fuller 'selfhood' for woman (for a relation between *I* and *she;* and for re-newed and re-newing relations between man and woman) must journey through not only the myths of man's selfhood, but also through the non-selfhood of woman upon which they are built – a simple-complex movement which is painful. Selfhood is only granted woman in the specular economy in a denial of selfhood; this is where her journey must in some sense 'begin'; it is the point to which it will repeatedly return. Woman's emergence into (fuller) selfhood is only possible within a 'new' economy; but the new economy itself must be based upon sexual identities for woman and man other than those (re-)presented in the specular economy.

The role played by transcendence in Irigaray's quest is critical and similarly complex. On the one hand, there is the sense in which Irigaray clearly seeks to transcend and surpass the present economy. On the other hand, this transcendence will not be on the terms of the specular economy. The desire to transcend the economy is rooted in (and gives rise to) an intuition that she and others, perhaps all of us, already transcend it: both on its terms and in contravention of them. We (women, bodies, outcastes) are the otherness that the all-seeing eye seeks to master in its attempt to convince itself that it can see and that it can master it/himself. We are the others (the 'counters') in account of whom (and not on whose account) the same can be the same (those who do the counting). But we are also the others who prevent and defy the mastery, through no intentional activity of our own but simply

---

3   The gestures of this introductory paragraph may be traced to the concise and lucid account given by Irigaray herself in the *Preface* prepared for the Japanese translation of *Passions élémentaires* and reproduced in the English translation under the sub-heading *Nuptial Quest*, Irigaray, L., *Elemental Passions*, pp. 1 ff.

in persisting in being. Irigaray's quest for her identity in love, therefore, will involve explorations of these different 'forms' of transcendence. It will also demand an attention to their crossings – in each other, in the present (specular) denial of identity, and in the newly emergent, more 'original', identity of woman.

Something of this chiastic structure is outlined in the Preface to *Elemental Passions*:

> *Elemental Passions* offers some fragments from a woman's voyage as she goes in search of her identity in love. It is no longer a man in quest of his Grail, his God, his path, his identity through the vicissitudes of his life's journey, it is a woman. Between nature and culture, between night and day, between sun and stars, between vegetable and mineral, amongst men, amongst women, amongst gods, she seeks her humanity and her transcendency. Such a journey is not without its trials. But these do not discourage her from her quest, as she attempts again and again to discover how I-woman can enter into a joyous nuptial union with you-man. She finds that this cannot occur unless *you* relates to *he* and *He*, and *I* relates to *she* and *She*.[4]

In this essay, I seek to understand something of the task and the event of transcendence as Irigaray conceives it. The elements of her work that receive my attention are: I reflect upon her reading of her body as found in comments and passages from a variety of her works, alongside her reading of the paradoxes and apparent tragedy of the feminine Christian mystic's "achievement" of "subjectivity" (gain of self in loss of self) in the central passage, *La Mystérique,* of her book *Speculum of the Other Woman*.[5] In this, my desire is to indicate the manner in which Irigaray reads, better, *interrogates*, the tradition and her body 'against' each other, in a hermeneutic of nature and culture which accepts the unavailability of their distinction and yet works, somehow between them, at understanding their relatedness.

First, I introduce some of the convolutions of thinking transcendence itself at all (in one sense the act of thinking thought as an event other than an act). I then consider the ways in which transcendence can be mapped to sexual

---

4   Irigaray, L., *Elemental Passions*, p. 4.
5   Irigaray, L., *Speculum de l'autre femme*, Paris: Les Éditions de Minuit, 1974. Translated by Gill, G. C. as *Speculum of the Other Woman*, New York, Cornell University Press, 1985, pp.191–202.

difference, before turning my attention to the question of a hermeneutics of the body and its representation in two receptions of Irigaray's work, describing my own approach in relation to them. I then proceed to a brief and suggestive exposition of woman's search for transcendence as I find it presented and imagined in Irigaray's texts, by way of a reflection upon each of four difficulties to be negotiated. I then return to the hermeneutics of the body and its place in Irigaray's quest, before turning to my concluding reflections upon the characteristic *traits* of her "sensible transcendental" and the suggestions it offers for a reconsideration of the theme of interiorisation from the western spiritual tradition and for contemporary understandings of grace.[6]

Talking of transcendence . . .

Transhumanising – its meaning to convey in words cannot be done;
but let the example suffice to whom grace grants experience.[7]

Dante's insight seems at once as obvious as it is strangely new. Humanity is suspended in a double bind, between the recognition on the one hand that our being has always something to do with *trasumanar* – with, that is, transcending human being – and the realisation on the other that, although we

---

6   Irigaray's term the *sensible transcendental* which emerges in Irigaray, L., *Éthique de la différence sexuelle*, Paris, Les Éditions de Minuit, 1984, translated by Burke, C. and Gill, G. C. as *An Ethics of Sexual Difference*, London, Athlone, 1993, is not readily glossed, for it designates a central theme of her work, inviting contemplation and discovery by its very tangible elusiveness. For helpful discussion, see Whitford, M., *Luce Irigaray: Philosophy in the Feminine*, London, Routledge, 1991: pp. 47 ff.; pp. 112 ff.; pp. 144 ff; and Tamsin L., *Irigaray and Deleuze, Experiments in Visceral Philosophy*, New York, Cornell University Press, 1999, esp. Chapter 6. The interpretation which unfolds in this essay, in terms of a 'hermeneutics of the body', is of a motif which points to the transcendent as always immanent, and the immanent as always transcendent to us. In offering such a 'translation' of Irigaray's thought I am mindful of the grief which other translations and misreadings have brought her, and of the fact that the remainder of translation is, in this case, not simply that which cannot be translated across the difference at stake (i.e. across sexual difference). My translation is an appropriation by another woman. In that Irigaray traces her painful journey of discovery of that identity, she teaches me much about my own journey and identity.

7   Dante *Paradiso* Book I, 70–72; cf. Dupré, L., *Passage to Modernity*, New Haven, Yale University Press, 1993, p. 107.

must clearly be able to 'know' something of this event (not least in order to intuit the recognition), we cannot properly or adequately talk or think about it. The question of transcendence, approaching as it does the 'limits' of human thought, is fundamental not only to questions of human being, but also to questions of knowledge, of interpretation, of the appearing of things in the world and, no doubt more 'fundamentally' still, to the question of being. There is a sense in which the 'theme' of transcendence is the theme, and the thematisation, of the unthematisable. It is precisely this rather strange recognition which generates the repeated treatment of this theme and refuses its consignment to silence. Far from postponing questions of interpretation and communication (questions of how to talk about this 'event' or 'question' of transcendence), the question of transcendence will always involve and raise them, in provoking not only thought of the 'beyond' of our world, but, as it were, the beyond of beyond, or the meaning of meaning.

But Dante's account of his journey, drawn ever onward, and ultimately upward, by his love for Beatrice, and the more so by her love for him, serves as a critical example of the fact that these various modalities of questioning (ontology, epistemology, phenomenology, hermeneutics) have been almost silently (and often unquestioningly) bound to the question of sexual difference in ways which have disguised and silenced that question. Among the characterisations which direct the choreography of these discourses there stand the differentiations between subject and object, active and passive, spiritual and material, external and internal, as they have been mapped to masculine and feminine respectively. In Irigaray's work, we meet, as if for the first time, the suggestion that sexual difference must be permitted to address us and be addressed by us as a *question* – indeed as *the* question for our times – in place of being over-deployed and over-determined as an answer.[8]

Transcendence, interiority and sexual difference

What happens when we reach beyond ourselves and cross our borders? Or is it rather that something happens which allows us to allow the beyond to reach in, to appear before and among us? What happens when we are caught up, for a moment, and admitted to the Presence, granted a flashing recognition?

---

8   Irigaray, L., *An Ethics of Sexual Difference*, p. 5.

We, human beings, are drawn and called by transcendence. Although transcendence remains always beyond our grasp and our description, and although, in matters of transcendence, as Dante suggests, the flimsy, fragile, often all-to- overwhelming, insufficient 'example' will simply have to suffice, we have found many ways of speaking of it. In particular, there have been many attempts to claim some particular thing, event or modality, as a universally 'sufficient' example of transcendence. It seems as if we are invited (compelled) to choose between different accounts, between, that is, different examples. Is transcendence to be thought of as an out-going ascent, a reaching above and beyond ourselves to something higher, a being caught up into another realm? Or is it rather an inward withdrawal, a descending plunge, deeper and deeper into ourselves, to find that our border is somehow in our middle, and that we are always crossing it, always transcending it?

It is, it would appear, remarkably easy to oppose differing accounts of transcendence across sexual difference, by means of a metaphorical-allegorical reading of (largely heterosexual) sex: the male, and therefore 'masculine' version of transcendence is thought of as an 'up' which goes 'out' of the self 'into' something heavenly; the concomitant female, 'feminine' (and perhaps feminist) version is more passive and receptive, a taking (up) into the self, and some sort of descent to things earthly and earthy. Both represent a particular configuration of internal-external relations, yet it can appear as if these are two fundamentally incompatible accounts between which we must choose: is transcendence like the "little death" or more like giving birth?[9]

But will this do? If a predominantly male-masculine tradition has apparently favoured one 'model' of transcendence over its rival, will it suffice for women, feminists and other 'others' to challenge 'orthodoxy' in reclaiming that 'other' model as sufficient, if not as good? Is this nothing more than the mere establishing of a new (inverted) orthodoxy in the image of the old? Or even a reinforcement of the old orthodoxy in accepting the predominant model and its choices? It is precisely the presumption of such choice (that this is a 'choice', and that this is 'the' choice) which Irigaray's development of the

---

9   Or, to illustrate the point with reference to the works of one of the most famous 'couples' from the western spiritual tradition (within which I offer this reading of Irigaray), and thus to indicate the inadequacies of perceiving the different accounts as different 'options': is the spiritual life that of ever greater exposure upon the mountainside (St John of the Cross) or of labyrinthine meanderings through many mansions, moving ever closer to the heart (St Teresa of Avila)?

sensible transcendental attempts to address and in some sense deconstruct in a *challenge* more worthy of the double sense of the name.

First hermeneutics of the body – a question of reading

In reflecting upon Irigaray's account of transcendence, I have had cause to draw upon and engage with two expositions of her treatment of this theme, the one more philosophical and the other more theological. They are: Christopher Fynsk's essay *An Exquisite Crisis*, which presents an attentive reading of "La Mystérique" at the centre of his remarkable reflections upon the simple fact of language in *Language & Relation: That There is Language*; and Fergus Kerr's more encompassing account of Irigaray's sensible transcendental in his incisive considerations of seven "versions" of transcendence conducted from the standpoint of a Christian, theological philosophy of religion in his *Immortal Longings: Versions of Transcending Humanity.*[10]

Both men are sensible to the difficulties and the importance of Irigaray's thought of the sensible transcendental, and they both offer 'sensitive' expositions of these. And yet, the significance – or rather the *manner* of the significance – of Irigaray's *body* for her discourse and for her discovery of her own identity and her own transcendence I find disturbingly almost absent from their texts.

Fynsk defends his reading on the basis of an hospitable pedagogic intent detected in the text. He does not pause to reflect that hospitality is to be expected of a woman, nor that his reading is conceived as a (masculine) 'entry' to her (feminine) text, finding a space in which to follow her between the narrating voice and a first person, between woman and "I".[11] He, like others before him, appears prepared to enter this gap and to follow, to descend, to the woman's place of non-subjectivity. But he, like they, does so as a means to an end, as a subject who has a subject to lose, without beginning to think what it must be not to have had an "I" to lose, and to have been deprived of intentionality as a means to another's end.

---

10 Fynsk, C., *Language and Relation: That There is Language*, Stanford, Standford University Press, 1996; Kerr, F., *Immortal Longings: Versions of Transcending Humanity*, London, SPCK, 1997.
11 Fynsk, C., *Language and Relation*, p. 162 f.

Kerr, reading in a different manner, in a different context, is likewise concerned to pay due attention to this utterly different account of self-transcendence. His translation of Irigaray's thought is particularly clear. But this clarity produces a single line of argument, with regard to which his loyalties are divided. He appears to have grasped something of the vastness of the re-thinking to be conducted in the wake of Irigaray's thought; he also appears to agree that there must be some breaking free from the grip of 'Hegel's story'.[12] But this vastness is reduced to a "Feuerbachian Theism" in which 'we' (especially women) have (i) to identify and symbolise the body differently, "in such a way that women would be no longer aligned with the corporeal and deprived of the mental-spiritual", a move with which he appears sympathetic and (ii) to "invent the divinities in whose image women may find themselves", a supposed "second", although necessarily "first", step which he finds more problematic.[13]

Both men – certainly both texts – appear to remain enamoured (if also critical) of the one who has been made to 'be' transcendence in a "specula(risa)tion of woman, who in her mirror seems always to refer to a transcendence".[14] In my own reading, I attempt a suspension of the questions of a 'line of argument' and of 'value'. This is no doubt demanding of and frustrating for the reader, but this suspension is what I find Irigaray's texts require. Thus, far from entering into the gaps (in particular between the various and often unmarked voices of her text) in order (supposedly) to 'follow' Irigaray (by chasing her out or invading her) and thus find my own voice or myself, I hope rather to trace the contours of the logics of difference which Irigaray exposes – with and in an intimacy which is by turns tender, urgent, soothing and searing – and thereby glimpse, hear, smell, taste, touch, feel something of an otherwise, indeed of her other ways, before I make my own way to 'follow' Irigaray in hers (or mine). This I conduct by way of a consideration of four difficulties to be negotiated in reading Irigaray's quest.

---

12 As he rightly points out we – human beings in 'the West' at this point in history – can *only* begin to grasp something: "Her whole point is that, in our culture, we are only on the brink of a massive shift in sensibility which will enable women to see themselves in their otherness from men, really for the first time. It is not clear how this will go". Kerr, F., *Immortal Longings*, p. 112.

13 See Kerr, F., *Immortal Longings*, pp. 111 f.

14 Irigaray, L., *Speculum of the Other Woman*, p. 201.

The denial of speech

One of the difficulties to be (en)countered in Irigaray's quest is precisely that of the denial of speech, which might be presented as the denial of subjectivity, of a legitimate feminine "I". That about which Irigaray would write (the specular economy) is precisely that which forbids, more fundamentally removes, her speech. This may be understood in many ways. That is to say, there are many suggestions in Irigaray's texts as to how this silencing is attempted and what it 'feels' like: it may be the insertion of another voice, another tongue, into her (my) mouth; it may also be a noisiness through which her (my) voice cannot be heard; it may be an inability to see, hear, recognise our voice(s) – our 'I' – *as* voice, as 'I' (except when we merely mimic man's).[15]

And yet the denial at stake also prevents me from achieving my ownmost silence. It is as if my proper place in the economies of thought is silence, but this silence (that is, I) can never come into being in this economy; for the place I am to hold is the holding place which maintains the economy by remaining resolutely outside it. The economy, then, is one which requires rigorous borders between inside and out – and a rigorous policing of them. This is the basis upon which transcendence as the crossing of borders is construed. It is also the basis upon which that which is other, not same – not I, not male-masculine – is consigned to the outside and attributed the designation 'transcendent'.

Approaching nothing

Also problematic to Irigaray's programme of thinking through sexual difference is the manner in which woman seems to threaten to elide with the void, as a single-sided envelope marking man's exterior, so that he can reassure himself of his all-encompassing expanse. The necessary outside to the masculine specular economy is nothing: the world stops at the mirror – his

15   See, for example, Irigaray, L., *Elemental Passions*, pp. 7 ff.; *Amante marine. De Friedrich Nietzsche*, Paris, Les Éditions de Minuits, 1980, translated by Gill, G. C. as *Marine Lover of Friedrich Nietzsche*, New York, Columbia University Press, 1991, p. 3; *Speculum of the Other Woman*, p. 13. See also Fynsk, C., *Language and Relation*, p. 165.

mirror – which marks its edge.[16]   This is the manner in which sexual difference has remained unthought – not simply as an unthinking differentiation of the world (into male and female, single and dual), but also in fact reduced to the non-difference of the same.

Woman is the other side of man; but man is all there is. Man makes (tries to make) woman a womb; but he does not make her *her* womb; he makes her in *his* image of a womb: a gap, a void, an opening, a space, a lack, an 'outside' in which he can come to be (himself, man) by fulfilling himself in filling it, in planting his seed and drawing back, or beginning as seed and filling out – promising, in fact, only ever emptiness and barrenness: empty promises of emptiness.[17] But the woman's womb is not like this.

And so Irigaray 'begins' her journey towards herself and towards love in sexual difference (and sexual difference in love) with the way in which her body 'speaks' against the mediation of herself to herself which she has received in man's language which has been designed to mediate himself to himself in her. She begins with un-knowing the self-knowledge with which the tradition has forced her to begin, working 'back' towards a self-knowledge from 'before', to a time, a place, a knowing 'before' the parting of lips in speech. This will always involve the painful recognition that what she is counts as and for nothing (except for everything) within the economies in which she has learnt to think.[18] It is what convinces Irigaray of the need to move beyond and away from any simplistic attempts to try to assert, insert or create a value for woman within the specular economy.

So she begins with the something that counts for nothing – her body – and will meditate, for example, upon herself as a being with two sets of lips, not one. No wonder, then, that her manner of speaking should feel violated when translated into the manner of the being who has only one set of lips. No wonder, then, that she finds that her speaking, the very witness of her existence and her body to themselves and to another otherwise, cannot be heard in the economy which refuses to recognise, to see or hear them. Or,

16 See, for example, Irigaray, L.: *Speculum of the Other Woman*, pp. 194, 199; *The Envelope* in *An Ethics of Sexual Difference*.

17 See, for example, Irigaray's reflection upon the man-child's relation to the womb in Irigaray, L., *Elemental Passions*.

18 See, for example, Irigaray, L., *Speculum of the Other Woman*, p.199; also *Ce sexe qui n'en est pas un*, Paris, Les Éditions de Minuit, 1977, translated by Porter, C. as *This Sex Which is Not One*, New York, Cornell University Press, 1985.

returning to the womb itself, she remarks upon its throbbing, moving thickness; the manner in which it does not – cannot – remain poised in empty space, itself a brittle, dry, thin, crisp, open, empty space, but is in fact a rich, damp, deep, dark collection of folds, always already fruitful; its not yearning for the arrival of self-recognition in the touch, the invasion, the greeting, the parting of another, but always already touching itself, knowing itself, much like the 'second' set of lips.

The forbidden touch

For Irigaray, drawing on her training in Lacanian psychoanalysis, patriarchal rule can be understood as a certain phallogocentrism. But this receives her own particular interpretation in the ban upon touch. "Do not touch!" as Fynsk argues, is for Irigaray the fundamental prohibition upon which phallogocentrism builds itself. "The prohibition bears on the body, *of course*", he remarks, but swiftly passes over any reflection upon this 'of course', eager to move on to issues he perceives as more 'fundamental', namely auto-affection and the articulation of desire.[19] Again he offers a potentially insightful translation: "The prohibition is 'don't touch yourself'", but this is immediately appropriated to the phallic economy as meaning, in effect, "don't touch language, don't touch the logos".

He thereby passes over the full weight of his own "of course" and thus misses the full extent to which the *ex-schize crise,* about which he is writing and in which he is following Irigaray, is not only exquisite but excruciating for woman. For, the assumption that auto-affection and the articulation of desire are "more fundamental" than any "bearing" on the body will continue to disable women from learning "to assert the feminine from the side of their own bodies – from the site of their own bodies".[20] Fynsk appears too ready to appropriate the tragedy of La Mystérique into a rejoicing in paradox, and the amorous economy of difference to the self-same logic of the specular economy, making this 'feminine subjectivity' at once more and less 'other' than Irigaray detects.

---

19 Fynsk, C., *Language and Relation*, p.161 (my italics).
20 Kerr, F., *Immortal Longings*, p. 94.

The economy built upon the prohibition "don't touch yourself" is in fact built upon the exclusion of woman, who cannot help touching herself. This economy will therefore also deny any woman who enters the economy access to herself: it will prevent her from touching (upon) her self-touching, upon her very being. In this way, for Irigaray, both transcendence 'in general' (an ecstatic relation to the self) and her own transcendence 'in particular' (the recognition of her own relationship to herself) will be denied her. But they will be denied her in a double move: in denying the form of her being, and in denying her access to that being. Contrary to what she has 'learnt' in this economy, woman does not need to be 'opened' (whether that is gently or violently, by invitation or by invasion, by herself or by another) in order to meet or become herself – truly woman, no longer maid.

And yet, of course, the ban itself betrays itself; just as woman's own persistent existence denies the identification of her as a 'nothing', her thickness denies her characterisation as a thin line, and the 'mystic's' discovery of God's surviving love for her becomes (is found to have been) her guarantee of her survival and thus of her existence, and of her prevenient and endurable lovability despite (precisely in) her degradation.[21] These are the paradoxes of the manner in which 'reality' and our experience not only transcend our experience, our language and our thought (precisely in that they require their 'mediation') but contradict them. They are the contradictions within which we can learn of how things are otherwise than the ways we have come to see them.

Self-relation and the feminine soul

But the crisis which Irigaray traverses is not merely that of learning a voice, accepting her own existence, and discovering her own way of being against the (almost invisible) laws she has learnt as "natural"; it is also that of achieving a recovery of her own self-relation, as (a) woman, to herself as (a) woman, from within (and therefore to some extent 'beyond') an economy in

21 "And if 'God', who has thus re-proved the fact of her non-value, still loves her, this means that she exists all the same, beyond what anyone may think of her. It means that love conquers everything that has already been said." Irigaray, L., *Speculum of the Other Woman*, p. 199.

which self-relation has been conceived as that of man to feminine, and of self-same to different, rather than of self to same.[22] For, paradoxically, the feminisation of the soul presents the greatest possibility and the greatest obstacle to be negotiated by a woman in search of herself and her (own) transcendence: in search, that is, of her soul.[23] This is for at least a double reason in the case of the 'subject' of La Mystérique which Irigaray considers in *Speculum*.

First, the 'feminine' soul 'belongs' to man. Man's relation to himself (his soul) has been construed in terms of sexual difference. To consider – and indeed to have a relation to – her own soul, woman must 'internalise' sexual difference in a different fashion from the man's interiorisation. Beginning from the assumption of himself as the same as himself – as male – the man understands his difference to himself, in himself, in terms of his difference to and from woman – the other. The woman, however, in learning to talk in man's language, 'first' learns herself as other to man (and not same to herself), and must then become other to her otherness if she is to 'enjoy' the same relation to 'her' soul as man enjoys to 'his' – which is the only relation to soul that the borrowed imaginary offers. The feminisation of the soul is a part of the identification of woman as / with transcendence within and against which Irigaray is working. In so far as woman is granted or gains access to transcendence in the specular economy, it is at the cost of losing (of having lost) her self.

This reflects the second manner in which the feminisation of the soul frustrates the search for woman's soul (her very own transcendence of herself, and not herself as transcendence / transcendent of / to another) in La Mystérique. In the Christological theme of *kenosis*, it can appear that, in order for the human being to become divine (on an inverted analogy to the becoming human of the divine), he (or more particularly she) must put off the self and leave subjectivity behind. This assumes a (divine) self to put aside – which of course the woman has not been granted. Thus woman is praised on account of the fact that she has been denied a self (and the Son of God is

---

22 "Her eye has become accustomed to obvious 'truths' that actually hide what she is seeking." Irigaray, L., *Speculum of the Other Woman*, p.193.

23 La Mystérique (both the passage in *Speculum* and that upon which it reflects) turns in an important ambiguity of subject – an undecidability between some un-named 'she' (a female mystic, for example) and the feminine soul. See translator's note in Irigaray, L., *Speculum of the Other Woman*, p.191.

deemed "that most female of men" in his mimicry of this being).[24] A veil is drawn over the utter contrast between the self-conscious, loving, salvific, 'selfless' *intention* of the divine *activity* of condescension and the sheer denial of woman's intentionality effected by another's intentions and the consequent removal of any activity from her part in her own selflessness and subjugation. Her selfless-ness (the selflessness to which she is 'called', which is her 'natural' vocation, her sheer being), her essential and critical 'lack', is idealised / idolised as 'pure' subjectivity – to be mimicked, in penetration, by men, who are in a position to intend selflessness and to act to put aside a self. We thus see that Irigaray's claim to a quest is in some sense the greatest outrage she 'commits' against the specular economy.

Second hermeneutics of the body – the thoughtful body

For Fynsk, auto–affection and the articulation of desire are 'more fundamental' than any bearing on the body. Irigaray's La Mystérique does, no doubt, offer us a lesson in the heights, the depths, the breadth and the costs of self-love and self-loathing, but neither this love of self, nor the staging of an attempt to articulate inarticulate desires, seems co-extensive with Irigaray's quest. She begins in search of love, and in search of sexual difference – in search that is of woman and herself. She is her own goal. But this, of course, is the last thing that woman has been permitted to be within the economy in which she has learnt the art of aiming, the measure of means and ends.

In the specular economy, woman is only ever another's – man's – means. In search of herself, then, woman follows man in following herself as a means. This route offers little hope of finding herself as an end. It does, however, offer ample opportunity for man to continue his use of her as his means to himself. This is the persistently negative side of the exposition of La Mystérique. The woman, like the soul, must "slip away unseen" – unseen in a different sense from the sense in which she remains always unseen, ever-gazed upon, in the specular economy – in order to learn to find herself, to follow the chains to her own unity, according to a different logic.[25]

---

24 Irigaray, L., *Speculum of the Other Woman*, p.199.
25 "The first necessity is to slip away unseen." Irigaray, L., *Speculum of the Other Woman*, p.192; see also p. 193.

Irigaray does not seek simply to place a little – or a lot – more emphasis on the body or the feminine within the economies as they stand at present. Nor does she attempt to present an alternative (the alternative) to the specular economy constructed according to the choices of its 'original' terms. She is in search of the ways in which present patterns of thought and paradigms of transcendence jar with the world, and, in that jarring, attempt to expel woman – and never quite succeed in doing so, an exception which harbours the possibility of redemption for all. In this, her body offers a new (a forgotten) discursive mediation of herself to herself. That body (she), therefore, is 'more fundamental' than either auto-affection or the articulation of desire. Her body, which has been the marker of the 'absolute' difference between inside and outside in the specular economy (in which interiorisation is achieved by – occasionally mutual – penetration) has become the *locus* of an undecidability, a convolution, a passage, a fold, a thick, dense, moving middle between the inside and the outside.

The significance of her body for Irigaray's text is that it can stand both for herself, and for her own way to and from herself, in a manner which promises to give her self to herself. Her body bears the memories and the marks of the understandings which she has interiorised, but it also bears the memory and the promise of other ways of understanding. Irigaray's body is the place (and for her the only place) for a re-thinking of the relations of the I to the self, of woman to 'I', of woman to woman and of man to woman, of 'you' to 'me', and of thought to the world. The undoing of an economy which demands a certain biological identity for woman must begin with a careful deconstruction (and no simple rejection) of precisely that identity.

In recognising that her body touches itself, that it desires, perhaps, to touch rather than engulf, and to be touched rather than penetrated; in understanding that the womb is not an empty space waiting to be filled, but has its own thickness, mobility and fecundity; in realising that her 'opening' – the parting of her lips – is a 'fold', rather than a 'hole' and an embarrassing, unspeakable 'lack' or 'nothing'; in finding that what has been understood as penetration is nothing other than a particular kind of touching in which she is not 'entered' and in which she does not offer her inside to be another's outside, but in which an outside meets another outside; in attention to her body, woman can learn another relation to herself, a 'new', more ancient, 'version' of herself, a relation to herself as an 'I'. And with these she can find new relations to man.

Inside and outside, active and passive, spiritual and material are not reversed or inverted, they are not simply 'crossed' but traversed , re-traversed, and re-aligned anew in their relation to each other.

Her body, then, is not simply a symbolic site for thought; it is the place in which thought happens.   Indeed, Irigaray's understanding of intuition is Platonic in the sense that we might suggest her point is that the body thinks (for me, as me) before ever 'I' do, and this is the intuition towards which my own thought is for ever working back.   And this intuition, in memory of – in the memory of – her body, Irigaray conceives as touching the self. For her, the self is self-touch; it is the relation of thought to itself, of thought to a body, and of thought to the world.

The blessings of touch
Concluding reflections on grace and the sensible transcendental

Irigaray's "sensible transcendental", then, for all that it appears in her texts as particularly associated with the new-ancient form of transcendence she desires for women, is not offered as a feminine alternative to the masculine paradigms of transcendence.   In her writings she does indeed contrast masculine transcendence with feminine immanence, but these are apportionments from the specular economy. The sensible transcendental is not a coded signal for the exaltation of feminine immanence alongside, above or in place of masculine transcendence. It is rather an indication that, just as that which touches is also always touched in a bewildering undecidability, so the immanent is transcendent and the transcendent is always immanent.   The "sensible transcendental" is intended to be both at once.[26]

Moreover, Irigaray does not 'choose' this model or version of transcendence; nor does she simply construct it. Rather, she finds she has been chosen according to a particular form of transcendence; she is her own example. Or, to put this another way, I do not find that Irigaray's programme is built on any *projectionism*, nor that it poses a choice for or against any such activity, as Kerr's interpretation suspects, and Grace Jantzen's, for example,

26 See Whitford, M., *Luce Irigaray: Philosophy in the Feminine*, p. 116.

eagerly welcomes, despite her rejection of the dualisms of western philosophy.[27]

Irigaray does not propose that we – you or I – choose or 'create' a feminine deity over a male one. Such a choice is the (false) choice forced by the specular economy, alongside the (false) choice between being and doing. Her programme is not a project to invent (a) God, although she is acutely aware of the ways in which we have excluded woman from divinity and confused man with it; it is not even the attempt to give us god in order to be able to give us ourselves. Rather, her project belongs, I suggest, firmly to the *discovery* of God – our search for God, and God's reaching towards us: a two-sided, asymmetric discovery to which we must carefully attend.

Reflecting on ourselves, listening to the echoes of our thought, tracing the shadow of our gaze, we must reflect upon how we have so pushed women out as 'other' that we cannot begin to understand the difference between men and women; and that this in turn causes and is caused by the thoughts we have made of God. We have dressed up our thoughts both of God and of woman in our differences and cannot begin to tell their own, proper differences (nor those of man). To *un*-learn these modes of thought is not projectionism; it is learning to throw a new glance in God's direction, or perhaps better on Irigaray's terms; it is about feeling anew for God in the world. A task which will of course be demanding of the imagination.

Thus, although Irigaray's construal of a feminine transcendence within the sensible transcendental begins with and from an 'otherwise' in and to the specular economy, she seeks ultimately to transform it, by appropriating it to a new, more ancient, 'higher' order and unity (significantly for Christian Trinitarian theology a unity which is precisely not the exclusive unity of the same) which the specular economy has expelled in its divisions of the world and in its failed attempts likewise to expel God and woman. With her, I suggest, we can discover again a sense of the God in whom there is ultimately *no choice between being and doing*, and so no 'secret' privileging of a proto-act (choice) over being (decisiveness), nor of activity over passivity, nor of going out over staying in and receiving.

The attention to touch will require a revisioning – a re-tracing – of the demarcations of interiority and exteriority. To think in terms of touch will not

27 See Jantzen, G., *A god according to our gender* and passim in *Becoming Divine: Towards A Feminist Philosophy of Religion*, Manchester, Manchester University Press, 1998.

absolve us of thoughts of insides and outsides, but it will direct us towards relations other than those which are pre-decided between them. For touch is when an 'outside' (skin or mucous membrane, thought or self) meets another outside (another one, or one that is more other). The explorations of touch will begin to question our assumptions as to what is outside and what is inside, and as to what same and different are. The sensible transcendental takes us 'back' to a time and a place before our self-made absolute divisions, to a recognition that the immanent is the most transcendent and the transcendent is the most immanent – more immanent, even, than ourselves. It refuses our alignment of one sex or the other with one side or the other of these divisions. Moreover, to re-trace thought as touch, rather than as sight, is to remind us that to know is in fact to be known, and that we only know and can only come to know truth because (and in so far as) we are 'first' truly known.

Similarly, the attention to touch, the re-construal of our relation to ourselves and to the world, and thus the very relation of thought itself, harbours an almost unprecedented *intimacy*. Here there is no 'safe' distance for apprehension or comprehension, no lofty remove from the world, but rather a bewildering, perhaps curious or desirous, immediacy, which is nevertheless always also a mediation, between us and the world, between our selves and ourselves, and indeed between ourselves and God.

Touch is in a sense the 'primary' irreducible – 'more ancient' – sense or relation; each of the other four physical senses can be reduced to it (for us to taste or smell, small particles must touch the relevant sensors in our mouth or nose; for us to see, light must touch the retina; to hear, sound must touch the sensors in our ears and be carried to our ear-drums). It can, therefore, direct us back (forward) towards a time and a place before such distance has opened in the world for us. The distance is clearly necessary in order for touch to become meaningful – where there is no parting, there is also no touching. But we must not allow this fact to propel us to the thought that the distance and distancing is 'more than' or 'prior to' the touching, in a reduplication of our attempts to privilege the other senses over each other, and together over their common element – touch. By the same token, however, it will also propel us towards thoughts of the divisions, the distinctions, the distance and the distancing which are part of our present forms of existence, and which form our only 'route' 'back' to any more 'original' intuition.

Thinking transcendence after Irigaray's suggestion of the sensible transcendental and her frank exploration of the cost of the near-impossible subjectivity to be granted, grasped, touched upon by and in *La Mystérique* from within the specular economy, I discover anew the suggestion that transcendence is a matter of pressing intimacy; that thought of transcendence will require a reconfiguration of interiority and interiorisation; and that, far from proposing that we invent a God to suit our needs and our desired subjectivities, it in fact invites a renewed attention to the manners in which we have 'always already' been found, called, seen, heard and touched by the God who created our inmost parts, who knit us together in our mother's wombs, from whom our bodies were not hidden while we were being made in secret, whose eyes beheld our limbs as they were fashioned day by day when as yet there was none of them.[28] This, in important senses, returns us to my opening quotation, and a remarking of the coupling of the transcendency of the mother with the transcendency of God. Only now we are – 'after' Irigaray – in a different time (and so a different place and a different identity), continuing – tracing – the journey 'back' to the 'before' of this coupling, not only in a 'new light' or from a new 'perspective', but in a new (more ancient) mediation, that of touch.[29]

That the specular economy Irigaray criticises fails in its totalising tendencies is the 'first' witness to all this; it also provides the possibilities for the (re-)tracing of such an otherwise. That the economy is so total in its tendencies is, however, what makes the labour of this re-tracing so immense and ineluctably painful.

---

28 Cf. Psalm 139. That these verses are immediately followed by the exclamation, "How deep I find your thoughts, O God! How great is the sum of them!" serves briefly to indicate the biblical resonances of Augustine's linkage of human transcendence to God in the doctrine of the 'image', in which the 'trinity' of mind – love, memory and understanding – is 'image' of God *only* insofar as it provides a three-fold 'imaging' of God in loving, understanding and remembering the One by whom it was made. Augustine, *de Trinitate*, XIV, XII, 15.

29 "My own transcendence has started before my time, in a strange sort of "before", in a strange quasi time that does not belong to human history . . . Perhaps the temporal 'metaphors' of 'before', 'past', . . . can be neither translated nor dropped when we try to speak about transcendence." Peperzak, A., *Ethics as First Philosophy*, London, Routledge, 1995, p. 190. And again, a 'return' to Augustine – one of the sources of the western tradition and his intuition that this God is indeed more intimate to him than his own intimacy; see, for instance, Augustine, *Confessions*, III, VI, 11.

Chapter Ten

On the Nature of Nature: Is Sexual Difference Really Necessary?

Laurence Paul Hemming

Feminism's generosity in the discourse of faith has been to demand the re-examination of who the God is that any one of us has faith in, and to show the extent to which gender ascription is located in understandings of God that masquerade as 'neutral' or objectively and equally true for all. This paper is really preparatory to a larger study, but asks about the link between cosmology and physicality – between our embodiment and our being ordered to a greater whole. I undertake this examination by reference to three different cosmologies: the emerging worldview of postmodern feminism; the rational universe founded by the Enlightenment; and the ancient cosmos, both as it is understood by Aristotle, and later by Eckhart. The question that guides this paper all the way through is what does it mean to be ordered to the whole. Has the whole disappeared, through the interstices of power and melancholia, or is the whole understood transcendentally, as providing the same possibilities for being everywhere within it, or is it finite and bounded, so that where I am in it will determine who and how I am at the same time? Each of the answers posed for this question reconfigures questions of gender, so that who 'woman' and 'man' might be in each is different. On the other hand, each is also constitutive for an understanding of God, so that how you think the world is made up will determine how you relate to God.

Increasingly, feminist theorists themselves have come to accept that not only divine, but also gender identity itself, has become more difficult to explain and understand. The very transition from speech about 'sex' to that of 'gender identity' illustrates how who, and what, you take yourself to be must include some gesture at least towards who you *think* you are, and are *thought* to be. Psychology has entered gender discourse as a constitutive moment for investigating self-understanding. And yet psychology itself is being turned inside-out: once a tool for revealing to me who I am as a subject, now in much contemporary discourse the subject is understood psychologically through the mechanisms of subject-formation, or what Judith Butler calls 'subjection'.[1] Following postmodern readings of Freud, there is no 'unrepressed' subject; rather repression produces the very subject it represses. This subject always becomes known to itself through and as the configurations of power that repress it to bring it about. Power here operates as a limit, that establishes the 'inside' and 'outside' constituting subjectivity itself, whilst also explaining how the subject is deprived of the autonomy it craves. Butler asks:

> Does the norm, having become psychic, involve not only the interiorisation of the norm, but the interiorisation of the psyche? I argue that this process of internalisation *fabricates the distinction between interior and exterior life*, offering us a distinction between the psychic and the social . . .[2]

The baleful consequence of this interiority is that even the white heterosexual male, the 'normal' subject – the subject that never needs to self-identify because its identity is already inscribed into the very fabric of sociality, so that wherever it looks, it finds itself affirmed in advance of itself – even this most 'natural' of beings experiences a disturbing melancholia that troubles and destabilises it.[3]

Butler's project is to destabilise the 'natural' by revealing it to be a fiction: however, it is a fiction in which each of us must be located in order to exist at all. My self-evident uniqueness to myself, my self identification as the self I know, exists in consequence of my being ordered to a whole that is simultaneously concealed from me, as the very alterity and process of subject-production and subjection that brings me into existence. Existence here indicates presence to self. The consequences of this view, for many feminist writers especially, have been disturbing. Butler explains my place in the universe through a process that has simultaneously positioned and

---

1   "An account of subjection, it seems, must be traced in the turns of psychic life." Butler, J., *The Psychic Life of Power: Theories in Subjection*, Stamford, Stamford University Press, 1997, p. 18.
2   Butler, J., *The Psychic Life of Power*, p. 19 (Author's italics).
3   See Butler's extensive discussion of this in relation to Freud in Butler, J., *Gender Trouble: Feminism and the Subversion of Identity*, Routledge, New York, 1990, pp. 57 ff.

individuated me. This is a psychic process, the process by which I gain a psyche; however, it leaves me both positioned and simultaneously decentred. Spatial position here has no intrinsic meaning, because although three-dimensionality (the positioning that enables my individuation to be seen) gives me a location, nevertheless every location is still potentially like every other. The interiority that produced subjectivity, the 'ideal space' of subjecthood, has been reconfigured as an exterior surface. Through the processes of power that enforce the psyche, Butler explains how gender is inscribed into the production and enforcement of social hierarchy: the very thing that feminism emerged to be the critique *of*, and which feminism as a politics most often seeks to overcome. Butler explains how I gain a psyche and so become ensouled, but she can give ensoulment no meaning.

Martha Nussbaum's at times intemperate critique of Judith Butler illustrates the extent to which there is discomfort with Butler's views. Nussbaum argues that "for a long time, academic feminism . . . has been closely allied to the practical struggle to achieve justice and equality for women".[4] She cites Nancy Chodorow, who, despite her writing on "the replication of gender categories in child-rearing", nevertheless believes that "men and women could decide . . . that they will henceforth do things differently".[5] We can *decide* means, henceforth, all 'real' sexual difference – sexual difference as it ought to be – is in consequence of will. She quarrels with Butler because for her the emergence of a gendered voice is always in view of a politics. She asks: "Butler . . . want[s] to say that we have a kind of agency, an ability to undertake change and resistance. But where does this ability come from, if there is no structure in the personality that is not thoroughly power's creation?"[6] Nussbaum is horrified at Butler's refusal to accept that a genuine feminist politics makes things *better*; Nussbaum cries out that "the big hope, the hope for a world of real justice, where laws and institutions protect the equity and dignity of all citizens, has been banished".[7] Nussbaum's enactment of woman is the action of women, women striving to

---

4 Nussbaum, M. C., *The Professor of Parody* in *The New Republic*, 22 February, 1999, p. 37.
5 Nussbaum, M. C., *The Professor of Parody*, p. 37, citing Chodorow, N. J., *The Reproduction of Mothering: Psychoanalysis and the Sociology of Gender*, Berkeley, University of California Press, 1999.
6 Nussbaum, M. C., *The Professor of Parody*, p. 41.
7 Nussbaum, M. C., *The Professor of Parody*, p. 45.

eradicate injustice and so restructure society anew. Women have discovered their access to power precisely through striving for something different.

This illustrates the extent to which the feminism that Nussbaum and many like her represent is entirely constructed on a post-Enlightenment, transcendental, ideal of subjectivity. The subject is not, contra Butler, enacted (by the interstices of power), but acts – it becomes powerful in order most to *be*. The 'ought', what *should* be, realises itself as the 'is', but in fact occurs prior to the 'is', as what has *already* been seen should be the case to make the 'is' appear. Power must be acquired and exercised in order to guarantee equality. Hierarchy must be levelled for the sake of that equality, because the levelling of hierarchy ensures that we all have the same access to power. For Butler, the question is left begging – power must be acquired from whom? Is not the very power to be acquired constitutive of who acquires it, so that women becoming powerful (as men are already powerful) thereby masculinise themselves through inserting themselves into the very power structures that produced 'powerful men' at all? Are those at a distance from power not forced to cite the power they cannot own through parody, as a way of indicating their own relation to power and their distance from it? Is this not, for instance, how camp relates to the masculine, simultaneously its euphoric and tragic stylisation – a style that inaugurates a way of being through reference to, and distance from, the very thing it parodies and cites?

For Butler, the differentiation of power, its distribution in and across the production and subjection of persons, constructs sexual difference. This is an understanding which takes seriously the question of embodiment, and asks how embodiment is constructed and given meaning as the very surfaces of the interstices of power. Nussbaum's horror at Butler is at seeing the very tool which she has raised to level the hierarchies of power simultaneously dispossessed in the process: if woman is the product of no inner reality, but simply an effect of the differentiation of power itself through its appearing – therefore, what it *looks like* and how it presents itself – then the levelling of power differences will abolish woman *in* her very self. Woman has no prior meaning, only superficial (i.e. as surfaced) meaning. This fluidity, which Nussbaum experiences as a horror, is understood by Butler as a congealment, which will not so easily wash away. The power difference which constructs the appearance of male and female will not liquify into nothing, but will endlessly reproduce both itself and its multiple parodic forms. Butler confronts Nussbaum and theorists of her type with an ultimate question, implicit yet never realised in the presuppositions of a politics that takes a transcendental equality and notion of freedom for granted. If the outcome and proper end of this politics is that men and women – all of us henceforth – will "decide . . . to do things differently", where is the difference between men and women to be located? Surely, you reply, the difference between man and woman is configured naturally (and so apart from power)? Even if we were to accept that there might be a 'natural' difference (not at all an easy thing to do: was it not argued that the 'natural' place of woman was in childbirth, and at the kitchen sink?), is this natural difference necessary? Is it essential – which might be put as: is it to be understood as an essence, or henceforth can we decide it differently?

Why can feminist theorists not simply appeal to essences, as naturally establishing sexual difference, thereby evading Butler's critique of power? The difficulty historically with essences is that the philosopher of essence *par excellence* is Aristotle, who subordinates the essence or nature of woman to man. Indeed, Martha Nussbaum herself has played an important, if not foundational, part in the feminist critique of Aristotle. It might almost be possible to argue that the very Copernican revolution undertaken in the establishment of the post-Enlightenment re-conception of the physical universe (a male, patriarchal arena) has had to be reiterated and re-cited in order to establish the voice of women against the patriarchal politics that the Enlightenment left intact; in other words, Nussbaum's critique of the effects of ancient cosmology, and above all Aristotle's place in it, is not in the least accidental, but necessary, as a further stripping away of its debilitating effects. Thus the nature of sexual difference must be detached from every claim to essences. The feminist critique of Aristotle has in large part grounded itself through an analysis of Aristotle's *Politics*, whilst finding supporting references in his remarks on the inferiority of woman in *De Generatione Animalium*.[8] Certainly Aristotle's assertions of the innate 'maleness' of the understanding and the natural inferiority of women are to be found there.

---

8   For the inferiority of the female to the male see Aristotle, *De Generatione Animalium*: I, XXI; II, I; VI, I (729a; 731b–732a; 765b). For Aristotle's assertions of the maleness of understanding, see *Politics*, I (1245b; 1254b; 1255a). See also Butler's critique of Plato in these matters (Butler, J., *Bodies that Matter*, p. 53 f.).

There is, however, a difficulty, which postmodern critique of the Enlightenment has highlighted: the very structure of subjectivity, upon which so much feminist ethics and politics are based, itself *always* proscribes hierarchy, because any conception of human personhood constituted hierarchically is a potential limitation on the transcendental subject; a heteronomous claim on its autonomy. Thus Susan Moller Okin notes that "[Aristotle's] entire universe, from the lowliest plant to the human race, and beyond the human race to the heavenly bodies and the gods, is arranged in a strict hierarchy, and it is this that enables him to say 'In the world of nature as well as of art the lower always exists for the sake of the higher'".[9] Regarding hierarchy, Okin concludes: "What Aristotle does, therefore, is to define the goodness of each thing and each person according to its function . . . but for Aristotle, human beings have functions just as much and in the same way as artefacts do, and only those at the very top of the hierarchy have a function which is defined only in relation to themselves and not to others".[10] Ignoring the place of the divine (τὸ θειῶν) and the celestial spheres (or taking for granted that the divine is a further inscription of the male), what Okin (and others) focus on is the strictly political consequences of the relation of male to female in Aristotle, which for her reveals the extent to which he buttresses the "status quo" of the political arena.[11] This subordinates Aristotle's cosmology to a purely post-Enlightenment politics, where it is bound to fail. This politics takes for granted the equality of male and female, which is at the same time the very equality it seeks to establish. This taking for granted abolishes the meaning of embodiment at the point where equality is to be decided, so that the meaning of embodiment will not be established *through* equivalence, but will be established *after* equivalence has been asserted. Embodiment as such has only secondary or subordinate meaning. The ideal realm of what ought to be triumphs again over our understanding of how things actually are.

---

9 Okin, S. M., *Women in Western Political Thought*, Princeton, Princeton University Press, 1979, p. 75, quoting Aristotle, *Politics* I (1265b).
10 Okin, S. M., *Women in Western Political Thought*, p. 85.
11 "We must acknowledge Aristotle's normative use of the word 'natural', and give the 'natural' . . . a distinct moral connotation . . . Thus Aristotle has established a philosophical framework by which he can legitimise the status quo." Okin S. M., *Women in Western Political Thought*, p. 80.

The subordination of embodiment, however, denies that being in a world, or cosmos, or universe has any primary meaning for what or who I *am*. I only enter the world *after* the establishment of my selfhood. 'Nature' here is deprived of any worldly referent. Nature is something I already had before I entered the world. More particularly, I could be anywhere in the world, and appear as any*thing* and still have the same nature. Here the 'inner' person, as what is most interior to her, is what is most real. The outer need have no bearing at all on the inner, and yet the outer is constantly driving to assert and express what the inner person knows is already the case. My inwardness, nevertheless, is always apart from yours, and I can have no access to it. We are forever apart, in interiorities that can mirror each other and yet never be shared. Transcendental autonomy establishes exactly this. The hidden exteriority that Butler traces (as what is to be interiorised through subjection) is never even available to the subjectivity postulated by Nussbaum. This interiority is simply the subject and recipient of external impressions – no wonder she delights in the work of David Hume.[12]

It would be possible to show, in a detailed analysis, how this approach overlooks Aristotle's fundamental philosophical position, and why it never really asks why Aristotle took the cosmos to be structured as he did. The answer is obvious: in order to inaugurate and consolidate his politics. Such an analysis would need, however, to overcome the question of Aristotle's unequal treatment of sexual difference. The hope might be that it is possible to elucidate a position which, whilst entirely relying on an Aristotelian cosmology, nevertheless subverts Aristotle's establishment of sexual difference, and establishes equivalence and difference through embodiment as such, thereby re-ordering the inner to the outer. Eckhart's treatise *von Abegeschiedenheit*, "On Detachment", provides just such a possibility.[13] Eckhart understands Aristotle in a way entirely differently from many feminist critics, and yet overturns Aristotle's description of sexual difference in such a way that he grounds it in an 'inner' and 'outer' that gestures towards Butler's definition of psyche, with one important difference. Through an

---

12 Nussbaum, M. C., *The Professor of Parody*, p. 40. "One afternoon, fatigued by Butler on a long plane trip, I turned to a draft of a student's dissertation on Hume's views of personal identity . . . Hume, what a fine gracious spirit: how kindly he respects the reader's intelligence, even at the cost of exposing his own uncertainty."

13 I am using the text based on the Kohlhammer Critical Edition in Largier, N. (ed.), *Meister Eckhart: Werke*, Stuttgart, Deutscher Klassiker Verlag, 1993, Vol. II, pp. 434 ff.

understanding of the 'natural' inner and outer of being human, he maintains a way to God, by emphasising Aristotle's understanding of the finitude of the cosmos. In this sense, Eckhart's notion of personhood never achieves 'autonomy' in the strict subjectival sense; it is always on the way to somewhere.

My aim is not to inaugurate a defence of Aristotle, but rather through proposing a return to what Aristotle was attempting to understand, to open (though not complete) a way forward for thinking sexual difference that appeals to cosmology, and so evades understanding sexual difference and human anthropology simply through transcendental subjectivity. My belief is that we must try to glimpse what it was Aristotle was trying to think *about*, which Aristotle himself is only *on the way to*. This means that, in the matter of sexual difference, I believe Aristotle's cosmology is prior to his understanding of sexual generation, because he enables us to understand the absolute location and meaning of persons.

This approach would 'locate' me in the cosmos, and so guarantee my uniqueness, whilst simultaneously explaining sexual difference in terms of what differentiates me. So far, however, a return to Aristotle would get us no further than Butler has achieved without him. My suggestion is that attempting to rediscover what it was that Aristotle was thinking *about* would have to overcome the dependence on subjectivity (as subjection) that Butler relies on, precisely in the matter of what she takes as the 'inner' and 'outer' of human being. My aim would be to point a way to how sexual difference could be accomplished without reference to the will that encloses the subject, and so constitutes the barrier between psychic and social, psyche and world, ψυχή and κόσμος, that will is. If Butler shows how through subjection I am 'willed as . . . ', and Nussbaum how through the exercise of will I *am*, Eckhart will point to what I am apart from will.

At the centre of Eckhart's treatise is a meditation on the meaning and person of Mary, through an understanding of what he calls 'detachment'. Detachment here translates *abegeschiedenheit* (or sometimes *gelâzenheit*). *Abegeschiedenheit* literally means 'the state of being cut off'. The detached soul is separated from things in their thingliness, so that what they are comes into view in an entirely different way. Detachment is an orientation on the cosmos which is different to any immediate preoccupation with things.

Eckhart says that love is to be praised above detachment, because whereas love compels me to love God, through detachment I compel God to love me. He argues: "I prove that detachment compels God to come to me in this way, because everything longs to achieve its own natural place. Now God's own natural place is unity and sheerness".[14] The intensive adverb *gerne* in this sentence means not the willing or striving of things for their proper place but indicates their naturally seeking after and being carried toward and attracted to where they belong, as a natural motion in them. Detachment does not, therefore, mean absolute separation from things, but rather, through finding the place to which I might naturally tend (rather than strive for through desiring and willing), the things around me will also tend to their natural place, in relation to me. *Abegeschiedenheit* is not, therefore, indifference to everything, a kind of withdrawal of the self into an absolute self-referential interiority but rather an ordering of the self to things in such a way that they are no longer desired or willed for what I want for and from them, but a relating to where they might be found in themselves.

Eckhart here makes a clear reference to Aristotle's understanding of place (τόπος). In Aristotle's cosmos there is no concept of space; all things are not in space, but rather have their proper 'place'(τόπος).[15] The place of things can be both relative to me in my being placed (θέσις), or absolute (τόπος as such), but place discloses the above-below, front-back, and left-right of things.[16] Thus how things look to me might depend on where I stand, but "on the other hand, in nature itself everything is for itself positioned in its own place".[17] The 'above' is not something arbitrary, but is the place toward which fire and the light are carried; in the same way, below is where the heavy and earthy are carried. Each of the elements has a proper place; anything combined of more than one element will find its place relative to its

---

14 Eckhart, *von Abegeschiedenheit*, p. 436. "Daz abegeschiedenheit twinge got ze mir, daz bewære ich dâ mite: wan ein ieglich dinc ist gerne an sîner natiurlichen eigen stat. Nû ist gotes natiurlîchiu eigen stat einicheit und lûterkeit."
15 For an extensive discussion of this, see Lang, H., *The Order of Nature in Aristotle's Physics: Place and the Elements*, Cambridge, Cambridge University Press, 1998, especially part I. A brief summary can be found in Lang, H., *Aristotle's Physics and its Medieval Varieties*, New York, SUNY, 1992, pp. 175 ff. Cf. also Heidegger, M., *Gesamtausgabe* Volume 19, *Platon: Sophistes*, Frankfurt, Klostermann, 1992, §15, b, α.
16 Cf. Aristotle, *Physics*, V, I-V (224a–229b).
17 Aristotle, *Physics*, IV, I (208b12-20). ἐν δὲ τῇ φύσει διώρισται χωρὶς ἕκαστον.

composition. Motion here is the expression of a need, of a desire of a thing to be where it should because it is not in its proper place. The motion of a thing when it is in its proper place is not therefore no motion at all, but the motion of being at rest. A thing in its proper place is moved by nothing. Which means *the* nothing is its desire: *nothing as such* moves it.

Beyond the above and below is the heaven, which is the place for all the things it contains. Contains here implies surround, since the inside of heaven is spherical and the below is itself in the form of a sphere. Everything heavy, in this sense, is carried to the middle. Aristotle notes that the universality of things in place is not the whole of the cosmos, but the inner limit of heaven, wherein all things have their place.

Eckhart is therefore immediately giving the reality of the human person within the physical cosmology of Aristotle a spiritual as well as a physical meaning, for he argues that through detachment I will be carried to my proper place. This is exactly his sense of *gerne*: if I have detachment I will compel God to come to me because I will be carried naturally to my proper place: the place where God is. Moreover, this is not through the exercise of will or desire, but rather in the abandonment of will and withdrawal from any exercise of the powers or desires of the person this movement will happen 'naturally'.

Why is detachment the proper place of God? Eckhart always stresses that *abegeschiedenheit* is unmoved. Thus "immoveable detachment brings a person into the greatest likeness with God. When therefore God is God, God has this from God's unmoveable detachment, and from detachment has God sheerness and simplicity and changelessness. And from there, should a person become like to God, as truly as a creature might have likeness to God, that must happen with detachment."[18]

Again, Eckhart is working within Aristotle's cosmology. The outermost limit of place, heaven as such, is not strictly speaking in place, nor is it moved. It constitutes the place of the movable (τοῦ κινητοῦ), the realm of things

---

18 Eckhart, *von Abegeschiedenheit*, p. 442. "Wan daz got ist got, daz hât er von sîner unbewegelîchen abegeschiedenheit, und von der abegeschiedenheit hât er sîne lûterkeit und sîne einvalticheit und sîne unwandelbærkeit. Und dâ von, sol der mensche gote glîch werden, als verre als ein crêatûre glîcheit mit gote gehaben mac, daz muoz geschehen mit abegeschiedenheit."

(which are all subject to motion), but is not itself moved.[19] There are neither things (bodies), nor motion, nor place beyond heaven.[20] Martin Heidegger, a commentator on Aristotle *par excellence*, notes: "Place is the *limit of* the περιέχον, that which encloses a body, not the limit of the body itself, but that which the limit of the body comes up against, in such a way, specifically, that there is between these two limits no interspace, no διάστημα".[21] This is important for Eckhart's interpretation of detachment. For he argues that nothing comes between the creature who has detachment and God. God is, in this sense, no-thing, so that the creature who wants to be likened (literally 'made-like') God must itself become no-thing so that "detachment is so close to nothing that there is nothing so subtle that it might hold itself in detachment other than God alone".[22] This 'become' means 'come up against' so that there is no interval, no distance between the creature and God. Eckhart says "detachment comes so near to nothing, that there may be not a thing between perfect detachment and nothing".[23] "Not a thing" means here both no things in general, and no distance or interval. If God is nothing, and I am next to nothing when I am in my proper place, then nothing has moved me there, and in being there nothing will continue to move me.

In *de Cælo*, Aristotle notes that the name 'heaven' (οὐρανὸς) is also that place where divinity is said to have its seat.[24] Later he takes the popular understanding of the immutability of divinity to be consistent with the name of eternity (αἰών), tracing the etymology of eternity as "being everlastingly",

---

19 Aristotle, *Physics*, IV, V (212b21–22). Καὶ διὰ τοῦτο ἡ μὲν γῆ ἐν τῷ ὕδατι, τοῦτο δ' ἐν τῷ ἀέρι, οὗτος δ' ἐν τῷ αἰθέρι ὁ δ' αἰθὴρ ἐν τῷ οὐρανῷ, ὁ δ' οὐρανός οὐκέτι ἐν ἄλλῳ.

20 Aristotle, *De Cælo*, I, IX (278b23–279a13).

21 Heidegger, M., *Platon: Sophistes*, p. 108. "Der Ort ist die *Grenze* des περιέχον, das, was einen Körper umgrenzt, nicht die Grenze des Körpers selbst, sondern das, woran die Grenze des Körpers sich stößt, so zwar, daß zwischen diesen beiden Grenzen kein Zwischenraum, kein διάστημα ist" (Author's italics).

22 Eckhart, *von Abegeschiedenheit*, p. 436. "Nû ist abegeschiedenheit dem nihte alsô nâhe, daz kein dinc sô kleinvüege enist daz ez sich enthalten müge in abegeschiedenheit dan got aleine."

23 Eckhart, *von Abegeschiedenheit*, p. 436. "Nû rüeret abegeschiedenheit alsô nâhe dem nihte, daz zwischen volkomener abegescheidenheit und dem nihte kein dinc gesîn enmac."

24 Aristotle, *de Cælo*, I, IX (278b15).

which is both without death and divine.[25] The later Mediæval tradition of Aristotelian interpretation had no problem with identifying this understanding of God with the idea of the prime mover in Aristotle's *Physics* and the understanding of the divine in *Metaphysics*.[26]

Although this is a spiritualisation of Aristotle's cosmology, it does not work through inwardness in the way we might expect. For at the heart of this exploration of detachment is a movement that involves a highest and a lowest within the cosmos. Detachment is a kind of highest, where the soul finds its proper place. Through detachment, which is the place of God, is, strictly speaking, the periphery and outermost limit of heaven itself, the place of nothing, of nothing. What is at issue with peripheries we shall see shortly, but first it is necessary to understand what this has to do with the soul.

A point of Aristotle's cosmology, central to Eckhart's understanding of *abegeschiedenheit*, is that the unmovedness of the heaven (which is what allows everything within the heaven to move and be moveable) is compared to the soul, in that both are unmoved accidentally (κατὰ συμβεβηκός).[27] Aristotle makes much of this comparison; indeed, it is precisely through it that he achieves the distinction between the nature of the soul and the nature of heaven (of the totality of all there is, τὸ πᾶν). For Aristotle the soul is the "first actuality" (ἐντελέχεια ἡ πρώτη) of the body.[28] Ἐντελέχεια means that which has come into, or reached, its limit – its fulness; that which has been

25 Aristotle, *de Cælo*, I, ıx (279a25ff.). κατὰ τὸν αὐτὸν δὲ λόγον καὶ τὸ τοῦ παντὸς οὐρανοῦ τέλος καὶ τὸ τὸν πάντα χπόνον καὶ τοῦ ἀπειρίαν περιεχον τέλος αἰών ἐστιν, ἀπὸ τοῦ ἀεὶ εἶναι εἰληφὼς τὴν ἐπωνυμίαν, ἀθάνατος καὶ θεῖος.

26 Aristotle: *Physics*, VIII, x; *Metaphysics* XII, VII. For the way in which Aquinas in particular achieved this synthesis, see Lang, H., *Aristotle's Physics and it Medieval Varieties*, pp. 163 ff. See also Randles, W. G. L., *The Unmaking of the Medieval Christian Cosmos, 1500–1760*, Aldershot, Ashgate, 1999, esp. p. 8.

27 Aristotle, *Physics*, IV, V (212b13–14). Τὰ δὲ κατὰ συμβεβηκός, οἷον ἡ ψυχή καὶ ὁ οὐρανός . . .

28 Aristotle, *de Anima*, II, ı (412a28–29). Lang translates this as "the entelechy, or form, of the body"; however, it is important to note that entelechy and form are not the same, and that there is no reference to form in the Greek text she cites (Lang, H., *Aristotle's Physics and its Medieval Varieties*, p 41, esp. note 31). See however, the argument at II, ı (412a19ff.). Here the equivalence is not between εἶδος or μορφή and entelechy (ἐντελέχεια), but between entelechy and substance (οὐσία). The εἶδος, or 'look' that the soul has, is of a body according to nature. Soul is therefore the appearing and being able to be seen of a natural body. Butler also mentions this passage in Butler, J., *Bodies that Matter*, p. 32 f.

perfected. As the limit and perfection of the body, the soul moves the body for which it is the actualisation. The soul itself is essentially unmoved. It has the capacity to move the body only because of its own unmovedness. Can the soul not also be moved? For Aristotle (in contradistinction to Plato) the soul is not self-moved, and is *essentially* (ἂν ἐκ τῆς οὐσίας αὐτῆς) unmoved, but can be moved accidentally (κατὰ συμβεβηκὸς).[29] This is in contrast to the heaven, which is unmoved both essentially and accidentally. Hence Eckhart relies on this distinction to illustrate how a created soul can achieve likeness to God and yet still be created.

How does Aristotle illustrate the distinction? He speaks of a sailor on the deck of a ship.[30] The soul moves the sailor across the deck of his ship, by means of walking. In this sense the sailor's body moves while the sailor's soul remains essentially unmoved. However, the ship also moves, by means of its propulsion or the movement of the waters. In this sense, the soul is moved by the moving of the ship, but accidentally (i.e. through no physical concern that the soul has with motion). By extension, the walking of the sailor is also an accidental, but not essential, movement of the soul. This example itself strongly parallels one of the central passages in Aristotle's *Physics* where he establishes the meaning of place (τόπος) overall. He takes the example of a vessel in a river.[31] The vessel can change place on the river, in terms of how it is perceived. But in reality, the vessel, in moving, has remained in its proper place. Its proper place is 'floating-moving-on-the-river'; the place given absolutely through its relation to the 'whole', the heaven-given nature of place. This is its 'proper' place, the place where the vessel is properly known to be what it is and how it is. Place *contains* the vessel and gives it its capacity to be. Aristotle comments, "just as the vessel is a moveable place, so place is an immoveable vessel".[32]

---

29 Aristotle, *de Anima*, I, III (406b14).
30 Aristotle, *de Anima*, I, III (406a6-11).
31 Aristotle, *Physics*, IV: III (210a24); IV (211b26–29, 212a8–21).
32 Aristotle, *Physics*, IV, IV (212a15). Ἔστι δ᾽ ὥσπερ τὸ ἀγγεῖον τόπος μεταφορητόσ, οὕτω καὶ ὁ τόπος ἀγγεῖον ἀμετακίνητον. Helen Lang sees the reference here to water, river, and sea as a reference to ᾽Ωκεανός, the surround of all the earth on which the sun moves as if on a river – often taken as the ancient name for the divine. She notes that Aristotle "emphasises that his account agrees with the ancients for whom 'the whole river' represents place". (Lang, H., *The Order of Nature in Aristotle's Physics*, p. 99.)

Eckhart relies on the distinction that Aristotle makes between the soul and the 'whole' of the cosmos – that both are essentially, that is 'naturally', unmoved, but gives it an important twist. He notes that "the masters say that in each person there are two sides of a person: the one is called the outer person . . . and the outer person works through the power of the soul. The other person is called the inner person, which is the innerness of the person".[33] It would be easy to overlook the meanings of inner and outer that are at work here, and yet they are in no way connected to the modern, psychological account of personhood found in Butler. I repeat, there is no sense in which 'inner' here denotes private, autonomous, or interior, either as the psychology of the subject or the consequence of the subject's subjection through the effects of power. To understand this, it will be necessary to make some further observations about Aristotle's understanding of place.

Heidegger notes that place must be understood as the "possibility of the proper therein-belonging of a thing", so that its 'nature' becomes visible.[34] Place in this sense is the "capacity (of things) to be present, a possibility which is constitutive of their being. Place is the ability a thing has to be there, where, in being there, it is properly so".[35]   What becomes clear from this understanding of Aristotle's notion of place (τόπος) is that a thing cannot really be understood in its proper being until it is seen to be in its proper place, the place which most belongs to it, and to which it too belongs. Place, therefore, is a kind of limit, distinct from what it limits, but conjoined to it in such a way that there is no interval between the limit (place) and what it limits (bodies in place).   Lang notes that "place and moveable body are not conjoined as two bodies in contact, but as a limit (place) and what is limited (moveable body) . . . The limit and the limited comprise one being".[36] This, as Heidegger notes, is the real meaning of the term οὐσία (normally translated

33 Eckhart, *von Abegeschiedenheit*, p. 448. "Hie solt dû wizzen, daz die *meister* sprechent, daz an einem ieglîchen menschen zweierhande menschen sint: der eine heizet der ûzer mensche, daz ist diu sinnelicheit; . . . würket doch der ûzer mensche von kraft der sêle. Der ander mensche heizet der inner mensche, daz ist des menschen innerkeit."
34 Heidegger, M., *Platon: Sophistes*, p. 109. "Der Ort ist die *Möglichkeit der rechten Hingehörigkeit eines Seienden* . . . Das Seiende der Welt als »Natur« im weiten Sinne hat seinen Platz."
35 Heidegger, M., *Platon: Sophistes*, p. 109. "Der Ort ist *das zum Seienden gehörige*, sein Sein mit ausmachende *Anwesendseinkönnen*. Der Ort ist das *Dortseinkönnen eines Seienden*, dergestalt, daß es, *dortseiend, eigentlich da ist*."
36 Lang, H., *The Order of Nature in Aristotle's Physics*, p. 93.

as substance or even essence), where the limit brings the limited to be known, and so 'be': "limit and end are that with which a thing begins to *be*. It is from that we must understand the highest term that Aristotle used for being as such, ἐντελέχεια".[37] Limit here is described in two further ways by Aristotle: as limit as such, πέρας and as end, τέλος; but also as the holding-in-limit, περιέχον, which is place. This holding-in-limit yields the appearance of surface, τὸ ἔσχατον, the outermost, or last. As outermost or last, it has no outer, but is the outermost that yields that there is limit as such. Paradoxically, therefore, it can be translated as innermost, or inner, because it is what brings what it holds within it to sight.[38] Τὸ ἔσχατον, strictly speaking, is the possibility of a thing having its disclosure or εἶδος, its 'look' or 'face'. As the inner, it allows the outer to be seen. Moreover, as the outermost, it can have no outer. It is what contains the outermost and holds it in place. As the inner, it is the disclosure or appearance of what is within; but as the possibility of *any* disclosure of what is within, it is really the inner *as such*, what Eckhart calls "innerness" (*innerkeit*); the outermost is held in place by interiority. It is in this sense that the soul, which is the essentially unmoved limit and entelechy of the body of which it is the soul, becomes thought of and is understood as 'inner' to the body to which it belongs. Most importantly of all, we are all held in place by the same limit, ἔσχατον, or "innerness". The limit, as interiority, is shared by, and is potentially visible to us all.

How can the distinction between limit and what it limits be better understood? Aristotle says that limit appears as a kind of surface. In order to understand this, it is important to focus on the appearing of a thing, rather than on its taking a 'surface' in order to appear (hence why τὸ ἔσχατον is so difficult to explain, as Lang notes), because the surface is only the εἶδος of what appears, which makes the thing available to be seen, but is not necessarily the only way it *could* be seen. Hence its surface can appear

---

37 Heidegger, M., *Gesamtausgabe*, Vol. 40, *Einführung in die Metaphysik*, Tübingen, Niemeyer, 1987 (1953), p. 46. "Grenze und Ende sind jenes, womit das Seiende zu *sein* beginnt. Von daher ist der höchste Titel zu verstehen, den *Aristoteles* für das Sein gebrauchte, die ἐντελέχεια."

38 Lang explicitly criticises this translation of τὸ ἔσχατον at *Physics* 212a20 by Hardie and Gaye. (Lang, H., *The Order of Nature in Aristotle's Physics*, p. 106.) But see note 39 below.

differently, whilst it itself really remains the same.[39] The appearance has to be taken together with what it is the appearance *of* in order for its οὐσία, its being, to be what *as a whole* 'is' there, in any particular place. Heidegger notes that all these determinations of being: limit; end; form; the 'look' that a thing has; all of these are brought to bear in the meaning of the term οὐσία, or more fully, παρουσία. He adds that "the usual thoughtless translation of this word with 'substance' misses its sense altogether. For παρουσία we have in German a corresponding term, *An-wesen* (presencing)".[40]

Having seen how deeply Eckhart draws upon Aristotle's cosmology in order to expound his understanding of *abegeschiedenheit*, it should now be possible to illustrate how precisely Eckhart subverts Aristotle's conception of woman in order to unfold what detachment is. If detachment is a being moved to the highest, it is disclosed by being the lowest. Eckhart begins by noting that "the masters . . . praise humility before many other virtues, but I praise detachment before all humility" because there cannot be perfect detachment without perfect humility.[41] Eckhart here takes the etymological reference of *humilitas* (which he quotes in Latin in the text, referring to the song of Mary, the *Magnificat*) as earthly, which of the four Aristotelian elements is the lowest. Mary's detachment is brought to light by her humility, which is why, according to Eckhart, she praises her humility in her song, and not her detachment. Detachment is silent, for Eckhart glosses the psalm "I shall hear what the Lord God will speak in me"[42] by noting that this requires silence so that God "comes in here to me". The identity of Mary's womb and the whole cosmos is being asserted, through the accidental identity of the unmovedness of place. Moreover, it is precisely because Mary is lower (in her perfect humility) that she has perfect detachment.

39 See Lang, H., *The Order of Nature in Aristotle's Physics*, pp. 106 ff. I remain unconvinced that she is really successful in explaining τὸ ἔσχατον precisely because she does not distinguish between μορφή (form) and εἶδος, the 'look' that form has. Consequently she does not fully bring to light the ambiguity in Aristotle's text that εἶδος is the two-dimensional 'look' that three-dimensional place has to take to be seen and so appear.

40 Heidegger, M., *Einführung in die Metaphysik*, p. 46. "Die übliche Gedankenlosigkeit übersetzt das Wort mit »Substanz« und verfehlt damit allen Sinn. Wir haben für παρουσία den gemäßen deutschen Ausdruck in dem Wort An-wesen."

41 Eckhart, *von Abegeschiedenheit*, p. 436. "Die *meister* lobent . . . dêmüeticheit vür vil ander tugende. Aber ich lobe abegeschiedenheit vür alle dêmüeticheit."

42 Eckhart, *von Abegeschiedenheit*, p. 440 (Psalm 84 [9] [Vulgate]). "Audiam, quid loquatur in me dominus Deus."

Christ wishing to become human does so by means of her humility, so that her detachment is undisturbed, for her detachment is immovable. Eckhart's point is that her perfect detachment compels God to come to her, because she has already attained the place wherein God is to be found; the silence of her detachment makes her available to receive God's word. God's coming to her can be seen, however, only through her humility. In this sense, the extent to which she is perfectly in place with God is seen through the most earthly of her virtues, humility.

Is there not a danger here, that we praise Mary's humility as a kind of submissiveness, which is therefore Godly because it is submissive? Eckhart would rule this out in two ways: first, Mary's humility is in consequence of her detachment, and not the other way round. She does not enter into detachment through humility, because this would be to desire, will, or even be willed as humble in order to achieve detachment. Rather, her humility is the consequence of her already having been exalted, which is detached; second, it is possible, Eckhart says, to have humility without detachment, but it is not possible to have perfect humility without (already having had) perfect detachment. In this sense, submissiveness, either desired, or enforced, would not be a way to God.

Detachment is without desire, as it is without movement. Eckhart says: "Perfect detachment has no looking up to, no abasement . . . and wills no sameness nor difference with any creature, [wanting] neither this nor that. It wills nothing other than to be . . . Whoever wants to be this or that wants to be something, but detachment wills to be not and nothing".[43] The Middle High German verb *willen* implies a lack, which does not desire something to possess it, but desires it in order to be possessed *of* it. I become what I am possessed by, which is why I am not free of it (which parallels Butler's understanding of how even distance from power is always forced to deflect and cite it, as an orientation towards it – even an orientation that seeks distance from the sources of power, though not, therefore, achieving distance from its effects. I am moved towards it in my wanting. 'Want' here has

---

43 Eckhart, *von Abegeschiedenheit*, p. 438. "Volkomeniu abegeschiedenheit enhât kein ûfsehen ûf keine neigunge . . . und enwil weder glîcheit noch ûngleicheit mit keiner crêatûre haben noch diz noch daz: si enwil niht anders wan sîn. Daz si aber welle diz oder daz sîn, des enwil si niht. Wan swer wil diz oder daz sîn, der wil etwaz sîn, sô enwil abegeschiedenheit nihtes niht sîn."

something of the older English meaning, as in 'he's been found wanting'. Wanting means I am moved toward what I want. To want for nothing is to be possessed by nothing, no-thing, and so be possessed by nothing, held in limit by nothing, and so to be full of God. To want nothing means to be unmoved, or rather to be moved by nothing.

Mary's outward being comes into an essential unity with God through her inwardness. This inwardness is precisely her identity with the outermost, her unity with the place where God is. What enables Eckhart to announce this interpretation, which relies so much on an understanding of 'nothing', is an interpretation of 1 Corinthians 1 [28]: "God chose what is low and despised in the world, even things that are not, to bring to nothing things that are". Eckhart relies again on there being nothing between limit and what is limited, between the outermost of body, which can be seen, and its 'inner' which by limiting enables it to be seen, so that this inner is the opposite of everything we now consider inwardness to be. Mary's humility indicates her detachment because it has nothing to do with will; it is neither desired nor enforced.

Eckhart asks what is the object or purpose of pure detachment: "Thereto I answer, and say, that neither this nor that is the object of sheer detachment. Its place is in a mere nothingness, and I say to you why that is: sheer detachment is from the highest place".[44] What is translated here as "place" indicates τόπος.

In consequence, Eckhart's understanding of detachment, as the meaning of redemption, and so the real meaning of being itself, is only possible through an understanding of the physics of the Aristotelian cosmos, the actual way it is structured. This structuring, does not, however, commit him in any way to accepting as real the valency of lower and higher to man and woman. Mary is in no sense here being posed as an unattainable ideal, separate from her sex, nor as unique in the scheme of salvation. On the contrary, the entire text implies, and the final section makes explicit, that anyone who wishes to come to God and to understand Jesus Christ will have to come to detachment in the way that Mary is already possessed of it. Redemption, whilst taking place within the structure of the cosmos, also reverses its apparent order into the

---

44 Eckhart, *von Abegeschiedenheit*, p. 450.   "Nû vrâge ich hie, waz der lûtern abegeschiedenheit gegenwurf si? Da zuo antwürte ich alsô und spriche, daz weder diz noch daz ist der lûtern abegeschiedenheit gegenwurf. Si stât ûf einem blôzen nihte, und sage dir, war umbe daz ist: diu lûteriu abegeschiedenheit stât ûf dem hœhsten."

real, natural order of highest and lowest that brings the soul to God. This bringing of the soul, however, is an already brought. As Oliver Davies has remarked, the whole structure of detachment is to become one with the intellective essence that God is. Moreover, the soul is already structured in the same way as the entirety of the cosmos, where the body of the soul is not already divinised, and so does not contain God, but is surrounded by and contained by God, first in the surrounding limit of the heaven, and second in virtue of the soul's identity with God in its structure and unmovedness. Where I would disagree with Davies is in his claim that this is in virtue of the attainment of a (private) interior state, for precisely the reason I have outlined.

Interiority means unity with the whole cosmos, not the unity *of* the intellective self.[45] In that God is immediately contiguous with the whole cosmos, but without it, so the soul needs to discover its detachment as a way of uniting itself with the whole cosmos, which will make it contiguous to God, with no interval or separation from God, and yet it remains distinct. Eckhart exploits the fact that the soul, even when it attains perfect detachment, can still appear and be moved accidentally, even though it has discovered the full meaning of its being *essentially* unmoved.

For Eckhart, however, the necessity of sexual difference is that it is only a woman who could have received the word and brought it to birth. It is Mary's capacity as one who can bring to birth that makes possible her humanity as the primary sign of the attainment of detachment for all of us, male and female alike. In this sense, but this sense alone, sexual difference is necessary, and simultaneously collapsed at the point of necessity. Here man is collapsed into woman and not the other way about. The question for Eckhart is not 'can a male God or saviour save women?', but rather, 'can a man be possessed of the place wherein we find this woman saved?'. The answer, moreover, is yes, because she gives birth to a man, the saviour Christ, a man. She *must* give birth to a man, because else we could be sure only of woman's redemption.

Moreover, this sexual difference is inscribed into the *final* structure of the cosmos. Mary's immediate being a woman is made possible and brought to light through her detached, and so fully true, being-with-God. Her being a woman is the 'natural' consequence of her place in redemption: its meaning

---

45 See Davies' helpful *Introduction* to Davies, O. (Editor and Translator), *Meister Eckhart: Selected Writings*, London, Penguin, 1994, pp. xxix ff.

is available fully only to faith. 'Natural' here, therefore, has none of the consequences that leads to its critique in much contemporary feminist literature. Natural is not immediately disclosive of an essence, only of an embodied difference. Eckhart, citing detachment as the means, quotes Augustine, saying that "the soul has a secret entry to the Divine nature, when all things become nothing to it".[46] Could it be that Eckhart has in mind the Latin etymology of 'nature', as that which is born, and emerges through birth, as the way in which the divine nature becomes known, through Mary, and in Christ, so that it indicates how through her nature Mary is shown to have attained the place of God?

To conclude: has what I have described here really been no more than a sleight of hand, which in effect refuses the critique of feminist thinkers in the arena of faith? I do not think so; in fact, to the contrary, I am certain that unless we pay most serious attention to the discourses announced by theorists like Judith Butler, we will lose any possibility of establishing understandings of difference that allow something akin to what Aristotle's understanding of 'place' is seeking to articulate. Difference establishes multiplicity and individuation, and more importantly explains it. For Butler, difference is not elided into a transcendental optimism that in the end cannot establish individuation, an optimism that imposes a metaphysical universality and sameness as an ideal postulate which in no way exists in reality. However, the interiority that all discourse based in a psychological constitution of the person establishes is inimical to a love of God, because it establishes God, and not the cosmos, as the true analogue of the human person. This either has the effect of proclaiming us all gods (rather than proclaiming a common home in God), or counterposing our own power to the power of God (which must result, as Nietzsche so deftly unfolded, in the death of God and the triumph of the will). My as yet incomplete and stumbling thesis is simply that precisely what Eckhart names as 'inwardness' (*inwendicheit*) means a turning away from all things that reveals the inner unity and purpose of the whole cosmos as its finitude and limit. Here nature does not mean 'purpose' or 'function', but 'being'.

---

46 Eckhart, *von Abegeschiedenheit*, p. 454. " . . . daz *Augustinus* sprichet: diu sêle hât einen heimlîchen înganc in götlîche natûre, dâ ir alliu dinc ze nihte werdent."

Chapter Eleven

The Grace of Being:
Connectivity and Agency in
John Macquarrie's Theology

Georgina Morley

The content of Christian believing issues in a shape of living which varies according to whatever doctrinal motif achieves dominance. For this reason, if for no other, the challenge of 'right believing' needs to be embraced beyond the bounds of neo-conservatism (whether Protestant or Catholic), and the danger of 'wrong believing' spelt out with radical attention to the constraint, prejudice and harm with which it colludes. Pastoral conversations with women who have found Christian faith dehumanising point to a whole host of doctrinal stumbling blocks which interact with, or emerge as, institutional and structural factors. So, for example, a robust 'two realms' theology coupled with a fear of contamination by The World issues in a kind of Christian ghetto; the expectations laid on a woman in this cautious world are ones to which many women find themselves obliged to live down. Equally, doctrinal millstones appear in psychological guise. An exaggerated monarchical model of God coupled with penal substitutionary atonement produces the affective result, "God is great; I am worthless. Everything good that happens is from God; everything bad that happens is my fault".[1]

---

1   The Western Fathers are routinely scapegoated for the introduction of Platonic dualisms into the Christian faith in such a way as to demonise woman as material temptress and justify her subjugation. Whilst the scapegoating reaches exaggerated proportions it is still the case that some women appropriate with frightening ease Tertullian's slur, "You are [each] an Eve . . . because of your desert, that is, death, the Son of God had to die", *Apparel of Women* I:1 1-2 in *Disciplinary, Moral and Ascetical Works*, Washington D. C., Catholic University of America, 1957, pp. 117 f.

It is little surprise that women leave a church which appears to perpetuate the doctrinal basis for such diminishment and damage. It is little surprise, too, that they turn most typically to person-centred and creation-centred spiritualities which emphasise the ways in which it is good to be human, and the fundamental connectedness of the cosmos.   Some, however, find weaknesses here, too. There is no summons from 'beyond' (beyond the self, beyond the natural), and there is no account of the always already given discipline of community. This means there is a very real risk that spirituality becomes reduced to preferential projections of my own aspirations, my own needs, my own prejudices. One of the persistent difficulties for women who remain within the church is the question of how to conceive of the otherness of God (indeed, how to submit to the summons of God) in such a way that it is experienced not as alien and domineering, but as the overwhelmingly demanding invitation of kinship. How can we give account of God and the human person so that God is 'big' enough, 'other' enough, to be worth our allegiance, and also that it is good to be human? How can we do this within the discipline of the Christian tradition and community?

It has become commonplace that feminist theologies which continue to operate within the broad context of Christian faith seek to redress the doctrinal balance, reclaiming less dominant strands of tradition, deconstructing and reconstructing and redeeming.[2]   But for what I shall argue shortly, it is important to recognise that it is not only feminist theologians who are engaged in this analysis and reconstruction, and to identify allies further afield.[3]   One

---

2   Rosemary Radford Ruether has been a key analyst in this respect, scrutinising the dominant tradition and identifying the needed reconstructions. Much of her work has been committed to uncovering by means of historical critique the dualisms which underlie the Western, Augustinian strand of Christian orthodoxy, and the dualistic anthropologies which emerge from them. See, for example, Ruether, R. R.: *Liberation Theology*, New York, Paulist Press 1972; *New Woman, New Earth*, Minneapolis, Seabury Press, 1975; *Sexism and God-Talk*, London, SCM, 1983; *Women-Church*, San Francisco, Harper & Row, 1985; *Womanguides*, Boston, Beacon Press, 1985, and a host of articles, particularly for this purpose *Dualism and the Nature of Evil in Feminist Theology* in *Studies in Christian Ethics*, 1992, Vol. 5, No. 1. The Irenæan tradition also receives criticism in Ruether's work, though in a less thorough-going manner, both because it has been less influential to Western thought and because the criticism tends to be more specifically focused on the issue of perfection in another time and the implied devaluing of the present.

3   At once, the sensitivity of this claim must be acknowledged since there are feminist theologians who would wish to establish a separatism between women's theology and the perceived male-dominated tradition. However, it is clear to me that women's theology must

such ally is John Macquarrie. There is significant common ground with feminist theologies in Macquarrie's concern that certain traditional formulations of Christian faith have diminished our understanding of what it means to be human and have objectified God into a distant, heteronomous and capricious monarch. For Macquarrie, as for feminist theologies, the theological task is to give an account of God which grounds the divine summons in an affinity between God and human being and the non-human created realm, so that the divine summons is not less than a call to and sustaining of responsible humanity. Within the wider theological arena, this project is located between, on the one hand, various liberal projects of re-conceptualising God into the realm of human constructs in order to safeguard the worth and dignity of being human from divine oppression; and, on the other hand, a conservative tradition of circumscribing human being in order to safeguard the worth and dignity of God from human presumption.[4]

Macquarrie works explicitly in the context of the exhilaration of later twentieth-century humanism, within the arena of liberal theologies, Barthian theologies, and the static, substance metaphysics of traditional natural theologies. He, too, acknowledges that it runs counter to the Judæo-Christian tradition to remove a properly metaphysical dimension from the doctrine of God, and thus from the whole systematic project. He agrees with Barth and Bultmann and the kerygmatic school that God must, as it were, be 'allowed to speak' to the human condition from beyond the human condition. And yet he acknowledges that an account of God *must* be able, at the same time, to give an account of the freedom and transcendence and responsibility of being human (as well as our need for direction, judgement, sustenance).

Macquarrie's theological life starts in earnest in the early 1950's with doctoral research on Bultmann's use of Heidegger, and he describes this

---

engage in critical *dialogue* with the tradition from which it arises, and must allow strands of common cause and insight to emerge from that from which it distinguishes itself. Without such dialogue, feminist theologies remain strictly alternative, and can have no renewing influence on the main streams of tradition.

4 On the relation between Macquarrie's theology and the pastoral effects of monarchical theism, compare Heyward, C. I., *The Redemption of God: A Theology of Mutual Relation*, New York, University Press of America, 1982, pp. xxi f. on radical loneliness as the affective result of the Augustinian-Barthian tradition of the goodness of God versus the sin of humanity.

period up to the early 1960's as "my 'existentialist' phase".[5] He pursues Bultmann; he translates (with Edward Robinson) Heidegger's *Sein und Zeit*.[6] And his work consists of characteristically existentialist concerns: he rejects categories of substance in favour of temporality to identify the nature of human being; he writes of the tension between our possibility and our facticity, of the authentic life to which we are summoned and the inauthentic life into which we fall, and of the irrefutable 'mineness' of my own existence and the call to decision and responsibility for it. And, theologically, following Bultmann rather than Heidegger, it is God who calls us to authenticity, and God who is the ground for hoping that the possibilities to which we are called are not incompatible with the facticity in which we find ourselves thrown. For, if it is not God, then we are left with Sartre's heroic pessimism.

Although for Bultmann existentialist philosophy finds its context in *revealed* theology (the address of God, the summons to an authentic life of faith, the lostness in the world which alienates us from our true selves and from God), for Macquarrie it also has a role in *natural* theology: in re-expressing theology for a non-theologically articulate age, by starting out from our shared humanity. Unlike classical natural theologies which start with an account of the objectifiable natural world, Macquarrie (in sympathy with feminist epistemologies) starts with the lived experience of being human.

From the existentialist analysis of human existence, being-in-the-world, Macquarrie shows how at least a formal expression of the word 'God' appears. Here is the fundamental polarity of human existence: our facticity and our possibility. We are thrown into an existence we can never fully grasp or get the measure of, and yet we are responsible for it, choosing for it in all the decisions we make. And in this precarious balance between finitude and responsibility there is "a radical alienation deep within our existence" which pushes us into imbalance, to immerse ourselves in freedom or in finitude: "we become untrue to the being that we are. We refuse to accept ourself as *at once* free and finite . . . we are estranged from ourself by our refusal to take upon

---

5   Macquarrie's doctoral research was published as *An Existentialist Theology*, London, SCM, 1955. See also Macquarrie, J., *Pilgrimage in Theology* in *Being and Truth*, Kee, A. and Long, E. (eds.), London, SCM, 1986, p. xiv.

6   Heidegger, M., *Being and Time*, translated by Macquarrie, J. and Robinson, E., Oxford, Blackwell, 1962.

ourself an identity which on the other hand we cannot completely discard, an identity which includes both the poles of our freedom and our finitude".[7]

Our alienation from ourself means that there can be no human solution to the problem of human existence, and this gives rise to two possibilities. Either we truly *are* confined to our own resources, in which case the logical outcome is the heroic despair in the face of absurdity (Sartre), or there is a possibility of *grace*, that is "a power from beyond us which can heal our estrangement and enable us to live as the being which we are, the being in whom are conjoined the polarities of finitude and responsibility".[8] Since we have found the source of grace in neither the world of things nor in other persons (though either might be a vehicle of grace) we are directed to a transcendent source, and to the question of God.

Although this is only a formal locating of the word 'God', it already contains a certain amount of content which is fruitful for our theological goals: it is directed to our *possibilities*, to our becoming who we are (it actively encourages self-transcendence); it is *integrative* of our facticity (it actively encourages self-integration in the context of our lived circumstances); it shows that the question of God arises from the constitution of human being not at some weak point but precisely at the point of our search for freedom and growth; and it suggests that grace can come from beyond us without demeaning or alienating us.

Macquarrie's thought can be summarised in the hermeneutical phrase 'the grace of being', which so far has two meanings. First, being human is *grace-full*, because it is in the very constitution of being human that the quest for God arises and is met. Second, God (as Being) is *gracious* to human being as our source, goal and support.

Even in his existentialist phase, Macquarrie has some hesitations about existentialism, notably its tendency to individualism and its inattention to ontology. These concerns largely shape the development of his work subsequently at Union Seminary, New York and at Oxford. During the course of some thirty-five years, his thought develops meticulously, extending his initial starting point in concentric rings, so that at first the grace of being encompasses the individual existent, and then the human community (church and society), and finally the cosmos, as human being becomes *the microcosm*

7   Macquarrie, J., *Studies in Christian Existentialism*, London, SCM, 1965, p. 8.
8   Macquarrie, J., *Studies in Christian Existentialism*, p. 8.

which sums up the life of the universe, and *the mediator* which brings it to a new level of personal being, rather than the personal individual who stands over and against the material realm.[9] By drawing on the fundamentally neo-Platonic tradition of dialectical theism, Macquarrie gives an account of the continuity of being, (material, organic and spiritual) which retains the summons into a fuller and more participative being, and which embraces rather than supersedes previous levels of being. In this mature form, 'the grace of being' elicits a third meaning. Human being is the vehicle of divine grace in the cosmos, the means by which the universe points beyond itself to a personal spiritual source, and the place in the cosmos where this source is disclosed. The resoluteness towards possibility in the context of facticity is no longer concerned only with my own authenticity, but with the perfection of the cosmos.

By retaining the summons to authenticity and responsibility of existentialist thought but relocating it in a framework of natural theology, Macquarrie mediates between the act of grace and the continuity of being. God acts, summons, invites, demands – but always as the source and sustenance and goal of our being, always from and to a radical ontological kinship. God redeems, not redeeming human being *from* the material cosmos, but redeeming the cosmos *through* human being. Human self-transcendence and capacity for God is not a sign of ontological difference between human being and the non-human creation, but of ontological affinity: the cosmos responds to the call into communion by producing from its own resources spiritual, personal being.

From the context of this theological ally, it is possible to raise a weakness that emerges in feminist theologies. Amongst those feminist theologies sharing Macquarrie's concerns with the dehumanising and alienating character of much traditional theological formulation, two particularly significant approaches emerge, each of which is concerned to redress the effects of dualism on the Christian tradition and human experience. Both strands are fundamentally concerned, therefore, with the *connectedness* of human beings with each other, the cosmos, and ultimate ontological reality, and with human being's (particularly women's) *responsible agency*. There is much common

---

9   See especially the trilogy, Macquarrie, J.: *In Search of Humanity*, London, SCM, 1982; *In Search of Deity*, London, SCM, 1984; *Jesus Christ in Modern Thought*, London, SCM, 1990.

ground between these two strands, though each has a different focus. The first has a purely socio-political focus, characterised by solidarity, and can well be considered as a type of liberation theology. The second includes the natural realm as well as the socio-political realm as its focus, and is characterised by a more organic sense of interconnectedness; I shall consider it as a type of process theology, albeit in a modified form. Although work within the two strands is not strictly sequential, the second strand is in some sense a development of the first, concerned to deepen the account of the relation between God and the world from a relation of 'suffering with' to a greater interdependence, and to ground praxis in its ontological framework. The relation between these two strands bears some parallel to Macquarrie's own cumulative movement from an attention to the social character of human being to the interconnectedness of the whole created realm, but is particularly of interest because whereas Macquarrie's own development is an integrating one, in an important respect which I shall return to below, the shift in feminist thought has a retrograde and fragmenting character.

Feminist theology shares with liberation theology a number of underlying assumptions and commitments, arising from its distinguishing characteristic, the theological notion of the 'option for the poor'.[10] Fundamental to liberation theology is the notion of the 'epistemological privilege of the poor'.[11] This means not simply the inclusion of the perspective of the 'poor' into the dominant conception of the human situation, but a radical reversal of perspective. The 'poor' become the true subject, from whose perspective alone a realistic understanding and assessment of 'the word and the world' can be made, since it is the 'poor' who are most accurately the representative of human experience as a whole.[12]

Accompanying the commitment to the epistemological privilege of the poor is the requirement for a renewed consciousness. Drawing on Freire's *Pedagogy of the Oppressed*, liberation theologians emphasise the need for a process of conscientisation which gives insight into the ideology of the prevailing culture and the way in which it operates to structure experience and

---

10 It is not my intention to evaluate liberation theology, but to highlight sufficiently those characteristics which allow feminist theology to be seen in its liberation dimension.

11 See, for example, Sölle, D., *Thinking About God*, London, SCM, 1990, p. 19.

12 This is the double hermeneutic of Jose Miguez Bonino. 'Poor' in this context means not only the materially poor but also those who are in all senses 'other' to the dominant history of human experience.

consciousness. Consciousness so structured will be false 'because value judgements are presented in it as empirical facts, because it maintains that a social phenomenon is really a natural phenomenon, or because it believes that the interest of one particular group is the interest of the whole society'.[13] The insight of the renewed consciousness operates as a powerful liberating force which issues in a critique of large-scale ideology and a demand for social transformation; as such, education is the "practice of freedom".[14]

Amongst feminist theologians, this commitment to transforming agency finds most vibrant expression in Sölle, for example in the notion of 'partisanship for life'. For Sölle, the commitment to praxis and the anticipatory freedom of human nature are intrinsically connected; human beings have the capacity for going beyond what exists, which means a capacity for transformatory righteousness.[15] In her commentary on Romans 6 [12-14] she writes: "We can put our members – i.e. our capacities, our potentialities, our vital energies – at life's disposal. We can make ourselves the weapons of righteousness, the instruments of peace whom God uses. It is not true that . . . we are at the mercy of the forces of circumstance which dominate us. For we are not subject to the laws of the imperialist structure of exploitation; we are subject to grace".[16] This 'partisanship for life' must be recovered from the trivialising effect of the prevailing culture – and this recovery is itself "conversion", conversion to our true possibility.[17] For Sölle, then, one of the "most godless statements" is "we cannot do anything about it".[18] Against the anticipatory freedom of human existence, passivity and helplessness has the quality of sin. Failure to make 'the decision for life' is sin precisely because it is a rejection of the eschatological vision and imperative.

The second strand of feminist theology under consideration is well regarded as a type of process theology, in so far as it is concerned with an organic relation between God and the world, in which God (as well as the

---

13 Chopp, R. S., *The Praxis of Suffering*, New York, Orbis, 1986, p. 42. This emphasis also characterises, for example, Ruether's work discussed above.
14 Freire, P., *Pedagogy of the Oppressed*, Harmondsworth, Penguin, 1972, p. 69. This is contrasted to the 'banking' model of education, by which deposits are made into the student mind, p. 45 ff.
15 Sölle, D., *Choosing Life*, London, SCM, 1981, p. 68.
16 Sölle, D., *Choosing Life*, p. 28.
17 Sölle, D., *Theology for Sceptics*, London, Mowbray, 1995, p. 113.
18 Sölle, D., *Thinking about God*, p. 58.

world) is conceived of as Becoming, that is, as changing as a result of the relationship. The insights of feminist liberation theology, and particularly the commitment to justice, are carried into this strand, but there is concern to strengthen the expression of the relation of God to the world and to ground connection more fundamentally in the nature of existence, not simply as necessary to justice. In this respect it attempts to address the effects of matter/spirit and temporal/spiritual dualisms with regard to the divine/world relation and the human/nature relation; the subject/object dualism is subsumed in radical immanence and, I shall suggest, the understanding of immanence shifts subtly so that liberating agency gives way to passive persuasive inter-dependence.[19]

Within the context of the rejection of dualism, process theology represents a shift of concern away from a static understanding of *being* and issues of essence/substance to a dynamic notion of *becoming* and the idea of God's participation in the temporal process. 'To be actual is to be in process' is a key motif, applied to God as well as to the empirical world. Reality is not a static entity but a process: 'actual entities' are 'occasions of experience' rather than 'objects', and are characterised by the activity of becoming. This means that reality is both fully temporal and also social: there are no absolutely independent individuals, but the universe (human and non-human) is a social process of becoming. Process theology is highly immanental, to the extent that God and the world are seen to be interdependent. God has a dual relation to the world. In an abstract, primordial aspect God presents to the world the total range of possibility in each moment of becoming, and is thus both the foundation of novelty in the process and the lure, the invitation, to becoming. God is "the lure for feeling, the eternal urge of desire".[20] In a concrete, consequent aspect God is the location, or the 'conscious receptivity' of all that has already been actualised in the world; which is to say that the concrete unity of the world is found in God's receptivity. God's means of action in the world is persuasive, rather than coercive, showing possibility and inviting voluntary co-operation and reciprocity, and is thus not perceived as omniscient

---

19 It is important to reiterate that I am not charting a *chronological* development here, but a *conceptual* one, in which the concern for relationality overcomes the drive to agency. In some respects this is a positive development, because it involves a much less stark dualism between oppressed and oppressor; but what interests me here is the pursuit of an inherent weakness.
20 Whitehead, A. N., *Process and Reality*, New York, Free Press, 1969, p. 406.

or omnipotent in the traditional sense. Omnipotence is sacrificed to goodness, including respect for the integrity of the creatures, and God's nature is completed in the world.

Mary Grey draws explicitly on process theology, exploring 'atonement in feminist process thought' in *Redeeming the Dream*.[21] Grey's intention is to uncover what interpretation of redemption has allowed the degradation of women, and to reclaim redemption from its "traditional meaning of the historical action of a patriarchal God through his suffering Son, who 'atoned' for human evil in a once-for-all humiliating death, to be copied throughout the unwinding of history by the endurance of suffering and injustice by all who followed him".[22] She argues that women have so absorbed the rightfulness of their being punished for their responsibility for sin that they have "assumed that their rightful place was just there, on the cross with Jesus!", and that their own suffering is somehow 'needed' for the continuing redemption of the world.[23]

Working inductively from women's experience of connectedness, Grey argues that the world is relational at its core, that "affiliation and mutuality" rather than hierarchical and adversarial individualism are the "raw material of the world".[24] Alongside the hidden strand of women's testimony she draws on systems theory and process thought to establish relation as the primary category of all existence. In this way she not only affirms the interrelatedness and interconnectedness of all things as a balance between integration and self-assertion, but also highlights the notion of process which makes relating dynamic and redemptive.[25] Grey's reformulation of redemption thus becomes 'dynamic mutuality-in-relating', not only between persons but in the whole of creation and as the very being of God: "If relationality is a basic category of existence, then it is also the basic dynamism of the divine nature, since all

21 Grey, M., *Redeeming the Dream*, London, SPCK, 1989, p. 169.
22 Grey, M., *Redeeming the Dream*, p. 153. Grey does acknowledge other models of redemption, but considers this to be the most influential and detrimental to women, and the most reviled by feminists. Note the significant shift from the political to the natural, and the criticism of a model dependent upon 'action in history'. This will re-appear in McFague's work below.
23 Grey, M., *Redeeming the Dream*, pp. 13; 119.
24 Grey, M., *Redeeming the Dream*, p. 31.
25 Grey, M., *Redeeming the Dream*, p. 32.

creation participates in the being of God".[26] This basic category is pressed further as the 'metaphysic of connection' in *The Wisdom of Fools?*, a 'connection theology' highly critical of the 'structured separateness' of dominant Western culture. Against the 'Logos myth' of dominant culture, Grey offers the "Sophia myth" of "connectedness, which conveys a sense of rootedness in the earth, with its changing seasons and rhythms, and a sense of interdependence, which sees human beings as vulnerable parts of a wider interlocking whole".[27]

Where Grey begins a move to a more inclusive, less anthropocentric stance, Sallie McFague in *The Body of God* makes a bold attempt at a thoroughly 'biocentric and cosmocentric' perspective.[28]   McFague acknowledges that Christianity is 'par excellence' a religion of incarnation, but suggests that the classical organic model expressed as the Body of Christ is highly problematic. Rather than encouraging a belief in divine immanence in the entire natural order, the model was early on spiritualised into a dualism of cosmos animated by Logos, and so separates head (rational controlling part) from body (physical, to-be-controlled part).   Further, the model is anthropocentric and androcentric whilst implying universalism, thus privileging sameness and conformity derived from the head and according to an idealised male body.   In so far as unitary wholeness is valued over autonomy and distinctiveness of parts, McFague suggests that in practice the 'Body of Christ' functions as a political model rather than as the natural model it purports to be.[29]

As a basis for a new organic model of embodiment, McFague draws on the "common creation story" to affirm unity (grounded in common history) and

---

26 Grey, M., *Redeeming the Dream*, pp. 126; 86. Grey acknowledges that this is 'perichoresis' in classical expression, though does not go on to ground her account in a Trinitarian model of God.

27 Grey, M., *Wisdom of Fools?*, London, SPCK, 1993, p. 6.

28 McFague, S., *The Body of God*, London, SCM, 1993, p. 48.

29 McFague, S., *The Body of God*, p. 37. Again, note the criticism of the political as against the natural. This negative assessment of the political and preference for the 'natural' underlies my argument that a shift from agency to passivity is occurring. The category of the 'natural' has been highly controversial in the feminist movement as a whole, due to the question of determinism. On the political nature of the body of Christ, see Mitchell, M., *Paul and the Rhetoric of Reconciliation*, Tübingen, Mohr, 1991: pp. 68 ff.; pp. 157 ff.; Martin, D. B., *The Corinthian Body*, New Haven, Yale University Press, 1995: pp. 3 ff; pp. 87 ff.

differentiation (as the process of evolution produces ever-increasing diversity), and to privilege embodiment: "The common creation story is the story of the physical universe, the story of embodiment, or, more precisely, the story of everything that exists on the matter/energy continuum".[30] In this model, the incarnation is not limited to Jesus of Nazareth, but applies to all bodies, so that in fact the cumulative world is God's body: "in the universe as a whole as well as in each and every bit and fragment of it, God's transcendence is embodied".[31] Contrary to traditional uses of the body metaphor in regard to God, McFague does not suggest that God relates to the world as the mind relates to the body, but as the spirit relates to the body – as "source, empowerment, vitality".[32] Not only does this undercut anthropocentrism (only a human being has a mind; spirit has a broader range), but it sheds a different light on the 'purpose' of creation, which is better expressed as empowerment – "fecundity, richness and diversity" rather than evolutionary direction towards a single prime species.[33] In this way, humans are radically decentred, but they are re-centred as the conscious aspect of the body, "as responsible adults, the only species on the planet that knows the common creation story and can assume (its) role as partners for its well-being".[34] The human task is to "stay in our place, to accept our proper limits so that other individuals of our species as well as other species can also have much needed space".[35]

30 McFague, S., *The Body of God*, p. 47. The matter/energy continuum denotes a point of contact with process thought here.
31 McFague, S., *The Body of God*, p. 133. Compare Macquarrie's understanding of the sacramental universe which culminates in Macquarrie, J., *Christ: A Guide to the Sacraments*, London, SCM, 1997.
32 McFague, S., *The Body of God*, p. 144 f. "Not only does this form of the analogy involve difficult, even dualistic, arguments concerning the mind/body correlation, but, just as important for our considerations, it implies that divine activity in relation to the world is primarily intellectual and controlling: God is Mind or Will."
33 McFague, S., *The Body of God*, p. 148.
34 McFague, S., *The Body of God*, p. 109. Again, the distinction between rational control and conscious influence is reminiscent of process theology.
35 McFague, S., *The Body of God*, p. 113. I have no argument with this as an ecological necessity; it is whether it constitutes a theological anthropology which addresses the feminist (and other) critique of the disempowering effect of monarchical theism which is at issue. It is revealing to contrast this ambivalence about space with Bonhoeffer's emphasis on the importance of taking up space in the public realm in order to be for others; see, for example, Bonhoeffer, D., *Ethics*, London, SCM, 1955, pp. 174 f. It would, however, detract from the main argument to undertake a critique of feminist process theology here.

This last sentence is revealing, and draws attention to a subtle but significant shift between these two strands of feminist thought. A liberation approach which endorses agency and the exercise of will is succeeded by a process approach which encourages passivity, dependency, rootedness in nature and 'staying in one's place'. Fundamental to this shift is a difference in the meaning of immanence between the two strands. In feminist liberation thought, the immanence of God is highly agential, working in history for the redemption of the poor, and this logically preserves the notion of the other, and of action as willed on the basis of a specific commitment to the other. But in feminist process thought, divine immanence is less agential, more receptive, persuasive. Otherness in terms of differentiation is asserted but not logically grounded, and the active will is put aside, ostensibly to give space to the integrity of creation's own process of becoming.

This has an important implication: the model of God, although not heteronomous, still tends to affirm women in exactly that covert exercise of manipulative power and the passive receptivity which feminist analysis has sought to expose. The primordial aspect of God models persuasive appetite, the covert urge by which the world is manipulated into a desired structure. The consequent aspect models extreme conditionality: the shaping of the self by the reaction of the world.[36] This is a classic double-bind for women: agency is sublimated into an evaluative sensibility which effects indirect influence, and avoids abstract, critical engagement. And yet the subject of this sensibility still receives her self from the complicated reactions in the public realm to her covert manipulations. Jean Porter draws attention to this in her article *The Feminization of God: Second Thoughts on the Ethical Implications of Process Theology*, in which she critiques Hartshorne's work with Ann Douglas's analysis of nineteenth century "virtuous woman".[37] Porter argues the 'uncanny resemblance' between Hartshorne's God and a nineteenth-century northern States ideal of a virtuous woman. Of significance to Porter's argument is the recognition that this was not a *neutral* ideal, but one which was manipulatively engineered "on the part of the increasingly powerless to consolidate power", and which continues to linger as a strategy.[38] Douglas's

36 Compare Whitehead, A. N., *Process and Reality*, p. 37.
37 Porter, J., *The Feminization of God: Second Thoughts on the Ethical Implications of Process Theology* in *St Luke's Journal of Theology*, 1986, Vol. 24.
38 Porter, J., *The Feminization of God*, p. 253.

analysis, on which Porter draws, traces the shift of women's fortunes with the industrialisation of North America's economy: "middle-class women carved out a social niche for themselves as the guardians of those qualities that society would like to preserve, even though they could find no place in its public life".[39]   Thus, Douglas notes, "they turned of necessity from the exercise of power to the exertion of 'influence'", principally by means of "emotional indispensability".[40]

Two concerns can readily be identified. On the one hand, this is an account of theism which "does not do justice to one of the central convictions of the Judæo-Christian tradition, namely, that God is not only an agent, but is indeed the supreme actor on the historical scene".[41] On the other hand, it is not an adequate ideal upon which to be human (for men as well as for women).[42] Not only does it prevent passivity from being identified as a possible form of sin, but it explicitly models covert manipulation as a 'good' form of action.

It is here that Macquarrie's thought will prove resourceful for further dialogue, because his theological project allows for both the agential aspect of liberation theology and the organic connectedness of process theology. His use of existentialist categories allows a strong account of committed personal agency, whilst overcoming the isolated Cartesian model of agent. The human/nature dualism of existentialism is corrected by his use of neo-Platonic categories of continuity within the cosmos. The question of God is thus raised

---

39 Porter, J., *The Feminization of God*, p. 253. As illustration that this was a strategic move, Douglas cites the stealthy advice offered in an 1828 edition of *Ladies Magazine*: "Authority over the men must . . . never be usurped; but still, women may, if they will, exert their talents, and [by] the opportunities nature has furnished, obtain an influence in society that will be paramount to authority". Douglas, A., *The Feminization of American Culture*, New York, Avon Books, 1977, p. 86. She refers to this as "the lure of total control found only in illicit authority", p. 88.

40 Douglas, A., *The Feminization of American Culture*, p. 90. Interestingly, as well as women she includes in her analysis of this aspect of American culture Christian ministers.

41 Porter, J., *The Feminization of God*, p. 256. Significantly, Porter concludes that classical theism with 'its concept of God as *actus purus* seems to me to contain at least a promising hint of a solution', p. 257. Her book *Moral Action and Christian Ethics*, Cambridge, CUP, 1995, provides a positive analysis of Aquinas' thought for contemporary ethical engagement.

42 Both Kierkegaard and, following him, Reinhold Niebuhr, attend to passivity as sin; compare Kierkegaard, S., *The Sickness Unto Death*, London, OUP, 1941, and Niebuhr, R., *Nature and Destiny of Man*, Vol. 1, London, Nisbet, 1941.

by the lure, even the demand, of our own self-transcendence, but significantly within the socio-political and cosmic matrix. God is, therefore, from the first, conceived of as dynamic, as the safeguarder of freedom and possibility; but that dynamism is framed not as the willed exchange between the individual believer and the divine monarch, but as the active summons to human being into fuller and more participative being within and for the cosmos. We are immersed in the grace of being; but the grace of being demands our responsible and resolute agency to bring ourselves and the cosmos into full possibility.

Chapter Twelve

The Power of Christian Innocence: Revisiting a Classical Theme

Anne Murphy

The power of Christian innocence and its redemptive promise has received renewed attention in recent theological writing. *The Heroic Face of Innocence: Three Stories by Georges Bernanos* has been reprinted as a volume in *Ressourcement*, a series aiming to make accessible some neglected classic texts in Catholic thought.[1] The 'heroines of innocence' treated by Bernanos are Joan of Arc, Thérèse of Lisieux, and the Carmelites of Compiègne, guillotined on 17 July 1794 during the French Revolution. Bernanos' central conviction is that the world is not saved by reliance on technology, political effort, or theological acumen, but by the heroism of the innocent. Bernanos is regarded by Hans Urs von Balthasar as the lay Catholic writer who has grasped most profoundly the heart of the Christian tradition especially in his treatment of redemption through sacrificial love.[2] It so happens that 1999 was the centenary of the birth of Francis Poulenc and a recent production of his opera *Les Carmélites* has been playing to packed audiences. The central theme of this opera (adapted from Bernanos) is the act of sacrificial 'substitution' in which the Prioress dies in terrible fear, having offered her life to enable a young sister to die in peace and serenity.

The novelist (Bernanos) and the composer (Poulenc) are entitled to take creative liberty with historical fact, though it needs to be recognised that both worked within the particular tensions of French Catholicism in the first half of the twentieth century. My interest lies in the 'downside' of an uncritical retrieval of this myth of redemptive, childlike, often suffering innocence, most

---

1   Bernanos, G., *The Heroic Face of Innocence: Three Stories by Georges Bernanos*, Edinburgh, T&T Clark, 1999.
2   von Balthasar, H. U., *Bernanos: An Ecclesial Existence*, translated by Erasmo Leiva-Merikakis, San Francisco, Ignatius Press, 1996.

usually projected onto young women. It appears yet again in John Saward's *The Way of the Lamb: The Spirit of Childhood and the End of the Age*, in which the 'mystery of childhood' is contrasted with the self-conscious striving for maturity in much of contemporary spirituality.[3] John Saward's book becomes a celebration of the gospel of spiritual childhood in contrast to what he claims is its rejection by Christian men and women 'come of age'. For him Jesus' unequivocal statement "Unless you become as little children, you will never enter the kingdom of heaven" is a truth by which the Church stands or falls.[4]

Few would deny that the grace of 'spiritual childhood' is a gospel value, drawing on the image of a child's capacity for intimacy, innocence and uncalculating love. Others would be quick to point out that in the real world natural childhood can be self-centred, manipulative, prone to tantrums; the child needs to be formed in patterns of responsibility for others as a basis for future maturity. However, many contemporary theologians are aware of that other saying of Jesus which immediately follows in Matthew's gospel: "But whoever scandalises one of these little ones who believe in me, it would be better for him to have a great millstone around his neck and to be drowned in the depth of the sea".[5] We have been made painfully aware of the part Christians have played in the adult betrayal and abuse of innocent children, of child-prostitution in our cities, child-soldiers in so many wars, and child-victims of AIDS and drugs.

Furthermore we are aware that an uncritical appeal to childlike docility and obedience can inhibit maturity, and has been particularly damaging to women in the long history of the Christian tradition.[6] I would like to explore the reasons why a retrieval of the redemptive power of the 'heroic innocence' of selected women is simply not credible unless accompanied by a 'health warning' and an awareness of the sustained questioning this and related themes have received from postmodern and feminist critics. Conversely, there is a need to challenge feminist orthodoxy by exploring the possibility of a

---

3   Saward, J., *The Way of the Lamb: The Spirit of Childhood and the end of the Age*, Edinburgh, T&T Clark, 1999.
4   Matthew 18 [3].
5   Matthew 18 [5].
6   See Sölle, D., *Paternalistic Religion* in Schüssler Fiorenza E. (ed.), *The Power of Naming*, New York, Orbis, 1996.

return to a 'second naïvety' by Christian feminists and how they might re-appropriate the (deconstructed) theme of spiritual childhood.

The context: French Catholicism

Bernanos' choice of Joan of Arc, Thérèse of Lisieux, and the Carmelite sisters of Compiègne as 'embodiments of Christian innocence' was not random or accidental, but rooted in the socio-political and ecclesiastical context of Post-Revolutionary France. In the early part of the nineteenth century the cult of the 'young saints of the Catacombs' became very popular in France especially among those with ultramontane sympathies. A new cult of St Philomena developed following the discovery of the body of a young girl in the Roman catacombs in 1802 whose real historical identity was unknown, but who gradually 'acquired' that of a young virgin, killed because she had resisted the sexual advances of the Emperor Diocletian.

The rapid spread of devotion to Philomena in France from 1835 onwards has to be understood "in the context of France's revolutionary past, the growing importance of the female religious vocation in the nineteenth century, and a widespread preoccupation with sexual violence in nineteenth century French society".[7] The narratives of Philomena's martyrdom, involving sexual danger and violence, were similar to the narratives of martyred female revolutionary and royalist 'saints' on both sides of the Revolutionary struggle. This included the story of the heroic deaths of the sixteen Carmelite nuns executed during the last days of the reign of terror (1794) which had a profound effect on Carmelite female spirituality. Devotion to Philomena and other heroic young martyrs was part of Catholicism's search for new forms of legitimacy as it struggled to heal the wounds inflicted on it in the aftermath of the Revolution. New shrines containing the relics of the martyrs of the early Church replaced those destroyed and desecrated during the Revolution. Female martyrdom, and the many meanings with which the broken and violated body of the female victim can be invested, has been very well

---

7   Ford, C., *Female Martyrdom and the Politics of Sainthood in Nineteenth Century France: the Cult of Sainte Philomène* in Tallett F. and Atkin N. (eds.), *Catholicism in Britain and France since 1789*, London, Hambledon Press, 1996, p. 117. I am much indebted to this article.

researched, and continues to raise many serious questions. Female martyrdom as a powerful symbol of chastity and purity under threat has a dark underside. What concerns us here is that nineteenth century French Catholics saw the female martyr "not as a powerless victim but as a resolute defender of her body and her faith".[8] As so often, the human body of one individual became a collective metaphor for the nation as a whole. Philomena's alleged resistance to the Emperor Diocletian in the early Church became an image of French Catholic resistance to the continuing threats of a secular and godless state. France had been violated by revolution and war. But the example of the heroic resistance of the innocent could engender hope, restore lost integrity and embolden those who continued the struggle.

From about 1850 onwards, the cult of Philomena and other young martyrs of the catacombs declined in the face of new archaeological evidence which provided proof that not all the bodies found in the catacombs could be identified as Christian. In 1881 Pope Leo XIII closed the catacombs and forbade further exhumations. The cult of the young martyrs "became a source of embarrassment rather than legitimacy".[9] By the early twentieth century Philomena had been displaced by two other young virginal saints: Joan of Arc (d. 1431, beatified 1909, canonised 1920) and Thérèse of Lisieux (d. 1897, beatified 1923, canonised 1925). Each represented young innocence, heroism and intense spirituality. Joan appealed most to those who linked the cause of throne and altar, espoused right-wing politics, and felt most humiliated by the loss of the Provinces of Alsace and Lorraine. She became the embodiment of French resistance to the enemy.

Thérèse captured the Catholic imagination of a whole era precisely because she both embodied and transcended the particular religious culture of her time and class, marked by the politics of ultramontanism and the piety of Jansenism. It is no accident that her favourite saint and role model was Joan of Arc, and that she wrote a play in her honour for convent recreation (1894). Thérèse desired martyrdom on a grand scale, but circumstances led her to accept the 'little martyrdom' of daily life including spiritual desolation and her terminal illness. Thérèse's autobiography appealed directly to young soldiers of the First World War, wounded in mind and body, lying powerless in

8   Ford, C., *Female Martyrdom*, p. 125.
9   Ford, C., *Female Martyrdom*, p. 126.

hospital wards. Her 'little way' spoke directly to their condition and helped them to make sense of their shattered lives.

Joan of Arc and Thérèse of Lisieux came to displace devotion to Philomena, and the cult of 'heroic innocence' was transferred and reshaped to fit their personal narratives in a new cultural context. This has both positive and negative connotations. The key point is: can their narratives survive the changes of the second half of the twentieth century and the questions posed by postmodernity? Or are they too deeply embedded in the master-narrative of the dominant culture which first constructed their heroism and power as role models? Is it possible, or even desirable, to de-construct and then re-construct the theme of 'heroic innocence' and/or spiritual childhood?

Loss of innocence

We live in a culture in which our perceptions of childhood and innocence have undergone recent and rapid change. The cruel murder of toddler James Bulger in Liverpool by two ten-year-old boys in 1993 shattered our belief in a child's innate goodness. The findings of the Waterhouse Report have revealed the persistence of adult abuse of children in care to a degree and extent which almost defies belief.[10] In fact the unwillingness of many to believe such things could happen, allowed it to continue undetected. A recent article suggests that we are "caught between two ways of knowing childhood. Our cultural ideal is cute and sentimental – all those pictures on cards and posters and biscuit tins, of little creatures with ringlets and dimples . . . And at the same time, our gaze is fearful and predatory and under it children have become erotically suggestive creatures".[11] The author goes on to say how "childish innocence often suggests its opposite: violation". So the well-known Miss Pears advertisement for soap had to be withdrawn when it was realised that it was no longer possible to present a cuddly girl with dreamy eyes and glowing skin, just like that. Yet the dust-covers of some recent books on Thérèse of Lisieux carry the photo of her as a golden-haired child of eight, rather than the more

10 *The Waterhouse Report*, London, HMSO, 2000.
11 Gerrard, N., *The Observer Review*, 14 November 1999, *Innocence on the Line*, p. 1.

usual one of her as an adult Carmelite nun.[12] This may be just sentimentality, but is also naïve and possibly dangerous. It certainly trivialises Thérèse's mature choice of her 'little way of spiritual childhood' by directing our attention to the so-called winsomeness of her natural childhood.

Our views on the passage from childhood to adult maturity have been shaped by our perceptions of the Myth of our first parents and the loss of Paradise in Genesis Chapter 3. In Jewish traditions the original adult 'sin' was the deliberate murder of Abel by Cain.[13] Then the evil of fratricide first entered the human race. The disobedience of Adam and Eve in Genesis 3 was sometimes interpreted as that of children who exceeded the boundaries laid down by a caring parent and suffered the consequences. Irenæus, drawing on Jewish sources, also saw Adam and Eve as immature children rather than as rebellious, disobedient adults.[14] God treated them mercifully, softening their exile with the promise of a saviour. Irenæus also saw human redemption in terms of *recapitulation*, or the summing up of all stages of human growth and development (including childhood) in the person of Jesus Christ. The choice of Adam and Eve thwarted, but did not destroy, God's plan for creation, and could only be reversed by one who lived through all the stages of human growth, renegotiating humankind's journey to maturity. In this sense Jesus was the Second Adam. Seeing the loss of Paradise as the result of an immature choice of an inexperienced young couple has received less attention in Western Christianity than the Pauline retrieval of the Adamic myth of rebellion and disobedience requiring a more drastic atonement.[15]

Some uncommon perceptions of Genesis allow us to see that the myth of Adam and Eve was a way of explaining the human condition *here and now*.[16] The reality of life in a primitive society was harsh: tilling the soil to produce

12 For example, Nelson, J., *Living the Little Way of Love with St Thérèse of Lisieux*, London, New City Press, 1999.

13 Genesis 4 [8-15].

14 For example: "God made man Lord of the earth . . . but he was small, being but a child. He had to grow and reach full maturity." Irenæus, *Apostolic Preaching xii*, in Bettenson, H. (ed.), *The Early Christian Fathers*, Oxford, OUP, 1969, p. 68.

15 Romans 5 [6-21].

16 See Primavesi, A., *From Apocalypse to Genesis; Ecology, Feminism and Christianity*, Guildford, Burns & Oates,1991, esp. chapter six. See also Bechtel, L. M., *Rethinking the Interpretation of Genesis 2.4b–3.24*, in Brenner, A. (ed.), *A Feminist Companion to Genesis*, Sheffield, Sheffield Academic Press, 1993, p. 107.

enough food to survive or facing the dangers of childbirth were the burdens of adulthood. In paradise Adam and Eve were shielded from such realities and so innocent – they did not know. The passage from childhood to innocence is about acquiring experiential knowledge; this is often, though not necessarily, related to the passage from moral innocence to personal sin. Popular language often equates loss of virginity or sexual innocence with the passage into adulthood. More generally it is understood as the loss of the 'sacred canopy' or protective shield which nurture requires before the child is ready to accept adult status and responsibility. At the head of the human race our child-parents made a harsh transition from Paradise to the real world and we have inherited both the necessity and the dangers inherent in making such a transition.

The rite of passage to adulthood

Those who advocate a return to spiritual childhood recognise (in theory) the inevitability of growing up and leaving natural childhood behind. Neither nostalgia for lost childhood, nor a childish refusal to grow up – the Peter Pan syndrome – are part of the Christian vocation. Thérèse of Lisieux remembered vividly the seemingly insignificant moment when she grew up:

> It was on December the twenty-fifth, 1886, that I was given the grace to leave behind my childhood days. We had just come back from midnight Mass. On such occasions there was a treat in store for me . . . I would go off to find my Christmas slipper in the chimney corner . . . [This night] Papa was tired after the Midnight Mass and the sight of my slippers in the chimney corner annoyed him. Imagine my distress when I overheard him saying: 'Well thank goodness it's the last year this is going to happen.'

Thérèse was about to burst into tears. Instead she pulled herself together, went downstairs and acted out the ritual as if she had heard nothing.[17]

Dorothée Sölle's rite of passage was more abrupt and harsh. During the Nazi persecution of the Jews, Dorothée's parents offered temporary refuge to

---

17 *Autobiography of a Saint: Thérèse of Lisieux*, London, Harvill Press, 1958, p. 127.

the Jewish mother of a friend. She lived in the guest room on the top floor of their home, and Dorothée often visited her:

> One day I expressed my concern about what might happen to her. "Don't think about it", she said, "they won't get me". She reached for her ever-ready purse, opened it, took out something and placed it in my hand. It was a small vial; how cold it felt to me! "They won't get me", she said. "Do you understand?" It was poison, and today I can still feel how cold the glass was on my palm. On that day I stopped being a child.[18]

The way in which a child first becomes aware of real evil, and the existence of a harsh and predatory world, can be crucial for life, but also for some understanding of the world's need of redemption and our "sharing in the sufferings of Jesus Christ".[19] Von Balthasar, normally an admirer of Thérèse, doubted that her life experience had given her an understanding of the sheer depth of sin and evil.[20] If the shattering of belief in the goodness of life is accompanied by physical and emotional assault, most usually by those who were trusted, the damage can be permanent. The abused can in turn become the abuser, perpetuating the cycle. This betrayal of innocence is what Jesus meant by being a scandal or stumbling block to the coming of the kingdom of God. On the other hand over-protectiveness or encouraging false dependence can also inhibit growth towards maturity. That is why the Church (as Mother) needs appropriate language to encourage the development of mature Christians: reiterating the metaphor of spiritual childhood or the virtues of docility and obedience may be harmful and counter-productive.

Youth, innocence and victimhood

Attaching special significance to young, virginal, heroic innocence is problematic for many other reasons. Both Joan of Arc and Thérèse were

18 Sölle, D., *Against the Wind: Memoir of a Radical Christian*, translated by Rumscheidt, B. and Rumscheidt, M., Minneapolis, Fortress Press, 1999, p. 2.
19 II Corinthians 2 [1-5].
20 See von Balthasar, *St. Thérèse of Lisieux: The Story of a Mission*, transl. Nicholl, D., London, Sheed & Ward, 1953, p. 271. Cited in Ford, D., *Self and Salvation: Being Transformed*, Cambridge, CUP, 1999, p. 238. Ford's short study of Thérèse in chapter 9 is very helpful.

young adults: they had made the transition from childhood but died comparatively young – Joan aged nineteen, Thérèse aged twenty-four. Would their narratives have been less significant if they had lived longer? It is hard to imagine Joan returning to her native village and 'normal life'. The future of Thérèse and her Carmelite sisters is more predictable:

> Thérèse would have lived her own text into old age. Entering the complex politics of community life and responsibility . . . and moving beyond the ardours of youth, she would of necessity have matured her life text. The stark, passionate, uncompromising holiness of the young might have been displaced by the complex, often misunderstood, battle-scarred holiness of age, harder to canonise but no less inspiring.[21]

Thérèse has been declared both a saint and a doctor of the Church, while John Henry Newman's cause may take very much longer: "One can only hope that those who proclaim her a doctor of the Church do not trivialise the intellectual life and scholarship of contemporary women theologians in the mistaken idea that Thérèse would not have continued to grow up, or that young adulthood is a sufficient role model".[22]

Underlying the choice of young, innocent women there is the preference for those who are the victims of undeserved suffering, deemed to be particularly redemptive. Two of the most significant strands which make up the Christian understanding of atonement articulate the belief that only an innocent victim can satisfy the justice of God for the enormity of the sins of the world (satisfaction theory) or can fully confront human beings with the depth of the evil into which they have fallen (moral influence theory). Only the sinless offering of Jesus Christ can fulfill both demands, but it has been extended to include those who form his body, the Church, and participate in his sufferings. The rich doctrine of the communion of saints – our responsibility for one another with and in Christ – has sometimes slipped into the harsh form of the doctrine of penal substitution. Here not only is the innocent Jesus seen to have borne God's wrath and punishment to atone for the sins of the world, but those close to him also make the 'heroic offering' of their lives as victims of justice: "Most perniciously it is the victimisation of

---

21 Fitzgerald, C., *The Mission of Thérèse of Lisieux* in *The Way (Supplement) 1997/98*, p. 88.
22 Fitzgerald, C., *The Mission of Thérèse of Lisieux*, p. 94.

women that is tied to a psychology of salvation".[23]   Women who do not deserve to suffer can become icons of holiness and salvation to others, or see themselves as Christ figures called to be victims with him. Little attention is given to the root causes of their suffering, or to the fact that much suffering should be eradicated rather than endured.

Many feminist theologians have come to believe that classical Christian theories of atonement and their influence on spirituality and practice have been damaging, especially for women.

"Because God suffers and God is good, we are good if we suffer. If we are not suffering we are not good. To be like God is to take on the suffering of all."[24] Women have come to internalise the qualities of being a victim/martyr. These include self-sacrificial love to the point of denying their own needs, passivity in the face of suffering, and a conviction that suffering is willed by God and *per se* redemptive. At its most radical, feminist theology rejects the Christian idea of atonement.

> Christianity is an abusive theology that glorifies suffering. Is it any wonder that there is so much abuse in modern society when the pre-dominant image or theology of that culture is of 'divine child abuse' – God the Father demanding and carrying out the suffering and death of his own son? . . .We must do away with the atonement, this idea of a blood sin upon the whole human race which can be washed away only by the blood of the (innocent) lamb.[25]

The doctrine of atonement will not be 'redeemed' for our contemporaries except by those who critically engage with the kind of argument outlined above. An uncritical re-articulation of the classical theme of the 'salvific power of innocent victims' re-enforces, rather than answers, such radical objections and ceases to be credible.

It is interesting to note that Thérèse, who certainly uses the language and rhetoric of being a victim of divine love, never casts herself as the victim of divine justice – despite its prevalence in contemporary French spirituality,

23 Helmut Thielicke, cited in Carlson Brown, J. and Parker, R., *For God so Loved the World* in Carlson Brown, J. and Bohn, C. R. (eds.), *Christianity, Patriarchy and Abuse: A Feminist Critique*, New York, The Pilgrim Press, 1989, p. 12.
24 Carlson Brown, J. and Parker, R. *For God so Loved the World*, p. 19.
25 Carlson Brown, J. and Parker, R. *For God so Loved the World*, p. 26.

deeply influenced by Jansenism.[26] However, she does use 'victimhood' as a way of expressing her rhetoric of love and generous self-giving. In our time the spirituality of 'interior victimhood' has been directed outwards to the victims of injustice in contemporary society. A recent study has linked Thérèse with Jean Vanier, founder of L'Arche and its work for the disabled. In the late nineteenth century, the Martin family in France and the Vanier family in Canada shared a spiritual guide and friend. But the 'little way of spiritual childhood', which he advocated, underwent a significant change as it was adapted by his protégées to meet the wants of a new age.

> St. Thérèse regarded her weakness as the springboard from which to offer herself as a victim to divine love. Jean Vanier's Christian vision . . . extends the meaning of love into the places where the weakness abides. What he has discovered is that if we open ourselves to receive from those who are weakest in our midst, they will transform us. And further, if we enter into the weakest and most broken parts of ourselves, we will find life.[27]

In its rejection of 'victimhood' because of its harmful associations, feminist theology may lose sight of the Christian paradox of weakness that can be a source of strength, and death which can be a source of life.[28] To reject classical theories of atonement, always provisional and shaped to suit a particular context, is to run the risk of rejecting what is essential to Christian belief. Understandably feminism is concerned with the 'empowerment' of women, especially the poor and marginalised victims of society. They need to be liberated from 'victimhood' and be enabled to stand up for their rights. As a form of Liberation theology, Feminist/Womanist theologies seek to be life-affirming and to reject what is oppressive. They are the antithesis of theologies and forms of spirituality which seem to canonise suffering, weakness, and passive child-like dependence. Feminist theology might be said to be semi-Pelagian in articulating a belief in the achievement of human maturity by one's own efforts. But it needs time and space to fully appropriate

---

26 See Matthew, I., *Thérèse of Lisieux: A Way for Today* in *The Way (Supplement) 1997/98*, p. 18.
27 Coady, M. F., *The Hidden Way: the Life and Influence of Almire Pichon*, London, Darton Longman & Todd, 1998, p. 122.
28 I Corinthians 12 [1].

a *via affirmativa* because of a long experience of the oppressive weight of a *via negativa*.

However, a Feminist/Womanist theology 'come of age' might look again on its accepted 'orthodoxies'. Traditional forms of self-denial can be damaging and need deconstructing. But self-giving as love must be at the core of human life and Christian salvation. The evil cycle of oppression and dependence and hurt can be broken "when someone chooses not to pass on the hurt but to 'absorb it'; not passively but in the most strenuous spiritual action possible".[29] Where there is a sense of true self-worth and respect, it is possible to understand again that before God we are creatures, completely dependent on grace, and that vis à vis other human beings we exist in a state of inter-dependence, relying on them and on ecological systems for our very survival. In time we might even be able to explore again the (deconstructed) metaphor of child-like (not childish) innocence.[30]

Conclusion

Heroic models are constructs – to a greater or lesser extent. The cult of Philomena became discredited because of lack of historical foundation. Joan was tried for heresy and witchcraft and sentenced to be burned at the stake by the Inquisition and the University of Paris – both of them Church authorities. It took four hundred years for the Church officially to recognise her as a saint, largely as a result of her retrieval as a patriotic icon of nineteenth century France. In the twentieth century the Maid of Orleans has been adopted as a champion of the left, the right and the feminist movement. Was the real Joan a heretic, a saint, a revolutionary, or a deranged fanatic?[31] The Carmelite sisters of Compiègne suffered the fate of many other aristocratic women; though personally innocent, they belonged to a hated *ancien régime*, for which the Church has to take much responsibility. Thérèse owed her initial popularity to the publication of an edited version of her autobiography. Recent studies indicate that it is possible to retrieve her story from the

---

29 Williams, R., *The Pivot on Which History Turns* in the series *Meanings of Christmas* in *The Independent*, 24 December 1999.

30 See Coakley S., *Creaturehood before God* in *Theology*, 1990, Vol. 93, No. 755.

31 See Lichfield, J., *The Many Faces of Joan of Arc* in *The Independent Review*, 21 February 2000, p. 7.

unpromising context of nineteenth century French, Jansenistic, *bourgeois* Catholicism.

However accurate and impeccable historical research and retrieval may be, it does not guarantee that the heroic 'myth' will live on in a new age.[32] The myth of the 'power of Christian innocence' and the models chosen to embody it raise many difficult questions for both theology and spirituality in a secular age. We may become convinced that certain texts or themes have no future. But if we do not engage with these questions, precious insights embedded in a discredited piety or in a culture no longer accessible to us may be lost forever and our tradition considerably impoverished.

---

32 However, for a very successful and positive feminist retrieval of Bernadette Soubirous, see Harris, R., *Lourdes: Body and Spirit in the Secular Age*, London, Allen Lane (Penguin Press), 1999.

Chapter Thirteen

Healing the Wound:
Discourses of Redemption

James Hanvey SJ

In 1995 the Superior General of the Society of Jesus promulgated the 26 decrees of the 34th General Congregation of the Society. Decree 14 took the title, *Jesuits and the Situation of Women in the Church and Civil Society*.[1] To the best of my knowledge it was the first time that a male religious order had formally addressed the situation of women in a decree of its supreme legislative body. The decree began by acknowledging and sketching the way in which prejudice, discrimination and injustice, though they took many different forms, was 'a universal reality'. The document was careful to insist that it was not a 'male discourse' about women but arose out of a careful, open, attentive listening:

> We do not pretend or claim to speak for women. However, we do speak out of what we have learned from women about ourselves and our relationship with them.[2]

The decree goes on to call for a process of conversion, the first step of which is a careful and courageous listening to the experience of women:

> Many women feel that men simply do not listen to them. There is no substitute for such listening. More than anything else it will bring about change. Unless we listen, any action we may take in this area, no matter how well intentioned, is likely to bypass the real concerns of women and to confirm male condescension and reinforce male dominance. Listening, in a spirit of partnership and equality,

---

1 *Documents of the 34th General Congregation of the Society of Jesus*, Institute of Jesuit Sources, St. Louis, 1995, pp. 171 ff.
2 *Documents of the 34th General Congregation*, §7, p. 174.

is the most practical response we can make and is the foundation for our mutual partnership to reform unjust structures.[3]

The problem of listening

If discourse intends to be a communication then it presupposes not only speaking but listening. Listening is an essential movement that constitutes an act of redemption. It also asks for a reversal. The male fiction is that it is women who speak and we who listen. Yet the deafening silence of women's voices through the centuries gives incontrovertible witness that this not the case. Even in theology the supposed subject is 'man' under which woman is subsumed as if there was only one experience and one voice. One senses that the turn to the subject that marks so much of theology's engagement with modernity is a disguised male subject, a detached *cogito* that speaks within a very male discourse. For all its existential reflection, the very fact that Rahner's human subject remains a disembodied consciousness suggests that it has neither the need nor the means to register difference.[4] Where the male voice is disguised in a disincarnate universal nature, the strategy can be one of *Pygmalion*. Women may speak but only when they have been tutored by men to speak like men. In this way the mythic hegemony of the universal subject is maintained. Alternatively, it may function like Lear, who in stripping Cordelia of her status and dowry makes her "that little seeming

---

3   *Documents of the 34th General Congregation*, §12, p. 175-176. The decree continues with the second act, discussing alignment in solidarity with women and enumerating eight steps which follow from this: 1. explicitly teaching the equality of women and men in Jesuit ministries, especially the educational establishments of the Society; 2. support for those movements which oppose the exploitation of women and encourage their entry into political and social life; 3. attention to the violence against women; 4. presence of women in Jesuit ministries; 5. their appropriate involvement in the consultative structures of decision-making in those ministries; 6. respectful cooperation with female colleagues in shared projects; 7. the use of appropriately inclusive language in speech and official documents; 8. the promotion of the education of women and the elimination of discrimination between boys and girls in the educational process.

4   While I would share with Georgina Morley's positive assessment of Macquarrie's 'grace of being', it seems to me to be open to the same criticisms as have been made of aspects of Rahner's thought. Granting its search for affinities rather than opposites, can it really sustain an appreciation of difference or must it instinctively suppress its destabilising force for the sake of irenic complementarity?

substance".[5] The issue is never just about language; it is about ontology and the space of existence.

The question of 'listening' is not, therefore, an easy one; yet the status of woman as 'listener' and receiver of the male word is one that our discourse imposes by the very act of its production. In the words of Judith Butler, in granting woman the status of subject she is placed in "subjection".[6]

> Let a women learn in silence with all submissiveness. I permit no women to teach or to have authority over men; she is to keep silent. For Adam was formed first, then Eve; and Adam was not deceived but Eve was deceived and became a transgressor. Yet woman will be saved through bearing children, if she continues in faith and love and holiness, with modesty.[7]

The word of women is untrustworthy and the ancient wound is played out in the legitimisation of their silencing. The Gospel's reversal of this teaching in the Magnificat and in Mary Magdalen's witness to the resurrection is also suppressed. Discourse that proceeds under this rubric is itself already a fallen speech.[8]

Too often the assumption is that listening is an act of passive receptivity rather than an act that proceeds from freely bestowed attentiveness that reserves the right of critical engagement and must speak in its own voice. The

5   Shakespeare, *King Lear*, Act 1. Scene 1 (lines 200-201). This is an important image in the play because it is precisely this process that Lear himself is to undergo and act out dramatically on the heath and in the final scene. It is a relentless stripping of all the borrowed substance of our creations to test the depths of nothingness.

6   *The Psychic Life of Power: Theories in Subjection*, Stanford, Stanford University Press, 1997. Cf. Laurence Hemming's discussion in this volume, *On the Nature of Nature: Is Sexual Difference Really Necessary?* A good example of the mechanism Butler describes is Marge Piercy's poem *The Friend* cited later in this chapter.

7   I Timothy 1 [11-15].

8   Rosemary Radford Ruether in her recent book, *Women and Redemption*, London, SCM, 1998, cites the First Letter to Timothy as a rejection of the 'baptismal realised eschatology' represented in Galatians 3 [27-28]. This eschatology is an overcoming of gender-difference and the hierarchy its supports. She argues that the tension in Pauline theology between a realised eschatology and a future completion was finally resolved in favour of the latter that reinforced traditional patriarchal relations. Clearly, there is a tension but Ruether seems not to take account of the radical eschatologies of redemption recorded in the gospels, especially Luke, where gender is not dissolved but rather becomes the very point at which the immanence of the Spirit of the Kingdom is manifest in power by bringing about a reversal. See pp. 38 ff.

act of listening presumes difference or else it is mere solipsism. It must be prepared for that difference to become delineated more sharply in the act of discourse itself. Listening, which is the result of an enforced silence, is an act of erasure.[9] It actively prevents any delineation of the uniqueness of the listener and the speaker. In this case the one who listens appears only in the voice of the speaker and for them to speak in their own voice is to threaten the totalising 'I' of the speaker thus destabilising the discourse. The threat of destabilisation may, itself, become a form of suppression, especially where the discourse is granted a quasi-ontological status of Revelation. In this way the listener is invited to collude in the production of the totalising magisterial 'I' of the speaker who endorses their act as virtue or faithfulness. If there is an intention to claim a universal validity, and within this are assumptions about the nature of truth which legitimates the discourse, then it must be a discourse that constantly requires assent. It achieves this through eradication of difference on the one hand, and the production of silence on the other: *Qui tacet consentire videtur.*[10] The listener is forced to sanction her own effacement; created as a 'nobody' in the very act of listening.

> I'm Nobody! Who are you?
> Are you – Nobody – too?
> Then there's a pair of us!
> Don't tell!
> They'd banish us – you know!

9   In what follows I am indebted to Lucy Gardner and Rachel Muers for their suggestive exploration of Irigaray's work. I would argue, however, that the transcendence which grounds interiority must be the living of the life of the Spirit. Interiority is a self-possession which comes through the *kenosis* of self in love. In what follows, it will be clear that the position I sketch is an attempt to move beyond the profoundly flawed anthropologies of Barth and von Balthasar who are committed to the specular economy by locating difference in a dialectic grounded in an ontology of monad-subject. For von Balthasar, woman is constituted in her generative receptivity. Though he attempts to escape the snare of making generativity conditional upon passivity and submission by developing a notion of her receptivity grounded in her freedom, he nevertheless ontologises a theory of women that is constructed out of her relation to man absolutised as Christ.

10 This is one of the *Regulæ Iuris* found in both classical Roman Law and in Mediæval Canon Law. It may be found as No. 43 in the list of 88 *Regulæ Iuris* at the end of the *Liber Sextus*, the collection of papal decretals that was promulgated by Pope Boniface VIII in 1298. I am indebted to C. Gallagher sJ for this information.

These lines of Emily Dickinson express the reality of women's silence but they are subversive also:

> How dreary – to be – Somebody!
> How public – like a Frog –
> To tell your name – the livelong June –
> To an admiring Bog![11]

Here, Dickinson assesses the cost of being "somebody", the pomposity exposed and ridiculed, while we are invited to join in the joke. In this act of exposure, "Nobody" steals the listener/reader demonstrating that, when claimed, the status of "Nobody" can be subversive. When forced into effacement, women, in Claudine Hermann's phrase, become *les voleuses de langue*.[12]

There are, however, moments when stealth is not enough: moments when the cost of not speaking one's truth is social and personal death. In such moments there can only be protest, an act of speaking out to claim life. Such moments assert difference and in so doing force a break in the ontology presupposed in a universal subjectivity. In these moments, even at the cost of suffering the pain of self-exposure, one must speak as in Alice Walker's poem, "On Stripping the Bark from Myself":

> . . . I know I could not live
> silent in my own lies
> hearing their "how nice she is!"
> whose adoration of the retouched image
> I so despise.[13]

Whether by theft or by protesting self-truth, these acts of resistance destabilise our understanding of 'listening' and expose the critical issue of the ontology of person and identity for theological discourse.

---

11 Dickinson, E., *The Complete Poems*, Johnson, T. H. (ed.), London, Faber and Faber, 1990, p. 133.
12 Hermann, C., *Les voleuses de langue*, Paris, Des Femmes, 1979.
13 Walker, A., verses from *Good Night, Willie Lee, I'll See You in the Morning: Poems*, London, Women's Press, 1987, p. 23.

Theological speech cannot be a partial speech, for God's self-disclosure and communication in Christ is not provisional or limited in its horizon. It is inevitably committed to the universal and the absolute even though it understands itself to be conditioned by time, culture, and the manifold of finite human existence. It is always a struggle to let the Word appear within the word and to understand the possibility of its speaking as grounded in the nature of its resistance to our speech. Theological discourse is, therefore, always forced to be intensely self-aware and self-critical if is to begin to accomplish its mission. The emergence out of silence of another voice is both grace and threat. Grace in that the discourse is enriched and shaped through difference but threat because its most fundamental assumptions about 'nature', 'person', 'subject', the universal claims and horizon of salvation and the meaning this must have for human reality, are brought into critical focus and their universal legitimacy questioned. If it can be shown that theology produces a totalising discourse which entails and requires the erasure or suppression of the feminine other, or indeed any 'other,' then it is a discourse that cannot serve the Gospel. It is radically flawed and in need of redemption that it may truly speak the Word. It will also happen that strategies of inclusion will not be sufficient to rectify this *vulnus profundum*. Thus, the discourse of theology, especially if it intends to be the discourse of the *ecclesia*, must itself be renewed and transformed.

Uncovering transcendence

In listening we give space for the other. In resisting our impulse to colonise either the place where the other is, or the language in which the other speaks, we wait for the other to emerge through their space and word. That waiting is already a creative act of humility which prescinds from the economy of power. It must be a deliberate self-forgetting, a holding back of all the impulses of exchange or control, at once a 'waiting on', a 'waiting for', a 'waiting with'. This space is not just external but also internal to us, for every act of listening is not just allowing the other their space and word but a granting of our space and our silence within which to be. It is an act of generosity, of grace, and when we do it the emergence of the other is a redeeming, a recovering of something which was lost, sold, given away, unseen, unvalued. The Spirit has moved over the void, the space becomes filled with a body, the silence with a voice, and light catches a face once hidden, the air vibrates with a personality. I am no longer in the presence of a nameless, though reverenced, 'other' but a person who meets me as one with me.

But this hermeneutic is too idealised. It is my myth. In truth I do not always graciously and gratefully give space or withhold my word. The one whom I will not see or refuse to hear confronts me, must struggle for their space, claim and hold it against all my strategies to supplant or control. When I force my discourse into their mind and voice then they must turn it back, strip it with irony and dissect away the masks, postures and all the sinews of the self that I import under cover of sympathetic attention. When the forensic 'other' meets me, challenging my intentions, questioning my motives, removing my disguises until I am naked and vulnerable, they become the enemy, the threat, the terror. Listening is never a simple absenting from self to attend to the other, but always an encounter with the self through the agency of the other. It is an encounter with the self, the 'me', which also needs to be redeemed.

If this discourse remains only within the dialectic of listening and speaking, the self and the other, then it will be locked in old spaces and ancient words; caught in the primordial ebb and flow of the battle for attention and the grammar of power. Something more is needed to free the discourse from its captivity; it must know itself to be within a bigger space, caught in a movement, an impulse, that simultaneously holds and nourishes while calling beyond. If listening is to be a redemptive movement it must take place in transcendence. It must allow transcendence to emerge from within and understand itself to be given space. In this act it also 'makes' space, new space, for God is the space in which we come to be. This space is created when we encounter the resistance of the Word to our speech. It is here, in this difference that cannot be erased, that incarnation takes place. It is the act by which God posits God's self in speaking the Word and thus establishes the space for difference to emerge. God's Word spoken breaks the logic of 'subjection' that the subject may appear in their space which God's act creates. This is a new ontology of subject, a new possibility from within speech, that establishes theology as the foundational immanent critique of human discourse through its resistance to all totalising strategies and subterfuges. It is the beginning of redeeming of language and the ontology which it produces. This is the reality of the Trinity. In God's Trinitarian life there is never an 'I' before a 'Thou' but always an everlasting life beyond the narrative and discourse of a binity. It is, therefore, a new way of being and of speaking, a new way of coming into language, of taking flesh.

In his discussion of the Western *filioque* and the Eastern insistence on the movement of the Spirit *ex Patre*, Lossky characterises the importance of the Spirit's procession "is an infinite passage beyond the dyad, which constitutes the absolute (as opposed to relative) diversity of the persons".[14] Whatever view we take regarding the merits of Lossky's case, the insight that the Spirit has a unique position *ad intra* the Trinitarian life that may provide a means of grasping the character of the Spirit's mission *ad extra* is an important one. In a significant way, Lossky's formulation identifies the Spirit as the reality of transcendence that is the Divine life and mediates it. As such, the Spirit is the absolute guarantor of God's presence *as God within* and to the finite, for the Spirit is the eternal self-possession of God, where the Word is reserved to God's self and self-articulation, and given within the finite in such a way that it can never be reduced to it: God never becomes a thing or an object, not even a subject. Though we are bound to use the language of 'self' and 'subject' we may only do so understanding that God is not an 'I' that comes to be posited within the dialectic of the 'thou' or over-against the 'other'.

The Spirit prevents and resists the blasphemy of this dialectic.[15] Instead, we are invited to a new conceptuality of a dynamic for which we have little capacity in thought or word. With this in mind we can, nevertheless, begin to explore how God as Trinity is incomprehensible and inexhaustible transcendence not simply in relation to the world but *in se*. The struggle to grasp and articulate this insight is a central issue in the formation of the Christian understanding of God as Trinity. Arianism strongly articulated the

---

14 Lossky, V., *A l'Image et à la Ressemblance de Dieu*, Paris, Aubier, 1967, translated as *In the Image and Likeness of God*, Erickson, J. H. and Bird, T. E. (eds.), New York, St Vladimir's Seminary Press 1974, p. 84.

15 It is precisely this point toward which much modern Trinitarian theology has been fatally inattentive. Its failure to work with a strong pneumatology and its insistence on converting relations *ad intra* into narratives of kenosis, while generating an appealing rhetoric, has run the risk of making theology a mythology. It has been too uncritical of Hegel's seductive logic of Divine becoming, and insufficiently attentive to the ghost of Feuerbach as it produced its Trinitarian drama. Theology must always resist the temptation to make God into a 'self', a golden calf with which it hopes to find solace in the desert of secularity.

'otherness' of God by locating it in the Father's unoriginateness. However, such a location is still locked within the false oppositional dialectic that cannot conceive of Incarnation; it thereby jeopardises the soteriological character of God's manifestation in Christ and the Spirit.

Transcendence is not just a point forever beyond, or a relation established in distinction from a given terminus; it is the very nature of God grounded within the perichoresis of the divine persons. When we begin to see this, then we can come to appreciate how God is present in and to all things as God, for transcendence is not a boundary. By its very nature it cannot be an 'other' that defines a 'not-other'. Occurring beyond this logic, its difference is of such an absolute character that it cannot be compromised by other differences; indeed, it becomes the environment and horizon within which difference emerges and appears without threat. It is the place where difference is given both the space and the call to become individuality and uniqueness. Yet, the very fact that because this is given within and through transcendence of God, it is sustained in dynamic generative relationality – a living *communio* in multiplicity that does not dissolve uniqueness into one or the *communio* into isolated singulars.[16] If we may use such bold imagery, the Spirit is the womb of God that is God's self.[17]

The thesis is a bold one. However, if we give it a cautious and tentative acceptance for the purpose of this essay, then we may begin to sketch the elements of a redemptive discourse that can only be the discourse of the Church. We can see how it is this Triune transcendence generates a discourse

16 It is only within a Trinitarian context that Macquarrie's understanding of the 'grace of being' could be developed, although one would need to be careful not to reduce the persons into transcendental categories of existence as in Rahner.

17 There is good precedent for doing so: Tertullian in his treatise *Against Praxeas* speaks of the production of the Word "from the womb of his (the Father's) heart". ["Ut ante omnia genitus, et unigenitus, ut solus ex deo genitus, proprie de vulva cordis ipsius secundum quod et pater ipse testatur, 'Eructavit cor meum sermonem optimum'" (Psalm 45 [1]).] Migne, J. P. (ed.), *Patrologia Latina*, Vol. 2, Tertullian, 2, *Adversus Praxean*, Paris, Petit-Montrouge, 1878, Chapter 7, Cols. 184-5. The Jesuit poet, Gerard Manley Hopkins, whose poetry should itself be regarded as pneumatological speech, plays upon the wind/Spirit as mother – "Wild air, world-mothering air/Nestling me everywhere", and Mary Immaculate, "merely a woman". The whole densely allusive poem has as its subtext the regenerative power of the Spirit through a feminine agency: "Be thou then, O thou dear/Mother, my atmosphere; / My happier world, wherein / To wend and meet no sin . . ." Hopkins, G. M., *Poems and Prose*, Gardner, W. H. (ed.), Harmondsworth, Penguin Books, 1978, pp. 54 ff.

constantly moving beyond the economy of dominance and subversion into a new realm of possibility.[18] If all discourse comes to know itself and its very possibility as grounded in transcendence of which it is also the fruit, then it must understand itself as given.[19] Hence, it must first become a listener in order that it may learn this new language. It must first become silent, attentive, waiting that it may listen to the God whose presence is the ever-greater silence of the Spirit in transcendence. This is not the existential silence of Wallace Stevens' man with the mind of winter who "nothing himself, beholds/Nothing that is not there, and the nothing that is".[20] Rather it is the generative silence of God's Triune life that both sustains us and draws us ever into it while purifying us of the cacophony of clashing egos and dominant orthodoxies that compete for our attention. The Spirit's presence is not the silence of suppression but that space from which speech is called forth; it is the inexhaustible plenitude of God that can never be contained in discourse. Neither is it simply the teaming silence of God's ever-creative life; it carries within it the dark and silent abyss of the Cross. Here is gathered all the silences of those who have been made into nothing, whose pain through all the centuries has found no voice, no one to hear.

18 It would also be possible to develop this thesis as a way of resolving the loss of difference which characterises modernity and its difficulty in maintaining the distinction of particular and universal – the problem of equality. It could also be developed to reclaim for the Church the space that Julia Kristeva awards to the therapist in *Extraterrestrials Suffering for Want of Love*, in Kristeva, J., *Tales of Love*, translated by Roudiez, L. S., New York, Columbia University Press, 1987. In both fields, the community of faith may understand itself to be the home of the human; itself, both witness to and already part of the immanent Kingdom of God as the healing of our woundedness. Our soteriologies are deficient if they do not account for our intersubjectivity, or, put another way, grace itself needs a community of grace.

19 The recently edited manuscript of Fessard, G., *Mystère de la société*, Bruxelles, Culture et Vérité, 1997, has a suggestive analysis of the dialectic between Man and Woman in terms of Hegel's master/slave relationship (pp. 203 ff.), which can only be resolved in the "gratuité de l'individuel" (p. 218). This 'gratuity' is a sort of recreation of the dialectic in love that issues in family and society. Fessard sees that is a societal *image de Dieu*. I approach this differently, seeing the very difference not as a dialectic which seeks resolution, but as the condition for the permanent 'grace of transcendence'. Of course, this would also ground the sheer gratuity (grace) of the individual without compromising intersubjectivity.

20 Stevens, W., *The Snow Man* in *Collected Poems*, London, Faber and Faber, 1987, pp. 9 f.

This great silence of God carries their silence so that when we begin to listen we come into their presence, the *desaparecidos* appear into truth.[21] In this way the unspeakable reality of God resists our claims to absoluteness and in so doing gives us the very power to speak always afresh, creatively and in truth. Such discourse is the immanent movement of the Spirit always present to us as God's mystery, the Triune freedom to be given without ceasing to be unpossessable. As such, it calls forth difference, for that difference is always the space in which the Other of the Spirit emerges. When discourse purifies itself of the closed logic of an I/thou exchange, it comes to understand itself as coming from and to the transcendent silence of God. It is then that it grasps how it is freed both to hear and speak truth, thereby realising itself as communication.

Only if language presupposes that it speaks the truth, or intends to speak it, can it be communication. Indeed the possibility of falsehood and the reason why it works is precisely because all language is ordered to truth. Integral to the appearance of truth in discourse is disclosure of difference as individuality, as a uniqueness that we cannot absorb, that stands before us as gift and possibility. Thus the Spirit appears in difference, realising the truth while forever being the immanent movement of transcendence. In this way it redeems relationship and the discourse that is simultaneously predicated upon it and shaped by it. Sometimes the Spirit will emerge as strangeness; sometimes as judgment, protest and cry of pain; sometimes as the very silence that forces its way between our words and their tissues of logic and grammar until they become exposed and separated, a destabilised and incoherent Babel. Then, when there is only the silence, are we cleansed of self and powerless so that we may appear again in new, more truthful, grace-filled ways. And so the Spirit moves over the void of our fallen discourses of power and domination, our strategies of silencing, colonising and subjection, to bring forth a redeemed discourse that has space for the other to speak and be heard.[22]

---

21 A Spanish term from Latin America, especially Chile, meaning 'the disappeared' – namely all those who have vanished without trace after being abducted by government agencies.

22 It seems to me that Susan Parsons' essay in this collection, *Accounting for Hope*, is correct in drawing our attention to the limitations of Ruether's approach. From the position I have sketched here, it would not be sufficient to understand 'redemption' as a historically immanent process of envisioning women and their stories to expose oppressive structures and reclaim the space to be and to become. To be sure, this must be part of any redemptive movement, but redemption is not redemption unless it moves into sanctification, into the

The strategy of the Spirit, therefore, lies in difference that calls us beyond the discourse of self and subverts its attempts at hegemony. Concretely, we encounter this in secular culture and the non-Christian world. The very multiplicity of languages in which humanity is thought, shaped, dreamed and celebrated compels us to listen, to purify, and to find new ways of speaking the Word we have been given. The Spirit will not let us take refuge in a ghetto-discourse, a dialect, or a private language. Within the Church, however, we may locate three ways in which the Spirit consistently works to renew the discourse of the community: tradition, prophecy, and the *sensus fidelium*. Magisterium and theology are also works of the Spirit in discerning, reflecting upon and stabilising the discourse so that it may articulate the whole life, experience, hope and faith of the *ecclesia*.

All discourses within the community that genuinely proceed out of the Spirit come to their truth and purpose in liturgy. There is a sense in which we may say that all Christian discourse is implicitly liturgical in so far as it seeks to become transparent to the δόξα of God. In the act of becoming liturgy, discourse is redeemed and sanctified. It is a gracious act that cannot be confected or manufactured by formula or will. The very freedom of the Spirit always guarantees that liturgy is no magic rite by which we seek to exercise power over God or creation. It is the Spirit's performative utterance that speaks *us*; thus we appear in God's presence. It is our εὐχαριστέω. Without dissolution of our uniqueness (indeed the contrary is the case) we become the act by which he is given, and gives himself to be Son, through our becoming one with Christ in his thanksgiving to the Father.

Tradition, if it is understood within the context of the Spirit, is the living voice that continues in the heart of the community. It is the way in which the community does not exclude and place one period, culture or voice above another. It is precisely the way in which the community allows the voices of the past to be present, still part of the conversation, that constitutes the Church as a community of redemptive discursivity. This dimension of the Church's reality is used by Helmut Peukert to revise Habermas' theory of communicative action. He argues that if subjectivity is dependent upon intersubjectivity, then the only way in which this can be grounded is through the way in which a society allows the discourses from the 'past' to be present,

Spirit's transcendent work of transformation. This why all immanent processes to be redemptive must understand their *telos* in the unclaimable horizon of the Triune life of God.

because the moment I begin to speak I enter a universal dialogue. This is central for resisting an 'amnesia' which holds open the question of theodicy and therefore the possibility of an acting God.[23] Although it is an important insight, if its argument is to be secure it must understand that tradition cannot be simply those who have been heard and claimed their place in the assembly. It has to be those who are not heard, who by their praxis of faith and presence, even when they have been silenced, have a voice. If this is not done, then the tradition remains a block to the Spirit, the perpetuation of an incomplete, imperfect and fallen speech. It is precisely against the strategies of amnesia that Spirit's work is *anamnesis*, the recovery of the memory of truth which requires the testimony of the silenced.

The Spirit 'brings all things to memory' and so it constantly calls us to a hermeneutic of retrieval. If, however, the voice of women has been silenced and only allowed to appear in and through the experience of men, then the Spirit must first find a voice outside the community that we may learn to hear the voice within it. From this perspective, it may then turn within to claim its own voice and freedom as the voice of the Church, the raising up of its own witness and hope. It will be the voice of prophecy in all its modes: visionary, mystical, critical, passionate for justice, crucified and resurrected. To silence or suppress this voice would be a sin against the Holy Spirit. Yet it is in the abiding eloquence of the *sensus fidelium*, that praxis of faith, hope and love, which informs the life of the community and brings its judgment on the adequacy of all our discourses, that the Spirit works to sift, test and refine. The *sensus fidelium* is the space that the Spirit reserves for itself. Ultimately, all discourse in the Church must stand before the *sensus fidelium* and the witness of life. It is in the practice of the Church's life that it bears its fruit and comes to be known. If the community comes to recognise itself in it, then it may become the speech of the *ecclesia*. For a time it may be possible to force acceptance or impose it, claim attention or create a fashion, but as the discourse is sifted through the Spirit-filled lives of faithful women and men it is either absorbed and purified, forming and shaping those lives Godward,

---

23 Peukert, H., *Enlightenment and Theology as Unfinished Projects* in *Habermas, Modernity and Public Theology*, Browning, D. S. and Schüssler Fiorenza, E. (eds.), New York, Crossroads, 1992, pp. 53; 55. The argument of this essay is set out in much more detail in Peukert, H., *Wissenschaftstheorie – Handlungstheorie – Fundamentaltheologie*, Düsseldorf, Patmos, 1976.

or it trickles into the vast desert of fallen discourses to become a language that the Spirit forgets. In this sense, every discourse that seeks redemption also knows that it is judged by the degree to which it builds up the community, enriches it and releases its potentials for new speech. If it is Spirit-filled then it will accomplish these things, but before the Spirit's witness in those faithful to Christ it can only be partial speech. Knowing, however, that it is always a work, a word, that is incomplete it must seek to free itself of any pretension to exhaust the discourse of faith.

A new heaven and a new earth

It is within this thesis of redemptive discourse that operates in time that I would locate the emergence of women's voices. Voices that challenge, disclose, rejoice and reclaim the gift of being a woman in the Church. This must have profound consequences for our ecclesiology. In the discourse of the Church the feminine has been a masculine construction, interiorised to become the passive, receptive soul before God or exteriorised in imaging the Church as virginal Bride and Mother. These are powerful positive images that develop in scripture and in the Fathers to express the eschatological nature of the community and its Spirit-given generativity. They point, however, to a strange paradox in the community's life: in constructing an ideal 'redeemed feminine,' in spirituality as well as ecclesiology, the actual incarnation of the feminine given in creation, namely a woman and women, is displaced. Moreover, women are forced to mirror this male creation and in so doing enter into service of male fantasies. It is interesting that once art moves from the static, stylised eternal Icon to the pathos of the human, images of women become increasingly subjected to male construction. The iconography of Mary, Mother of God, and Mary Magdalen as it develops through the centuries increasingly becomes the creation of images of womanhood that regulate and purify male desire. It is safe to admire and desire the silent wrapped virgin in Fra. Angelico's Annunciation or to seek the company of naked, reformed and eremitical Mary Magdalen in the *legenda* of the Basilica of St. Francis in Assisi. 'Woman' is constructed and disciplined through the visual. In the great flowering of humanist art 'woman' emerges only in relation to male desire and anxiety; the ancient strategies of either exciting temptation or restraining are played out. 'Woman' is not permitted to have a body of her own.[24]

It is not surprising, then, that as feminist discourse breaks out into public speech, one of its first tasks is to reclaim 'the body' against the sustained displacement and disembodiment that has shaped the dominant discourse. We can grasp something of the range of this experience in two poems: one, by Susan Wicks, the other by Marge Piercy.

The vivid and disturbing treatment of the Annunciation by Susan Wicks inhabits a different world of earth and experience from Fra. Angelico:

This was no time to wonder if she knew Him,
if He was the father of someone close to her,
no time to gasp, or cry out – before He was on her
like a robber, pinning her wrists and burning

His precious liquid into her
like acid or molten metal or the swarming points of hot starlight.
This was no time to wonder if she knew Him,
if He was the father of someone close to her,
no time to gasp, or cry out – before He was on her
like a robber, pinning her wrists and burning

His precious liquid into her
like acid or molten metal or the swarming points of hot starlight.

The body is possessed, overwhelmed, subjected to a sort of rape. Yet there is an ambivalence in the image and emotion which comes from the disembodied nature of the Divine perpetrator: "She bit down on His tongue, and found her mouth full of nothing . . ." What takes place is an ecstatic dispossession but is she left with a transformed self or something that she inhabits but no longer recognises?

---

24 Van der Weyden's painting, inspired by the *devotio moderna*, is an interesting contrast. He consistently parallels Mary's life with Christ, most notable in his portrayal of *The Deposition of Christ*. Here, Mary physically enacts the pose of the dead Christ. Once again, she becomes the hermeneutical key to the interior disposition the believer seeks in relation to Christ at this point. It is interesting how Mary as access to the interior mystical-devotional world is displaced at the reformation, and taken up either by anonymous voices or ordinary persons, as in Bach's 'musical paintings' of The Passion and Easter narratives.

Now she can sing
her magnificat – sing each morning
as she bends over cool basins,
her hair sticking to her cheeks, her new body
shaking, as if it did not belong to her.[25]

The sense of dispossession and the ambivalence of the creative appropriation of the body leaves the self as stranger to itself. This tension, held in such disturbing tension by Wicks, can descend into a darker resolution in Piercy's poem ironically entitled *The Friend*. Here, the logic of the male 'I' and the female 'thou' is exposed:

We sat across the table.
he said, cut off your hands.
they are always poking at things
they might touch me.
I said yes.

The poem contrasts a desperate notion of 'love' that proves itself in passive surrender to mutilation. The form is conversational, but one voice is compliant and the other is the emotionless voice of domination. Systematic abuse has been substituted for sexual gratification and power for relationship.

I love you, I said.
that's very nice, he said
I like to be loved.
that makes me happy.
Have you cut off your hands yet?[26]

Perhaps the most powerful image of all is in Toni Morrison's *Beloved*.[27] The ancient wound that marks Seth's back takes the form of a tree. Is it the mark of the Fall or the Cross? Certainly it is the mark of her oppression. In this novel, through the disembodied figure of *Beloved*, Morrison is able to give voice to all the lost and disembodied women that are there, calling through the

25 Wicks, S., *First Coming* in *Open Diagnosis*, London, Faber and Faber, 1994, p. 57.
26 Piercy, M., *The Friend* in *Circles on the Water: Selected Poems*, New York, Knopf, 1982, p. 39.
27 Morrison, T., *Beloved*, London, Vintage/Ebury, 1997.

centuries, carried in the silent, secret history of suffering and seeking love's redeeming.

Combined, these images from women are the Spirit's witness and they open up the question of embodiment which a writer like Judith Butler pursues in a different key.[28] They are creating a new and rich discourse: one that is not confined to critique but opens up new avenues for theological work. This is especially true in the case of our understanding of the incarnation. As Rosemary Ruether observes, "there has been a remarkable persistence in attachment of Christian feminists to the Jesus story".[29] It is understandable that feminist theologians will seek to find ways of understanding the event of Jesus that break the fallen strategies, that suppress and silence women. Part of this must also entail a reclamation of the person of Christ within categories that are liberating for women as a part of a more complete soteriology. Some of these attempts have been more successful that others; most have been partial, perhaps too dominated by the stance they have been forced to take to free themselves from patriarchal and kyriarchal structures. It seems to me, however, that the work of feminist thinkers in uncovering the discourse of body and gender offers a significant resource to a renewed Christology. If the critique of discourse we have been exploring is correct, then that critical clause of the Nicene Creed, *ex Maria Virgine*, understood within the language of the tradition, has been deeply flawed and insufficient. We cannot grasp the true nature and meaning of this event until we have a fully developed articulation of feminine difference and experience. This must, in consequence, bring about a radical shift in our discourse about 'maleness'. The redemption of the discourse is necessary if the Church is to come to a deeper understanding and experience of the Lord whom it confesses. This is a fundamental task for theology which is only just beginning.

These voices and the experience they articulate pose a deep and radical challenge to the community's way of characterising itself. If the bodily experience and reality of women is suppressed or evacuated of its earthliness for the sake of a male version of what it should be, then creation itself is mutilated. If these images are further deployed as part of the Church's discourse of self-understanding, serving to shape both our dispositions to the

---

28 Cf. Butler, J., *Gender Trouble*, New York, Routledge, 1990, esp. Part Three, *Subversive Bodily Acts*, and the section *Bodily Inscriptions, Performative Subversions*, pp. 128 ff.
29 Ruether, R. R., *Women and Redemption*, p. 275.

ecclesia and determining the range of permissible relationships to it, then we continue to risk disfiguring the community. The emergence of the voice of women about women, while it cannot be any more absolute or definitive than the voice of men about men without falling into the trap of hegemony, calls for a profound reappraisal of our ecclesiology. Too often this can be reduced to skirmishes about language and office. These are important, but the re-visioning must be pursued to another level that touches upon the foundational images (ontology) that encode our concepts and affections. This reappraisal will not be complete unless it requires a radical reflection upon the Church's redemptive mission. The community cannot effectively respond to the task it has been given without first seeking a more honest and complete grasp of its own nature. It can only achieve this if it is willing to examine the strategies by which it colludes in suppressing the discourses of the Spirit which keep it open to the transcendence by which it lives. In the same way, with courage and boldness it must bring these insights into its dialogue with other religions where the strategies of suppression are also at work.[30]

In this brief concluding essay I have been able only to sketch a response to that which I have heard in the voices of this collection. The reader is always a guest, sometimes unexpected, but invited nevertheless to participate in that complex act of hearing and speaking through which a space has been created for exploration and new possibilities. Some may find it strange, perhaps even scandalous, that a man should have the concluding word. If so, that would be an unfortunate lapse into the logic and discourse which *Challenging Women's Orthodoxies* is resisting. In a redeemed discourse there is no 'last word', for that belongs to the Spirit.

---

30 Ayçegül Baykan argues that the situation of women in fundamentalist religions is not the result of historically fixed traditions and cultures, but produced and sustained by contemporary global political, ideological, and economic movements. Baykan, A., *Women Between Fundamentalism and Postmodernity* in Turner B. S. (ed.), *Theories of Modernity and Postmodernity*, London, Sage, 1990.

Index

abegeschiedenheit 162-4, 166, 170
Abel, murder of 196
Abelard 125
abusua 104-8
action and active agents 14-15;
   see also communicative action
Adam 28-9, 113, 196-7
All-Africa Conference of Churches
   93, 101
Ammah, Rabiatu 106
'amorous economy' 135-6
Amu, Ephraim 92
anamnesis 217
Angelico, Fra 218-19
Anselm 125
'answer' to man, woman as 112-19
   passim
anthropocentrism 27, 186
Arianism 212-13
Aristotle and Aristotelianism 44,
   48, 155, 159-74
Asante culture 99, 104
atonement 126, 175, 184, 196,
   199-201
Augustine, St 29, 174
Auschwitz 73, 79, 82-7

Bam, Brigalia 95, 107
Barth, Karl 109-20, 177
Baudrillard, J. 13
Baumel, Judith Tydor 76
Berkovitz, Eliezer 84-5
Bernanos, Georges 191, 193
Blackfriars theology 63, 65
body 141, 144-6, 148-50, 219-20;

   see also embodiment
Briggs, Sheila 66, 70
Brock, Rita Nakashima 126
Brown, R. 125
Bulger, James 195
Butler, Judith 155-62 *passim*, 168,
   171, 174, 207, 221

The Canterbury Tales 124
Carlson Brown, J. 200
Carmelite sisters of Compiègne
   191, 193, 202
Les Carmélites 191
Catholic Women's Network 54-6,
   58-9, 63
de Certeau, Michel 113
Chaucer, Geoffrey 124
childhood *see* spiritual childhood
Chodorow, Nancy 157
Christ, Carol 107
Christian feminism 54-61, 65, 69-
   70, 111, 123, 128, 192-3, 221
Circle of Concerned African
   Women Theologians 90-91, 95-
   8, 103-6
civilising mission of women 55
Coakley, Sarah 129
Cohen, Arthur 84
Cohn-Sherbok, Dan 79
Collins, Diana 56, 59-61, 68-9
communicative action 216
communion of saints, doctrine of
   199
Condren, M. 62-70 *passim*
connectedness 180-81, 184-5

contextual theology 91
cosmology 155, 159-73
Court, Gillian 57-8
creation, doctrine of 6, 28-9, 112, 185-6
cross, the; *see* theology of the cross

Daly, Mary 70
Dante 138-40
Darwin, Charles 27-8
Davies, Oliver 173
Des Pres, Terrence 80
detachment 162-6, 170-74
dialectical theism 180
Dickinson, Emily 208-9
Dickson, Kwesi 93
dignity
  human 6, 24, 26, 30
  of living creatures generally 34
Diocletian 193-4
dispossession of women 68-9
Donatello 40
Douglas, Ann 187-8
Dowell, Susan 57-8, 68-9
duties, non-human-centred 22

Eagleton, Terry 47
Earth system science 21-34
ecclesiology 218, 222
Eckhart, Meister 155, 161-74
ecological consciousness 25-7, 30
Ecumenical Association of Third World Theologians (EATWOT) 91, 95-7, 100-102
Ellis, Marc 86
embodiment 8, 155, 160-61, 185-6, 221; *see also* body
empowerment 14, 201
England, Rivka 78
Enlightenment thought 5, 44-8,

155, 159-60
environmental ethics 22-3
equality before God 6, 52
equality of women 38-9, 44-8, 62, 68, 160
essences 159
ethics 1-2, 15, 45; *see also* environmental ethics; feminist ethics
Eve 63-9, 107, 111, 125, 196-7
  rehabilitation of 56-61, 67-71
evolution
  biological 27-9
  of the planet 31-2
existentialism 178-80, 188

Fackenheim, Emil 84
faith xii-xiii, 4, 20
Faith and Reason (encyclical letter) 3
feminine virtue, ideal of 46
feminisation
  of the Church and society 62
  of the soul 147
feminism
  and the academic community 46-8, 51
  'legislative' 46
  'philosophical' 47
  wisdom of 65;
  see also Christian feminism; naturalistic feminism; post-Christian feminism; postmodern feminism; radical feminism
feminist ethics 40-41
feminist orthodoxy 121, 129, 192-3, 202
feminist theology xiii, 2, 4-18, 35-6, 51, 60-63, 66, 69, 109, 111, 121-32 *passim*, 176-7, 180-83,

200-202, 221
  and the Holocaust 74, 76, 81-2
Field-Bibb, Jacqueline 61-5, 70
Florence, statuary in 40
Frank, Anne 78
Freire, P. 181
French Revolution 44, 191, 193
Freud, Sigmund 156
fundamental theology 2-5
Furlong, Monica 57-8
Fynsk, Christopher 141-2, 145,
  148

Gaia theory 21-2
Gawronski, Raymond 111, 116
gender, discourse of xiii-xv, 7
gender identity 155
'gender wounding' 75
'gendered social reality' 39-40
gerne 163-4
Gill-Austern, B.L. 127
global community 25
God
  death of 18, 174
  and detachment 164-6
  as a dimension of the Self 50
  discovery of 151
  in dual relation with the world
    183
  encounters with xi
  image of 58, 64, 70
  immanence of 187
  and Mary 171-2
  monarchical model of 175-7,
    189
  otherness of 176, 212-13
  patriarchal model of 73-4, 85,
    184
  relating to 155, 173, 178-81,
    182-9
  Word of 64, 211-14

Goddess religion 64-5, 67
Goldenberg, Myrna 75
grace 182, 210
  of being 179-80, 189
Grey, Mary 184-5
'growing end' of theological
    tradition 25, 28, 31, 34
Gutiérrez, Gustavo 104

Habermas, J. 108, 216
Hampson, Daphne 36-52
Harvey, Susan Ashbrook 57-8, 66,
    68
Hayter, Mary 70
heaven 165-7
Heidegger, Martin 110, 165, 168,
    170, 177-8
Hermann, Claudine 209
heroic myths 195, 202-3
Heythrop College xiv
Hilberg, Raul 75
Hillesum, Etty 78
historical consciousness 24-5
Holocaust, the 73-87
hope 2-7, 9-11,16-20
Horowitz, Sara 75
human being, characteristics of 11-
    12, 16, 177-80
humanism 5, 7, 9, 13-14, 177
Hume, David 161
humility
  intellectual 49-50
  of Mary 170-72
Hurcombe, Linda 57-8, 68-9

identity 13, 44, 155
immanence
  feminine 150, 152
  of God 187
  radical 183
'innerness' 169

innocence, Christian 191-203
instrumentalism 49
interiority 135, 139-41, 153, 156-
    7, 161, 169, 173-4, 218
Internet, the 25
intimacy 152
intuition 150, 152
inwardness 172-4
Ireland 67
Irenæus 196
Irigaray, Luce 12, 111, 118, 135-
    53
Islamic fundamentalism 106

Jansenism 194, 200-201, 203
Jantzen, Grace 150-51
Jawort 115-16
Jenner, Judith 62, 65, 70
Jesuits 205
Jesus Christ 6-10, 14, 32-3, 51-2,
    62, 70, 103, 130, 171
  imitation of 123-4
  innocence of 199
  as the second Adam 196
Joan of Arc 191-5, 198-9, 202
John Paul II, Pope 3
justice 19, 183

Kansas 28
à Kempis, Thomas 123
kenosis 129, 147
Kerr, Fergus 141-2, 150
kerygmatic school 177
King Lear 206-7
Kroll, Una 60-62, 68, 70

Lang, H. 168-70
'last wordism' 35-7, 222
Laub, Rega 78
Leo XIII, Pope 194
liberalism in politics and

    philosophy 6, 44
liberation theology 102, 181-3,
    187-8, 201
listening 208-16
  to women 205-7
liturgy 216
Long, Asphodel 67
Lossky, V. 212
love 19-20, 130-31, 148, 163, 220
Lovelock, James 21
Luther, Martin 122

McFague, Sallie 185-6
MacIntyre, Alasdair 7, 44-5
Macquarrie, John 176-81, 188
male constructions of images of
    women 218-21
martyrdom 78-9, 193-4, 200
Mary, mother of Jesus xi, 57-8, 66-
    8, 110, 115-20, 125, 162, 173-
    4, 218
  humility of 170-72
Mary Magdalen 207, 218
Mary Michael, Canon Sr 54, 56
masculine and feminine approaches
    and values 41-3, 116
Maybaum, Ignaz 84
Maza, Bernard 84
Mengele, Josef 75
Mertes, Kate 69-70
Methodism 101
Midgley, Mary 21-2, 49
missionary religion 90, 103, 106
modernity xiii-xiv, 1, 5, 9-14, 35,
    38-44 *passim*, 50
Moltmann, J. 123
moral consciousness 25
moral influence theory 199
morality and rationality 45-6
Morley, Janet 58, 63-4, 71
Morris, Joan 61

Morrison, Toni 220-21
Moses xi
motherhood 98-9
motion 164-8
Movement for the Ordination of
    Women 57
Murray, John Courtney 24-5
muteness 109-16 *passim*
La Mystérique 137, 145-8, 153

Naess, Arne 22
Nassibou, Janice 106
natural theology 178, 180
naturalistic feminism 7-8
Nazism 80-81, 84-6
Newman, John Henry 199
Nicene Creed 221
Nielson, Martha Lynne 66, 68
Nietzsche, Friedrich 16, 45, 174
nihilism 17-18
Nussbaum, Martha 157-62

Oduyoye, Mercy 89-108
Oduyoye, Modupe 94
Okin, Susan Moller 160
omnipotence 184
omniscience 183
ordination of women 54-61
    passim, 66-9
original sin 67
orthodoxy xiv, 11, 16-20, 37, 140;
    see also feminist orthodoxy
Oxford Christian Feminist Network
    63, 65
Oxford Women's Liturgy 64
Oxford Women's Theology
    Seminar 59

Parker, R. 125, 200
Parsons, Susan 36
'partisanship for life' 182
pastoral theology 127-8

patriarchy 5, 38-45, 50-51, 60-66,
    74, 80-86, 98, 125, 131, 145,
    159
personhood 162
Peukert, Helmut 216
phallogocentrism 145
Philomena, St 193-5, 202
Piercy, Marge 219-20
Pieris, Aloysius 97
Pinsent, Pat 58-9
place, concept of 167-9, 174
Plaskow, Judith 107
Plaszow labour camp 76
Plato and Platonic thought 8, 150,
    167
Pobee, John S. 93
poor, the, 'epistemological
    privilege' of 181
Porter, Jean 187-8
Post, Stephen 1A23
post-Christian feminism 10
postmodern feminism 155
postmodernism 4, 10, 13-19, 37,
    50, 160, 195
Poulenc, Francis 191
power 6-7, 13-16, 156-8, 171
    discourse and language of 14-16
prayer 19-20, 23
process theology 181-4, 187-8
Programme for Christian/Muslim
    Relations in Africa 106
projectionism 150-51
psyche, the 156-7, 161-2
purity of women 57-8

Quaker Women's Group 59

radical feminism 35, 65-6
Radical Orthodoxy 4
Rankka, K.M. 131
Rapley, Chris 23, 26
reciprocity in male-female relations

42-3
redemption, doctrine of 7-16, 73-
    4, 81-3, 123, 133, 149, 172-3,
    184, 206, 213, 218; *see also*
    atonement
religious freedom 24-5
remembrance 132, 217
representation and over-
    representation 7-8, 12-13
repression 156
Resurrection, the 49, 52
revelation, doctrine of 23, 31-4,
    38, 49, 208
Ringelheim, Joan 76-7
rites of passage 197-8
Rozenzweig, Franz 31-2
Ruether, Rosemary 6, 9-18, 221

salvation 29-30, 69-70, 199-200
Sartre, Jean-Paul 178-9
satisfaction theory 199
Saward, John 192
Schmitz-Moormann, Karl 28
Schüssler Fiorenza, Elisabeth 18-
    19, 62, 70
science, status of 49
self-identification 156
self-relation 146-7
self-sacrifice 121, 124, 127, 130-
    31, 200
selfhood, denial of 136
'sensible transcendental' 150, 153
sexual difference 7-8, 139-40,
    143-4, 147-8, 157-62, 173
sexuality, women's 56-61, 68, 125
Shekhinah 74, 81-5
silence 127, 143
    of Mary 118-19
    significance of 109-10, 112, 118
    of the Spirit 214-15
    of women 111-20, 125, 206, 209,

217, 221
skenosis 93
Smith, Carol 69
Society for Research and Education
    in Earth System Science 21
Sölle, Dorothée 126, 182, 197-8
Sophia myth 185
Soskice, Janet Martin xiv, 59
soul, the 29-30, 136, 146-7, 166-9,
    172-4
South Africa 122, 133
space exploration 25
specular economy 135-7, 143-53
speech, denial of 143
Spirit, the 212-18
spiritual childhood 192-9, 201-2
spiritual womanhood 55, 58
spirituality 38, 176, 200
Stevens, Wallace 214
subjectivity 156-60
suffering
    experience of 132-3
    glorification of 124-5, 200-201
    problem of 122-3
    of women 126

theological discourse 210-18
theological freedom 33
theology
    in Africa 96-7
    of the cross 122-4, 126-7, 130;
    see also contextual theology;
        feminist theology; fundamental
        theology; liberation theology;
        natural theology; pastoral
        theology; process theology
Thérèse of Lisieux 191-203
    passim
torture 113
touch 145-6, 151-3
tradition xii, 216

transcendence 135-43, 146-53,
186, 211, 215, 222
transcendental autonomy 161
transcendental subjectivity 162
trasumanar 138
Trible, Phyllis 85-6
Trinity, the 212, 215
truth in discourse 215
'two-winged theology' 98-9,
107-8

ultramontanism 194
United States 44
universal values 9, 17

Vanier, Jean 201
Vatican Council, Second 24
victimisation and victimhood 125-
7, 131, 199-201
'virtuous woman' 187
von Balthasar, Hans Urs 109-20,
191, 198
vulnerability 131

Walker, Alice 209
Waterhouse Report 195
West, Angela 59, 61, 63-5, 129-30
Whittier, J.G. 114
Wicks, Susan 219-20
Williams, Delores 126
Windle, Ruth 59, 68
Wollstonecraft, Mary 44
Womanspirit movement 64, 67
womb, the 144-5, 149
Women in Theology
network 55-6
women
position in the churches 53-6
social situation of 38
Woodhead, Linda 128-9
World Council of Churches (WCC)
93-6, 100-102

Yamoah, Charles Kwaw 91

Zechariah 110, 119
Zehnnerschaft 76-9